DAVID ELYAN

SERENDIPITOUS TALES

CONTENTS

Spanish Family Crest

INTRODUCTION

To save you rushing for your dictionary, serendipity is the making of happy and unexpected discoveries by accident; and my life seems to have included far more than its fair share of such discoveries. This book was originally intended to be autobiographical but it was soon evident that long stretches of it would be extremely boring, both for you and me – so instead I have concentrated on family and personal history and a collection of episodes of an anecdotal nature along the way.

My initial thought was *Anecdotage* as a title, based on the fact that I might soon be suffering from memory loss and a fear that I might have forgotten most of the anecdotes before I had a chance to put them in print. My mother began to suffer from memory loss from the age of 80 and I am not far off that now. The stories that follow sometimes describe periods of only one or two hours while others deal with 50 or more years. As all have been written as stand-alone chapters, there is inevitably a small amount of repetition for which I apologise.

Some of the pieces have previously appeared in print: *The Story of School Prints* and *Work that remained in progress* were both published by the Whittington Press (Matrix Nos. 10 and 14, 1990 and 1994 respectively) while *Memories of Princess Diana* appeared in the *Malta Sunday Independent's* "First Sunday" in September 1998. *The Elyan Collection* was first published as part of "A Bibliography of the David Elyan Collection" by Malta University Press, 2000.

A version of "Yesterday" is reproduced by kind permission of the late Sir David Willcocks, 1976.

There are references in the text to "Whiskey" and "Whisky". Cognoscenti will know that the former is Irish and the latter Scotch.

1

Thanks are due to my cousin Tamar Hodes for her advice and to John Randle of the Whittington Press for his suggestions, including the removal of exclamation marks!

David Elyan

EARLY MEMORIES

First a word about my parents – before my 'memories' began. They were both born in Cork: my father Max on 12 October 1908 was the fourth of six children to David and Sarah Elyan; and my mother Freda was the fourth of five born to Sam and Dora Gremson on 18 July 1918. They married on 6 June 1939 – a very brave decision at an inauspicious time I always thought, with the likelihood of a World War just around the corner, and I arrived a year or so later on 4 October 1940.

Having been born at Mrs Harvey's Nursing Home in South Terrace, Cork, my earliest memories are of childhood at 'Derrynane' where we lived for the next ten years. The house was opposite the Lough, pebble-dashed and semi-detached, rather typical of the 1930s when it was built and unattractive, but the best that Dad could afford at the time, costing £1,500. The nicest feature was the view towards the Lough itself at the front, a nature reserve even in those days with swans, ducks, coots and moorhens as well as some passing seagulls. The birds lived in a marshy island area in the centre which was just as well as they were then out of reach of small boys such as my little friends and me.

I am writing of my recollections some 60 years later from memory and it may be that some of them are inaccurate or exaggerated. To a small boy a man of 47 is little different from one of 74, in the same way that a hill is a small mountain.

A considerable advantage of the area was that there was a large space in which to play safely. There was not much through traffic and of course there were not nearly so many cars about as there are today. Apart from the Lough opposite, if you went out of the house and turned left, past some other houses and turned left again, you were in a lane with some further houses on either side and eventually arrived at what I remember as an open area of waste land with trodden paths and hillocks with wild flowers, lots of weeds, butterflies and dragonflies. It was here that we played soldiers, Cowboys and Indians or hide and seek. We caught butterflies when we could; and gathered birds eggs and blew out the insides with pin-pricks so we could keep the shells for our collections. It was all so typical of William in the Richmal Crompton books which I read avidly at about that time.

I vaguely remember that some of the older boys would catch frogs, put grass straws up their rear ends and blow until the poor little things exploded. We didn't see anything cruel in what was done. At the Lough we used to fish for sticklebacks, known locally as 'thornees', and roach. The sticklebacks when caught were put in jam jars and brought home. If they were lucky, the fish were put back in the water later to continue their lives, but otherwise they died in the jars and were thrown out when the smell got too bad. Very occasionally some council workers would turn up with a rowing boat to tidy up the debris in the water and, if our luck was in, they would take one or two of us to the island in the middle. This was like visiting a tropical island as there were reeds and rushes and birds' nests among the undergrowth to be explored.

As little boys we had stone-throwing competitions from the edge of the Lough where the object was to try and hit one of the birds in the water. I don't recall anybody ever hitting anything of interest but we did make the ducks and moorhens scoot hurriedly away from us with wings and legs going as fast as they could.

One day during a stone-throwing exercise, I had thrown my stones and missed as usual. As I was gathering up some more for a further assault on the ducks, somebody's larger-than-usual stone hit me on the temple just behind my right eye. Blood spouted everywhere and I could hardly see. I ran towards home crying but was intercepted on the way by a neighbouring lady who was doing some gardening at the time. She brought me in to her kitchen and washed me down so 'your mother won't faint with the shock when she sees you'. I think I was taken to hospital later that evening to have the wound stitched and retain the mark to this day.

Later when I was about 10 we moved about a mile away to 'Croata' on Glasheen Road and my bucolic days were over. Funny how it always seemed to be sunny then. I can't recall what we did when it rained. There was of course no TV so it was probably reading books about William or Biggles, or the *Children's Newspaper* that Mum used to buy me every week.

At 'Croata' life became much more ordered. There was homework and studying to be done, tennis of a sort at the Church of Ireland sports ground after school and cycling. Sometime later there were rabbits (who kept on breeding) to be looked after and then the arrival of a dog. Paddy was a wild and quarrelsome Irish terrier who had to be taken for walks after school. His only enjoyment in life seemed to be fighting – particularly larger dogs such as Alsatians – and it was quite a relief to all of us when Dad gave him away.

Though I can't remember what we did when it rained at 'Derrynane', I do remember what we did when it was very cold and freezing. The Lough iced over and when the ice got thick enough people would turn up and skate. We were not allowed on the ice on our own but we would venture on to it with Dad at weekends. We couldn't skate but we certainly knew how to fall over, which we did with great regularity. One memory is of Marshall Hutson, head of the Art College and a friend of Dad's, who was something of an expert skater, and who looked so graceful with his beard as he waved to us gliding past.

On my last visit to the Lough some years ago, it was much tidier than I remember it and a proper nature sanctuary with signs describing all the different birds to be seen there. To me all those years ago there was only one sort of duck.

Me aged Four

In the garden at Derrynane

Dad made the horse!

Doreen

Derrynane, The Lough, Cork

The Lough at Cork

FAMILY BACKGROUND

It might be useful if I jot down some information about the Elyan family background and, in particular, about my father while I can still remember the facts.

According to family research – as far back as we can go – the family lived in Spain contentedly for some hundreds of years under Spanish and then Moorish rule. As the Moors were driven out and the Spanish returned to power, before long the presence of Jews and Moslems remaining in Spain was seen as a threat to the stability of the nation and led to the Spanish Inquisition of 1492. As Jews, life was never easy, particularly living in Ayllón in the province of Segovia, roughly halfway between Madrid and Burgos, where I imagine the men would have farmed and studied the Talmud (Jewish law) while the women cooked, mended and helped with the other tasks. At a time when very few people could read or write, the Jews were among the better educated in that they spoke two or three languages and could read and write them. Also, they had learnt book-keeping or simple accounting from the Moors, so that their services were often in demand and a number of them rose to quite high positions in government. They were the first in Spain to produce wine, olive oil and textiles.

After 1492, however, life suddenly got very much more difficult when Jews were required to convert to Catholicism or, if possible, flee. The family managed somehow to continue living at Ayllón until the 16th century, presumably having changed religion as required – at least on the surface – whilst continuing as Jews in secret. Many did this and were called 'conversos' but God help them if they were found out: death and torture were certain, usually in the cruellest possible way. We know that

Paul and Issabella Ayllón were burnt at the stake in 1562 for returning to Judaism, and their son followed a year later. Those who converted – the New Christians, they were also called – on baptism were released from the social segregation of the Jewish quarter and were permitted to engage in a wider range of occupations. But, as Jews were nevertheless regarded as dissenters from the Catholic faith, it was feared that their heretical and rebellious ideas were always likely to threaten the ideals of religious conformity as set out by Thomas Aquinas in his *Summa Theologiae*.

In France, the situation of the Protestant (Huguenot) minority was just as bad. On 24 August 1572 thousands of them were slaughtered in the St. Bartholomew massacre, and 26 years later Henry IV (of Navarre) introduced the Edict of Nantes in 1598 whereby Protestants were granted freedom of conscience.

However, in 1685, his grandson Louis XIV revoked the Edict and his French Protestants were again effectively removed from society with the drastic restriction of their rights for much the same reasons as the Jews in Spain: they had become too successful.

The Pope at the time (Innocent XI) thought the revocation to be an act of folly but Louis had his reasons. He was concerned that the Dutch, his Protestant enemy, were in contact with the Huguenots and by removing their status he would eliminate the 'enemy within'. As a result most of them fled to Germany, Holland and England, all very much to the detriment of France.

Having been particularly interested in English history of the 16th century, I was familiar with the fate meted out to William Tyndale in 1536 and to Thomas Cranmer some 20 years later as a result of religious intolerance in England at that time. Indeed I was a member of the William Tyndale Quincentenary Committee which had organised the 500th anniversary celebrations in 1994 of William Tyndale's birth, including services at more than 40 cathedrals and churches throughout Britain and abroad, but little did I realise then that my own ancestors had also met such grizzly ends at about the same time.

Two years before Tyndale's untimely but foreseeable death, Sir Thomas More had fallen out with Henry VIII over his dalliance with Anne Bolleyn.

In 1534 Henry had declared himself to be the supreme ruler of the world and above everyone else including even the Pope. He required all citizens to accept this "fact" by taking an oath of supremacy. Thomas More, a devout Catholic who had been knighted by Henry, refused and was charged with treason. Found guilty, he was beheaded in 1535 and missed out on the satisfaction of seeing himself canonized some 400 years later.

Referring back to Thomas Aquinas, he had not completed his 'Summa' at the time of his death in 1274, and although his theories were debated at length during his lifetime, and for 200 years thereafter, it was not until the work was published in book form in 1485 that his ideas were circulated to a much wider public.

From Spain the family and others would have gone into France and on to Italy (Livorno) and Greece (Salonika) before ending up at the opposite end of Europe in the Moslem Ottoman Empire, which at the time welcomed Jews. In fact when the Ottomans had conquered Spain and a large part of Europe, Jews had lived relatively peacefully under their rule and, as mentioned above, were permitted to occupy senior positions in government and in the professions.

Eventually they made their way to the Grand Duchy of Lithuania, which again at first welcomed Jews, although their activities there were very restricted. They were banned from the professions, universities and most occupations which is why so many of them had to engage in menial trades such as shoemaking or tailoring. Some 300 years later there were over 200,000 Jews in Lithuania and exceeding 300,000 in the Baltic countries overall, and by then, under Russian rule, antisemitism again became rife with, at first, occasional pogroms and then more frequent outbursts.

The Lithuanians and the Jews welcomed Napoleon when he led his troops there on their way to Moscow in 1812 and it is said that the Emperor consulted successors to the famed Vilna Gaon, the leading rabbi and sage, about their prospects. As Napoleon continued eastwards, the advice given must have been doubtful.

Later in the 19th century there were two major uprisings against the Russian oppressors which were savagely quelled by Czar Nicholas I and his son Alexander II, resulting in the closure of all Lithuanian newspapers and publishing houses in 1864. Towards the end of the 19th century the Jews realised that there was another world outside of the pale, or in their case the ghetto, and it was called America. However, there was one problem: how to get there when you had no money. Some managed to pack up and got as far as the British Isles where, since Cromwell's days, Jews (but not Catholics) were almost welcome.

My great-grandfather, who was married with some young children, decided to make the move in 1880 from the Lithuanian-Latvian border where they lived and found himself in Cork, which was a staging post for New York. Though most others had left Lithuania intending to travel via Germany to USA, Canada or South Africa, they lacked the funds to go all the way and got as far as Britain, finding employment there and hoping eventually to carry on their journeys to a new utopia.

The family name up to this time moved from the Spanish to the Greek and then to the Russian alphabets before reverting back to "English" on reaching the British Isles. And on the way numerous variants appeared: Illion, Aelion, Elion, Iljon and some others – but they are all related, if somewhat distantly, to the Elyans.

Those who arrived in Salonika from 1500 onwards were again made welcome by the Ottoman governors of Macedonia, who were made up of a series of Turkish pashas, and they all prospered for the next few hundred years.

While they did so, the original 20,000 who were invited to locate there grew steadily to 80,000, which was about 50% of the total population; the other 50% being made up equally of Christians and Moslems. It appears that these Jews never spoke much Greek or Turkish but continued to converse in Spanish and their own dialect of Ladino in their everyday life whether in banking or dock-working.

As my ancestors eventually moved on to the Grand Duchy of Lithuania, we became estranged from those that remained who were to experience great extremes of success and tragedy. Eventually the Greeks retook Macedonia and expelled the Turkish population (in 1923/24), while their attitude to their Jewish neighbours was not quite so benign as under the Ottomans. Many left for Egypt, particularly Alexandria, where the family name was changed to Aghion (causing even more confusion to historians) though the family prospered in the cotton trade until the 1950s when Colonel Nasser seized power and overthrew the Egyptian monarchy. Not long before, the majority of the dock-workers in Salonika (by now called Thessaloniki) emigrated to Haifa, in the new state of Israel established in 1948, and began to provide the same port-side services as they had done for centuries in Greece.

Those who stayed behind continued in the same occupations as previously – bakers, bankers, shopkeepers, etc., though there was a slow but steady stream of emigration to USA, Canada, Australia, Israel and other parts of Europe. Then in 1942 the Germans invaded Greece and proceeded to round up the 65,000 remaining Jews. They had been told they were to be "rehoused" in Poland and were to be dispatched there by train at the rate of 2,000 per day so that all of them would be removed within one month. Believing this to be true, a number of the families went out to purchase new, warm clothing because it was going to be so much colder up in Poland, while almost all of them left their house keys with neighbours until such time as they would be allowed to return home.

One relative I met in Thessaloniki in the spring of 2019, 94 year old Moshe ha-Elion, was dispatched by train with his family to Poland and, on arrival in Auschwitz, he was then separated from his parents and siblings. He never saw them again and later discovered that they had all been sent to the gas chambers within days of their arrival.

According to the records at the museum in Thessaloniki, some 240 "Elyans", whatever the spelling, were sent northwards, never to return.

The story of Moshe's survival is a most remarkable tale in the face of adversity and is described in a book he has written. He still remains a considerable celebrity in Thessaloniki and, despite his venerable age, he continues to be active, writing poetry, composing music and lecturing to students about his amazing experiences in the death camps.

CORK

The early days in Cork were not easy. There was a small Jewish community there which needed a minister which was a role the Rev. Meyer Elyan could fill. However, the community was very poor and they could not afford much in the way of payment, so he had to find some additional means of supporting his family. These new arrivals spoke little if any English though they were conversant with German, Russian and Polish. And they spoke Yiddish among themselves, which wasn't much use in the English or Irish countryside.

Though many of them had skills – as tailors, cabinet makers, furriers and even herring picklers – they needed to earn money quickly. They did not of course have the resources to start a business, so they took the only course open to them: they became pedlars. They managed to obtain goods, usually shoes and lengths of cloth, on credit from the wholesale warehouses in Cork, which they would then sell to customers in the villages and small towns in the countryside where there were no retail drapery or shoe stores. The goods themselves were sold on credit to customers who made weekly repayments. Those who sold the suiting material took the customers' measurements and had the lengths made up into three-piece suits which were delivered the following week. Surprisingly, they were able to make a living from these activities. Usually a number of these 'traders' would hire a pony and trap to get around the villages and my great-grandfather was allowed to join them provided his goods did not compete with theirs. As he was neither a tailor nor a shoemaker, he had to find something else that could be sold – so they decided he should stock up with holy pictures and rosary beads. As he had a long beard, he must have looked quite a sight.

The earliest immigrants, when they had managed to save some

money, then went on to open shops of their own in fields such as confectionary and tobacco, stationery and 'fancy goods', groceries and clothing. Despite the hardships and handicaps, they prospered at a modest level; and by hard work, their appreciation of learning and the need for a good education, their ambition was to ensure their children were enabled to attend university or to enter the professions. The Reverend Meyer did not stick to the pony and trap for very long as an early trade directory indicated that he had established his own (presumably small) business as a general merchant in Cork in 1881.

My two grandfathers came from Lithuania and Belarus (formerly White Russia) respectively and dealt in clothing on weekly terms on the one hand and in animal furs on the other. The male children became a civil servant, a chemist and a cabinet maker on the paternal side and a doctor and dentist on the maternal. Dad had to leave school in his early teens owing to his father's ill-health and became apprenticed to a cabinet maker in Cork. It is interesting to note that despite having little or no secondary education, he was able to quote poems learnt at junior school and great chunks of Shakespeare until old age.

The family grew up in Monerea Terrace, a row of small red-bricked artisans cottages opposite the gasworks in Cork, where money was so tight that Dad used to be sent out to collect lumps of coal that had fallen from the coal-carts on their way to the gasworks. I don't know how they all fitted into number 5 which had three bedrooms, no bathroom and one outside toilet at the end of a small garden which I can still remember. By the time Larry, the eldest, had passed the civil service exams and gone off to work in London, that still left Grandma Sarah, a widow, and five children as well as a lodger (who was essential to provide some regular cash each week). There were occasions at weekends when, to earn a little extra money, Dad was taken to the races by a kindly horse trainer, not to gamble or as a jockey (though he would probably have been small enough then) but to help look after the horses while the training staff were otherwise busy readying a horse for the next race. He got paid 6d, or about two-and-a-half pence for a full day's work. One of his memories was of old or sluggish horses having fistfuls of tobacco shoved up their backsides by the trainer so that they would look lively and frisky on entering the parade ring. The equine experience stood Dad in good stead later on when he befriended a local grocer who allowed him to borrow his horse and trap at weekends. I have recollections of us going out in the trap on a Sunday and it was great fun for a little boy (of about five or six) being up so high.

Looking back on those days between the two World Wars (before I was born) it is hard to believe that the seeds had already been sowed for one family member to become MP for Preston in 1945, defeating Randolph Churchill in the process, for a cousin to become Chief Justice of the South African Protectorates in 1955 and get a knighthood in 1970 (Sir Victor Elyan); for another cousin in USA to be awarded a Nobel Prize for medicine in 1988 (Dr Gertrude Elion); and for two more to become among the first life peers (Labour and Liberal) with seats in the House of Lords. Sam Segal (1902-1985) became Lord Segal of Wytham and was appointed a deputy speaker of the House of Lords while Basil Wigoder, QC (1921-2004), a chairman of the Liberal Party, became Lord Wigoder of Cheetham.

As I was growing up we didn't have a car or a telephone at home and TV sets didn't exist. I remember when we first got a phone on a line we shared with neighbours, perhaps about 1947, the sound of it ringing used to terrify my sister Doreen who would run screaming from the hall

5 Monerea Terrace (left), Cork

where it was located. The shared line meant that we had to wait for the neighbours to finish a call before we could make ours (and vice versa).

By this time Dad had set up a furniture making business in Adelaide Street and he used to cycle there from home at the Lough. When I started at the Grammar School, Dad made a wooden saddle which he fixed to the crossbar of his bike and used to take me to school before going on to work. I can't for the life of me remember how I got home.

Our first car was acquired in 1950 – a second-hand Ford Anglia – which Dad bought from a family friend after her husband died. I think it cost £250 and, believe it or not, I can still remember its number – PI 9510. It had a fabric panel on the roof that used to leak a little when it rained but we didn't complain and put up with the occasional drip.

There were no driving tests in those days and no driving schools so Dad arranged to have a few lessons from a lorry driver friend of his before acquiring the 'new' car. After some weeks we were due to go to Dublin to stay with Uncle Larry who now worked in the Irish Civil Service at Dublin Castle. Dad was a bit apprehensive about driving in the heavy traffic of Dublin so he brought his driving instructor along just in case we had any problems with the car or he couldn't find his way to Larry's flat in Fitzwilliam Square.

It was such a novelty to go out on car journeys at weekends and on the traffic-free roads of those days with Dad singing the popular songs of the day and the rest of us all joining in.

When Mum and Dad married in 1939, they bought a new semi-detached house at the Lough in Cork called 'Derrynane'. At that time Dad also owned a bungalow which he himself had built with friends at Crosshaven, a seaside resort not far from Cork, some five years previously. However, before the outbreak of the war, in which Ireland was neutral, there were still British troops stationed in Cork and at Fort Camden in Crosshaven. Unfortunately the bungalow's proximity to the Fort meant that it became out-of-bounds for safety reasons for the duration of the war and then, when it was recovered, it was sold so that the proceeds could be used to finance Dad's furniture premises in Adelaide Street.

In 1950 'Derrynane' was sold and we moved to a house called 'Croata' on the Glasheen Road, just in front of the Church of Ireland sports grounds where we used to play tennis and hockey. The house was purchased from Professor Tadgh O'Donoghue of the University College who had written books in Irish under the nom-de-plume 'Torna'. About a decade later we moved again to a new bungalow, 'Hillside', that was largely built by Dad on a site he had purchased on Rochestown Road. I think most of the woodwork was prepared at the factory. This was our last and nicest home in Cork. My sister Doreen had her engagement party there and my friends from Trinity College would come down to stay during the holidays. We were particularly busy entertaining during Dad's presidency of the Rotary Club. Of the many visitors who called I particularly remember the Christmas visits of the writer Frank O'Connor who had long been a family friend. Indeed a number of his short stories were based on humorous tales told to him by Uncle Larry.

Dad had always been interested in football. He played as a youngster but then work got in the way. As I was growing up he brought me regularly to see Cork Athletic play at the Mardyke and he got to know all the players and management. When in 1953 Cork Athletic reached the FAI Cup Final at Dalymount Park in Dublin, I was made the club mascot. It was a particularly unusual event that year as the opposing team was Evergreen United, another team from Cork, and that was the only time before or since that two Cork teams contested the final. The match ended as a two-all draw and unfortunately I could not attend the replay as I had to go to school. However, Cork Athletic won the match and afterwards there was a parade through Cork, with me and the team on the back of a lorry, and then appearances in Cork cinemas with the cup and a celebratory party at our house. The star of the match had been Raich Carter, who was a famous England international and who achieved notoriety when he was "signed on" by Cork for an enormous fee reputed to be £50 a week. As I write this, numerous footballers playing in England receive payments of more than £50,000 a week. C'est la vie.

Having I thought completed this chapter, I discovered a history of football in Cork by Plunkett Carter (2009) in which he referred to Raich Carter's fee as £50 per match plus his travel expenses, which compared with the Football Association's maximum of £14 per week at that time. "He helped Cork to the league and cup double in 1953... (and his) colossal wages were, it is believed, paid by Mr Elyan, who had a cabinet making business in Adelaide Street. Carter's appearances paid rich

The Rev Meyer Elyan
(Pastel by Sister Monica Kiersey)

David Elyan
My Grandfather

Marriage of David Elyan and Sarah
Hodes, Cork August 1901

Larry (back), Ray, Dad and Ethel
1909

dividends as attendances trebled whenever he played, and most importantly his brilliance ensured Cork Athletic's fourth consecutive FAI cup final appearance in 1953".

Now I had never heard that my father paid Carter's wages, though his generosity knew few bounds, and I am sure that if he had been asked he would have contributed willingly. Dad lived for a further 49 years and he never mentioned any contributions to me, though I do know that he remained in contact with Raich after he retired from football and, in 1994, wrote to Mrs Pat Carter, on Raich's death to express his sympathy: I have her reply. If the story was true he probably kept his secret from my mother also as she would have complained, quite justifiably, about his unnecessary extravagance. Cork Athletic went out of business four years later in 1957 due to "financial difficulties" and were succeeded by a new club named Cork Hibernians.

Mum and Dad's wedding. Cork June 1939

With Mum, Dad and Doreen, at
Youghal 1950s

Back: Dad, Hemmy and Arthur
Front: Ethel, Larry and Ray c. 1980

THE GREMSONS

Mum always considered herself to be better class than Dad. Her family, she used to explain, didn't live in a terraced house in 'Jewtown', but on higher ground in Rockboro Road. Her family were cultured – and they had an inside WC. Their cousins included the multi-talented Wigoder family of Dublin, Manchester and Leeds.

Mum's father, Sam Gremson, was born in Nevel Vitebsk, in White Russia, nowadays Belarus, the home town of Marc Chagall. Sam was born on 10 January 1887 and Marc on 7 July 1887. As both families were Hassidim (orthodox Jews), it is more than likely that they and their families would have known each other. Sam's father was a scribe, one of those devout individuals who spent their time in the laborious task of producing documents such as the Torah (five books of Moses) in the Hebrew script.

Sam probably arrived in Cork in about 1909 and by 1916, already married to Dora (née Clein), he had become a British subject. I have his original naturalization document which indicates that his former surname was Viazminsky. We will never know how he came to change it to Gremson, nor do we know how it became Viazminsky. Freddie Rosehill, a contemporary of Mum's, told me that his father Harry arrived in Cork at the same time as Sam. Freddie did not know his father's former surname and wondered how he came to be Rosehill. We do know that Sam's signature was witnessed by S. Spiro, JP. This Mr Spiro owned a jewellers shop and was known locally as 'Shmeryl'. He was the grandfather of Sir Jonathan Miller, the well-known theatre and opera director.

Sam was described as a general merchant and I remember that he traded in furs and pelts, which were used to make fur coats and stoles, from a former church (St. Peter's) in North Main Street.

Mum's mother, Dora, after whom my sister Doreen was named, was one of a number of daughters of Hersha and Feiga Clein who had settled in Cork in the 1880s. They were known locally as Fetta Hersh and Mumma Feiga; and Mum was called after Feiga, who was a Wigoder before she married. She was also a redhead.

Dora and her sister Eva were the only two of a number of Cleins to remain in Cork, while two other sisters emigrated to Atlanta, Georgia, where they married and provided me with Hoffman and Parkes cousins.

After Eva married Joe Levin, they went to live in Eva Villa, off Donovan's Road, very close to the University College. I recall going there for tea as a child during and after the War, and remember some rather frightening bamboos and bullrushes in the garden which were much taller than me. Grandma Dora was diabetic and one day, while going to visit her sister on the bus, she had a fatal heart attack on the Western Road. (My father's father died equally unexpectedly while attending a football match at the Mardyke). Uncle Joe Levin died not long afterwards, at which time Auntie Eva came to live with us at the Lough until her death in 1949. The Levins did not have any children of their own which probably explained why they could afford a car – and they doted over Mum as the daughter they never had. After Eva died, Grandpa Sam took her place and joined us at the Lough until he died little more than a year later. I used to visit him during his final illness at the Bon Secours Hospital in College Road.

The Gremsons always seemed to have a cousin or two to stay at Rockboro Road while they attended University College Cork (UCC). These were the Lentins whose home was some 60 miles away in Limerick and at least three of the boys – Jack, Louis and Micky – all managed to study medicine while staying there. Mum was closest to Micky and they studied together as well as practicing the violin.

As a small boy I remember meeting Max Gremson, who was Grandpa Sam's nephew, but who was actually older than his uncle – something I just couldn't get my head around – and which they found most amusing. With much smaller families these days, I expect that sort of thing is now far less likely to be encountered. My father's mother, for example, was the eldest of 13 children and as a teenager she acted as surrogate mother for her youngest siblings.

Max appears to have been something of a Russian intellectual. He became friendly with Professor Alfred O'Rahilly, President of UCC, with whom he played regular games of chess, and in addition Max taught O'Rahilly some Russian while the Professor taught him some Irish. Max arrived in Cork from London in about 1917 and became a fervent Irish nationalist. Mum recalled that he was also thought to be a member of the IRA, which was probably true, as there was a ladder kept in the back yard, propped against a wall, for his escape if the British army or the local police came looking for him.

It was amazing that from a meagre income Sam managed to send four of his five children to university. Harry studied medicine, Percy dentistry, Ray commerce and Sadie science. Only Mum, the fourth, did not attend despite the fact that she was considered to be the most academically gifted of the five. Instead she married Dad and always regretted her lack of further education, though she acknowledged that Dad had offered to finance her through a degree course some years later. At Rochelle School, created by the descendants of Huguenot settlers in 1829, Mum was a gifted pupil who won many prizes (a number of which I have retained). She also played hockey and tennis for the school and won some medals for her swimming. There is a nice photograph of her in the Rochelle School history when she was in the 5th form (1934).

As a teenager Mum played the violin in the Cork Symphony Orchestra and, later, was a member of the committee of the Cork Orchestral Society. I don't ever remember her playing the violin and believe she gave up after Doreen was born when she was seriously ill. However, she gave me every encouragement to learn the piano, but I think I was too young at the time or perhaps far more interested in football (encouraged by my father). Still, when it was decided I should give up the piano as a waste of my time and their money, she persevered with my musical education and brought me to concerts and particularly operas whenever possible. For this I shall be eternally grateful. It gave me the greatest pleasure years later to be able to reciprocate in some small measure and arrange for her and Dad to visit London to hear Luciano Pavarotti sing at the Royal Albert Hall; and for them both to return there to celebrate Mum's 80th birthday on 17 July 1998, the first night of that year's Prom season, for a rather special performance of Gounod's "Damnation of Faust" featuring Bryn Terfel and Ann Murray.

A special surprise was managing to arrange to have supper during the interval in the Royal Retiring Room – just four of us – but please don't tell Her Majesty: she might not be pleased or amused.

Sam Gremson's love of education and his considerable sacrifices to enable his children to attend university would be stupendous by today's standards but they were nothing out of the ordinary at the time. Other Cork families (or at least the Jewish ones) did the same. The Newmans and the Marcuses were just as education minded and sent four or five children to university from equally meagre resources.

Solly Marcus had a small picture-framing business in Adelaide Street and of his children Brammy (Abraham) studied medicine, went on to become medical correspondent of *The Observer* and, later, established a successful medical magazine publishing company; David studied law, became a barrister and then literary editor of two national newspapers in Dublin – *The Irish Press* and *The Irish Independent.* He also founded two literary magazines – *Irish Writing* and *Poetry Ireland.* Their sister Nella studied music and became secretary to Sir Ted Lewis, chairman of Decca, while Jakie-Lou (Louis) got an arts degree and became a film-maker with Gael-Linn in Dublin. When she was 60, Solly's wife Fanny had an article published in *The Irish Times* on the subject of turning 60. A day or two later Dad met Solly in the street and congratulated him on having so many writers in the family. Solly retorted: 'I'm still the only one, Max, who can write a cheque.'

Other families of note were the Schers and the Birkhahns. Isaac Scher was a successful dentist in Sydney Place with an amazing collection of glass and a suit of armour in the hall which fascinated us children. His four sons all qualified as dentists also, and two of them additionally as doctors. The eldest, Eric, went on to become professor of dentistry at Queen's University, Belfast. The Birkhahns who lived in McCurtain Street were almost as unusual. Father Joe, a dentist, also had four children: two boys and two girls with one of each becoming a doctor or a dentist. Joe's own father came from Lithuania where he had trained in the Baltic fish pickling business. Arriving in Cork he soon set up in the same line at Bantry, some 56 miles west of Cork. He and his wife both lived until well into their late 90s.

Mum's two older brothers, Harry and Percy, were almost inseparable from their school days although I never thought they looked like brothers, one being very fair and the other quite dark. After they qualified in medicine and dentistry respectively, both went to work in Manchester. Some years later they both volunteered for military service in World War Two. As Ireland was neutral, they could not be conscripted but like many young Irishmen at the time felt it was their duty to 'fight for their country'. Harry was sent to the Far East and Percy to Palestine. While in Burmah, Harry contracted a disease and had to return home on a stretcher. Although he recovered somewhat and recommenced working as a GP in Prestwich, he never regained good health, developed angina and died before his time.

Percy met Lilly, a Sabra, while in Palestine, married at her family home in Tel Aviv and they too later settled in Manchester. As children Doreen and I used to stay with them in Great Clowes Street over the dental practice. Sadly Lilly died in her late 30s and Percy of a heart attack at 60.

Auntie Ray, Mum's older sister married Joe Toubkin in 1937. Joe was London-born and a Cambridge educated engineer who spent his entire working life overseas with Shell in places such as Romania, Norway and South Africa. They retired to Australia but later moved to Knightsbridge where they remained until their respective deaths in the 1990s. On one of their regular visits to Cork, when they realised that I had become interested in classical music, they went out and bought me two long-playing records: Mozart's No. 41 symphony (the Jupiter) and Sibelius's 2nd. The first would have been an obvious choice perhaps but the second was something of a rarity and therefore amazing. I simply loved it, and almost all of Sibelius's works which I subsequently discovered. On a visit to Helsinki some years later, I just had to visit Ainola, Sibelius's home from 1904 until his death in 1957, so that I could pay my respects to the Finnish master.

Auntie Sadie, Mum's younger sister, went to Matlock in Derbyshire after graduating where she taught science in a convent for some years. After Grandpa Sam died in 1950 she came to live with us at the Lough during the school holidays and acted as my second mother, spoiling me terribly. After a few years at Matlock, during which time her family must have concluded that she was not likely to meet the right sort of Jewish boy in a convent, she was persuaded to emigrate and went to stay with her Aunt Ada Hoffman in Atlanta. There she met and married Herman

Zager, a Latvian-born photographer, and together they moved to Cartersville – not connected to Jimmy Carter – where she remained until her death in 2003. She and Herman are buried alongside each other in Rome, Georgia.

Mum died in hospital at Newport, Isle of Wight, aged 88 on 22 August 2006, four years after Dad, having suffered for some years with dementia. She was the last of her generation and is buried next to Dad in the old Hebrew cemetery in Cheltenham. A restful place if ever there was one.

Painting of Mum (oil by Tilly Willis, 1992)

Gremson home at Rockboro Avenue, Cork

Grandpa Sam, Grandma Dora, Auntie Eva and Uncle Joe (Levin), Youghal, 1940s

Marriage of Sam Gremson and Dora
Clein, Cork April 1911

Back: Percy and Harry
Front: Mum, Sadie and Ray c.1930

Uncle Joe and Auntie Eva at Eva Villa, Cork, 1940s

EDUCATION

It is usual, I understand, in a book of an autobiographical nature, to include some paragraphs about one's education and schooling. It might not make for a long or an interesting chapter.

My schooling commenced after the war in 1945 at Cork Grammar School, then located in Sydney Place, Cork, up St. Patrick's Hill, and filled with Georgian houses full of doctors and other professionals. When you got to the top of the hill, and stopped to get your breath back, there were superb views looking down over the city. However, all I can remember of the building was the entrance which had an arch of ironwork and the date '1881" placed in the centre.

After some years the school moved to a new location when the Incorporated Society for Promoting Protestant Schools in Ireland purchased a detached old house called 'Ashton' in some acres of grounds at Blackrock, on the outskirts of Cork. As the school was never very large, usually having 120 to 150 pupils, it was able to expand in its new home which had the added attraction of hockey and cricket pitches as well as a number of tennis courts. I think my parents chose the school on the basis of its small size. While there I played all three games without distinguishing myself at any of them. At 16 I passed the Intermediate Certificate examination with honours and the Leaving Certificate two years later. My only real achievement there was in art where I won a national competition sponsored by Caltex, a Canadian petrol company. I don't know what became of my original artwork, although I have retained the award certificate most carefully.

At 18 I went to Trinity College, Dublin, to study for a commerce degree (B.Comm). This was called a professional degree (along with the likes of medicine and engineering) and was a four-year course similar to the Scottish system.

Confronted by so many non-Irish students, who were mostly older than me, it was apparent that I was going to have to work quite hard if I were going to pass my end-of-year exam the following June. Many of these older students were British and following schooling were required to do National Service. By the time they had completed this they were already in their twenties and in some cases had then to attend a "crammer" for a year to obtain the grades that would get them to university.

Trinity College in those days was very much a "Protestant" university, created by Elizabeth I in 1592. In Catholic Ireland of the 1950s and 60s, the "liberal" teaching and attitudes of the university were anathema to the Catholic church, so much so that the Archbishop of Dublin, John Charles McQuaid, banned Catholics from attending. The only "let-out" for Catholics who wished to study there was for lapsed Catholics to ignore the Archbishop's diktat and risk going to hell. Alternatively, those educated at Catholic schools in England, such as Ampleforth or Downside, were able to claim that as they had not studied Irish, they would not be able to gain admission to any of the other Irish universities. (It was discovered later that the bigoted Dr McQuaid had for many years turned a blind eye to the physical and sexual abuse of children by his clergy in Dublin and elsewhere).

In those days Trinity was largely funded by private benefactors and bequests, most notably from members of the Guinness family, but with increasing costs it was becoming practically impossible for private individuals to continue in this way. Thus it became necessary for the Irish government to meet the shortfall and this of course came at a price – which was that the university should become much more 'Irish'. Today more than 80% of undergraduates are both Catholic and Irish.

Having worked diligently in my first year and having passed the exam, supposedly the most difficult of the four years, because we were told it enabled the authorities to weed out the poorer students, I felt I could relax somewhat and take an interest in the many other activities that were available. I had hoped to play cricket but ran into a difficulty in that the season started after Easter and I had to take the annual exam in June, some two months later, so no hanging about then in the outfield.

I joined the college newspaper *Trinity News* and soon found myself writing a weekly column which I continued for nearly three years. It was a social column called 'Four and Six', which had been created before I arrived on the scene. The name came from the fact that the Gents toilets in Front Square were located at No. 4 while the Ladies were at No. 6. The column consisted of the latest gossip and reports on parties and, although my articles were written anonymously, it didn't take long before people knew the name of the author. Though I denied any involvement, the news did me no harm and my social life improved greatly because would-be party givers generally liked the idea of reports appearing in the paper. I should mention that in those far-off days invitations were almost always printed and some were even gilt-edged as well.

Around the same time as I started on *Trinity News*, I also joined a literary magazine called *Icarus* which was all about poetry, short stories and book reviews with occasional articles on exhibitions and performing arts. My job was business manager, which meant I had to go around the city soliciting adverts from bookshops, pubs and restaurants to keep us afloat. It wasn't an easy task but I was helped by the fact that our advertising rates were very low and, in general, the managers of the businesses approached were well disposed towards respectful students.

In 1961 I and some others decided to launch a new literary magazine which we called *The Dubliner*. We raised a few hundred pounds as working capital to get us started and to my amazement the publication continued in existence for some 13 years. It was moderately successful and although we never made any money, we were, thankfully, guaranteed against loss by the Irish Arts Council (whose secretary, Mervyn Wall, happened to be a friend of Uncle Larry). There is more about this under "Work that remained in progress".

Other activities in which I participated were the College Historical Society, believed to be the world's oldest debating society – again more about this under "The Hist" – and the DU Gramophone Society founded by my good friend Russell Telfer who was able to tell any of Beethoven's symphonies or concertos from hearing a couple of bars of the music.

My summers were spent partly on holiday jobs to earn money which would then enable me to spend the remainder of the vacation abroad. The first of my jobs was working for Eskimo Frozen Foods in Cleethorpes where I donned a blue boiler suit and packed frozen peas. After six or so weeks of wearing the same boiler suit, without washing it, it did rather smell somewhat, but then so did all the others. I'm not sure if this had any effect on the packed peas.

The work in Cleethorpes involved very long shifts, mostly of 12 hours or more but we didn't complain because we knew the money would build up while we couldn't spend it. Our only indulgences were taking out the factory girls we worked alongside. Many of them were quite pretty though we had the greatest difficulty understanding their accents. Still, on our time off, all that was forgotten when we took them out, usually to a pub or two followed by a visit to the aptly named Pleasure Gardens before returning "home". Home was usually a room in a small terraced house run by a fisherman's wife, whose family were at sea for most of the week. We paid two pounds ten shillings for bed and a cooked breakfast.

At the time (1960), Grimsby, a couple of miles down the road, was reputed to be the world's biggest fishing port. When I visited the docks there soon after my arrival I was amazed by the rows and rows of hundreds of small black trawlers which were harbour-bound over the weekends. Having a need to visit the Gents, I was surprised to see a sign above the urinal which said in large letters "VD CAN BE CURED". It was probably not so surprising in the world's biggest fishing port to see that somebody had written underneath in pencil "and so can kippers".

Holidays afterwards were spent travelling by car to Denmark via France, Belgium, Holland and Germany in Russell's new pale blue Triumph Herald. We discovered that almost all Danish girls were blonde, wore dark blue pullovers and jeans, and cycled everywhere. At least that is my memory of them – and our training with the Cleethorpes factory girls came in very useful. Subsequent holidays were spent on the French and Italian rivieras – areas I have adored ever since.

The following year at Eskimo I received a promotion and had a deskbound job following up on invoices that had been queried. No more smelly boiler suits – and we were allowed to continue working long hours including over weekends when there was nobody in the offices apart from a couple of dozen students. On one Sunday we decided to have a cricket match in one of the long open-plan offices, so all the desks and tables had to be moved to one side of the room to prepare for the bowlers run-up. After the match ended we replaced the desks as best we could, which of course was not very well, so that when our supervisor arrived for work the following morning she was horrified by the state of the office and exclaimed 'anyone would think you had been playing cricket here.' If she only knew the truth…..

Having graduated in 1962, my father wanted me to study accountancy but I had discovered that I would prefer to become a chartered secretary – not an occupation that had ever been mentioned by the careers officer at school or the appointments office at Trinity. The exams were somewhat easier and I would get paid, whereas if I had gone for Chartered Accountancy I would have been articled to a principal who would receive a premium which would then be repaid to me over three years. I knew my father would have supported me willingly but, having financed me at university for four years, I thought it was time for me to attempt to stand on my own two feet.

We arrived at a good compromise because I found a job with a firm of accountants in Dublin where I could do some accountancy and auditing work while simultaneously taking charge of the firm's company secretarial functions and, in the evenings, attend classes at Rathmines College of Commerce. So unused was I to full-time work after four years of a leisurely existence that I frequently nodded off during the lectures. I think the lecturers must have been used to this happening because they never said a word to me about my somnolence.

In order to qualify as a Chartered Secretary I had to enrol as a student of the Institute which would lead to the ACIS qualification. A few months' later I noticed that there was another similar organisation in existence, the Corporation of Secretaries, whose syllabus was very similar to that of the Institute and whose qualification was the ACCS. For very little extra effort and some additional fees I could work towards obtaining both qualifications. So far so good. Eventually I passed both sets of exams and received my two certificates – but a few years later, to my dismay, both of the organisations decided to merge and I've ended up with one qualification.

After graduating from Trinity and before moving to London at the beginning of 1966, while working in Dawson Street and studying in the evenings, I managed to have an enjoyable social life.

There were race-meetings on Saturday afternoons at a number of racecourses close to the centre of Dublin, which meant you could have lunchtime drinks and a sandwich in a Dublin bar – Jury's, the Dolphin or the Shelbourne hotels come readily to mind – and at that time on a Saturday many of the customers at these establishments were knowledgeable about or (better still) involved with racehorses, so that 'tips' were readily available.

Then when the racing was over, it was back into Dublin again for yet more drinks at the above or other bars and eventually on to somebody's party. Luckily there were friends with cars to get me there. Sometimes, when the car-owner decided it was time to get going, we had just begun to drink the next pint of Guinness. As there was not time to 'knock it back', we'd take the pints with us and drink them in the car on the way to our destination – and then leave the mugs in our host's or hostesses' kitchen. They must have wondered in the morning how all the empty pint mugs had got there.

It reminds me that when somebody once said to Brendan Behan that the wealthy Guinness family were very good to the people of Dublin, he replied 'yes, but you must remember the people of Dublin have also been very good to the Guinnesses'.

Apart from the racing, it was easy in those days to get tickets for rugby internationals at Lansdowne Road or for tennis tournaments at the Fitzwilliam Lawn Tennis Club. After Wimbledon, a number of players would turn up in Dublin to play in the much more relaxed atmosphere of the Irish Open and as the spectators were so close to the players, you could almost touch them from your seat. The player I particularly admired was the Brazilian Marie Bueno who not only looked so elegant on court but who also went on to win 19 grand slams.

In 1965 I began to 'step out' with Jinnie Mahon, daughter of Sir George Mahon, head of the Guinness & Mahon merchant bank in Dame Street, Dublin. As she was an attractive and classy girl, for our first date I thought I could not possibly take her to a Dublin pub where, very likely, we would bump into friends and get jostled about in a crowd. So instead I thought I'd take her to dinner in the Shelbourne Hotel. In those days the Shelbourne had a very popular burger bar – with a fried egg on top of the burger – but they also had a very pleasant up-market restaurant so I booked a table there.

When we arrived and entered the dining room, I was a little surprised to find the head waiter welcoming Jinnie like an old friend. As he led us to our table at the far end of the room, there were some little old ladies having dinner alone and each one greeted my companion like some long-lost friend. Jinnie said to each 'lovely to see you Mrs O'Reilly' or perhaps 'how nice to see you again Miss MacDonough'. I was understandably puzzled as to how she knew all of these people and, when we got to our table, asked 'how come?' She replied that the Shelbourne was owned by a company called Trust House Forte Ireland and her father just happened to be its chairman. Every Christmas he invited all the permanent residents in the hotel to join him and his family for dinner at their home in Castleknock on the outskirts of Dublin.

Before and after leaving Dublin for London, I was invited to be best man at the weddings of three of my friends and a prospective brother-in-law within a relatively short period of time: Russell Telfer married Isobel in Dorset, Peter O'Clery married Caroline at Chelsea Old Church, Quentin Crivon married Louise in Belfast and Harold Woolfe married my sister Doreen. I remember the services very well indeed, something of the receptions, but not a word of any of the speeches. Perhaps it had something to do with the post-nuptial drinks. What do they say about always a best man but never a groom, or have I mixed my metaphors? In any event I must have been good at something even if it was only keeping wedding rings in my pocket during the services.

Graduation Day, 1962

Marriage of Peter and Caroline O'Clery
at Chelsea Old Church, Sept. 1966

Marriage of Doreen and Harold Woolfe,
1965

With Russell Telfer at Woolland, Dorset, August 1979

SCHULL

As mentioned elsewhere, as a family we spent some of our summer holidays at Schull, on the coast about 70 miles west of Cork, where we stayed at O'Driscoll's East End Hotel. Despite the beautiful local scenery, there wasn't a lot to occupy a schoolboy of 15 or 16, either at the hotel or in Schull itself, and at the same time the parents must have wondered what to do with me for a whole week or more.

As luck would have it, Dad discovered that a local trawler owner was willing to take me off his hands for a day or two by arranging for me to join one of his boats. The price seemed to be 6 bottles of Guinness for the crew who would have to put up with my getting in their way.

Departure time was to be 4 a.m. from the quayside with the return approximately 12 hours later.

Getting up early has never been a problem for me and going down to the quayside from the hotel, just as the sun was thinking of rising, there wasn't a soul in sight. Returning would be very different: the harbour wall would be crowded with hoteliers, housewives and vans awaiting our arrival, to see what the trawler had collected from the sea before the bulk of the catch was transported by road to fish merchants in Cork, Limerick and Dublin.

After we set off to the fishing grounds – indicated to our skipper on his radar screen, probably a novelty in those days – we motored for a couple of hours before slowing down so that the nets could be trawled behind us and I could watch while the crew were busy getting ready to welcome the catch after some further hours of drifting.

Then the excitement really began. The nets were winched aboard loaded with wriggling masses of all sorts and sizes of fish sparkling in the sunlight. As the catch was unloaded on to the deck I noticed mackerel, monkfish, octopuses and many other sorts that I didn't recognise. They were being sorted out into those that were wanted and those that were surplus to requirements. The wanted ones were put in appropriate boxes bearing the fish merchants' names and packed with ice. The unwanted were thrown back in the sea while all the gulls in the area wheeled and screamed overhead in excitement.

Among the undesirables were ugly catfish and dogfish – I didn't and still don't know the difference – and for a joke a couple of the crew dared me to kill a catfish and handed me a spade with which to perform the execution.

I brought the spade down with all my might on the unfortunate creature but after the impact, which would probably have killed a human, it kept on wriggling as if it had merely been tickled. Ever more furious as the crew laughed at my efforts, I tried even harder with the spade but eventually had to admit defeat. A crew member showed me how he would do it. He picked up the fish and tore off its ears at which point thick, dark red blood dripped on to the deck and the fish was no longer alive.

Not a pleasant tale perhaps but part of a day's life on board a trawler which remains in the memory.

As I left my new friends to head back to the hotel, I was given a large brill which was freshly cooked for us that evening and shared with some of our fellow guests. It was so delicious that for many a year now I have been looking for one as enjoyable.

Another recollection of the time was being impressed that the local Church of Ireland rector was actually called Bishop Jagoe, but I couldn't understand how a Bishop could be in charge of such a small church in such an out-of-the-way place. At the time one of my sister's best friends was the daughter of the Bishop of Cork, George Otto Simms, who went on to become Archbishop of Dublin and Primate of All Ireland, and he and his family lived in a rather grand if dilapidated palace overlooking St. Finbarr's cathedral in Cork.

The answer was that Jagoe had previously been the Bishop of Bermuda before taking up his appointment in Schull where he retired to a country house nearby.

With the advent of the annual Schull regatta I was asked if I would like to join the crew of Teddy Pope's yacht for a day's racing. I jumped at the opportunity.

The racing was pretty uneventful with competitors travelling from as far as Belfast and Dun Laoghaire as well as more locally from Cork and Crosshaven; and though we did a lot of rushing about, which probably deserved some reward for effort, we didn't exactly cover ourselves in glory on that occasion, nor did we win any prizes. Probably having me on board didn't help though I hope my extra ballast might have come in useful.

At the end of the day we all adjourned to O'Keeffe's Bar, just down the road from the East End Hotel and, as you can imagine, the place was heaving with 30 or 40 sailors in smelly jumpers and jeans, making a most enormous amount of noise with everybody shouting at the tops of their voices.

Teddy and his friends thought it was great fun having me along as, strictly speaking, I was too young to be allowed to drink in a pub and they knew that my father would have been none too pleased. Nevertheless even at that tender age I had begun to develop a liking for Guinness which hasn't left me to this day.

After we had been there for an hour or so and the noise couldn't have got any louder, the door suddenly opened and a short, plump man with a moustache entered. He was in shirt sleeves, wearing a tie and yellow braces, and seemed so out of place among a crowd of sweaty sailors that he could only have been a foreigner.

His sudden appearance reminded me of one of those Wild West films where John Wayne would enter a saloon bar via the swing doors with his hands on his guns while the locals drank, danced or played cards. Suddenly the music and the dancing would stop and all was silent while Wayne strolled up to the bar counter in his inimitable way.

Well, O'Keeffe's Bar was just like that. Everybody suddenly froze while the newcomer pushed his way towards the counter while dozens of pairs of eyes watched him silently.

When he reached the bar counter he addressed the barman: "I say, would you possibly have a bottle of Beaujolais in stock?" he enquired in a frightfully English accent.

The barman didn't answer but turned around and faced some shelves which were loaded with wine bottles. He looked for a while and then picked one out, turned towards the customer and asked "will this do oo, sir?". The Englishman replied "that's absolutely splendid. How much do I owe you?". "That'll be seven and six pence, sir", and with that the visitor paid and departed without a further word being said.

The local population wasn't known for Saturday evening dinner parties and I wondered if he was going to be a guest of the Bishop and Mrs Jagoe on the outskirts of the village.

As soon as the door closed behind him the noise level got going again. Some shouted at the barman "would oo have another bottle of that Bojolly stuff, Michael?"

It was as if the school teacher had left the class momentarily while he went outside for a fag.

I can't think why that story has stuck in my memory for so long when there were so many much more important events to remember later on.

AND AFTER

In the meantime at the end of 1965 I had decided to move to London because the employment possibilities were better than in Dublin. My ideal job would have been in book publishing but all opportunities in that area seemed to go to family friends of the directors of publishing companies or family members of their favourite authors – and I had no such family contacts. Instead I found a property development company which needed an assistant company secretary and, as this was better than nothing, I grasped the job and started with them at the beginning of 1966. In fact it was far better than nothing because the company, Stock Conversion, was quoted on the London Stock Exchange, which gave me very useful experience of dealing with a 'listed' company; and the job offered accommodation in one of the company's apartments in the West End of London which was destined to be redeveloped at some stage. I was given a choice of three: Berkeley Square, Dover Street or Wigmore Street, from which I chose the latter and remained there for two years, opposite the wine merchants Findlater, Mackie and Todd – best known for their "Dry Fly" sherries. It was about a 20 minute pleasant walk from there to the company's offices in Jermyn Street.

The flat was above Plato's Greek restaurant and had come available due to the demise of Mr Plato who, I discovered on moving there, had been a habitué of a number of London casinos and for many months later invitations (still printed) continued to arrive inviting him and a guest to dinner. These were willingly accepted and greatly enjoyed by me and girlfriends while they lasted.

Stock Conversion was created as a property development company by Robert Clark and Joe Levy in 1958. The story goes that Robert Clark, born in Paisley, studied law at Glasgow University and while there founded the Glasgow University Film Society. On graduating he became a trainee solicitor with the Glasgow firm of Maxwells. However, after failing some exam or other, he was summoned to a meeting with the senior partner 'to discuss his future'. During the discussion Mr Maxwell mentioned that there was an opening in his family cinema business for a manager – would Mr Clark be interested? He was; so he left the law firm and joined the film business. With the enormous expansion of cinema in the 1920s and 1930s, the business grew to be one of the largest cinema chains in the UK with more than 400 outlets at its peak in 1951. The company by then was called Associated British Picture Corporation, it had become a public company, and included British Pathé News, Elstree Studios and ABC TV – one of the first commercial TV companies in the UK. Somewhere along the line Mr Clark had married one of Mr Maxwell's daughters.

Joe Levy on the other hand had been born in the East End of London and established a successful estate agency business with his brother David – DE and J Levy. Clark and Levy worked very well together despite their differences. Levy was described by Oliver Marriott, in his book "The Property Boom" as 'a small jovial man'. He also had a loud raucous voice. His estate agency offices were in the same building as Stock Conversion and whenever he took the lift up to our floor, we could hear him even before the lift doors had opened. He was very much the showman. He had two Rolls-Royces, JOE 8 and JOE 30; and he spent his weekends at his Henley-on-Thames home called "Up the Creek". Clark on the other hand was as quiet as Levy was loud and he occupied the Chairman's suite at the top of the building. On the few occasions I had to visit him there I was surprised to find him, quietly, reading French poetry.

Stock Conversion undertook some major developments in London, often through jointly-owned companies with the likes of George Wimpey, Friends Provident and some investment companies. The best-known of the developments in my time was Euston Centre which included the Euston Road underpass. The total site area was over 20 acres and it took more than 20 years to piece it together, with land purchases often being made through small companies to avoid undue attention. Although many of these companies had Scottish names, presumably chosen by Clark, the more interesting names had been chosen by Levy. One of them was amusingly called CTFOL Ltd. – standing for Changing the Face of London Limited. A few weeks after I joined the company I was appointed secretary of a few of these subsidiaries and one of my first meetings was at 117 Old Broad Street, the headquarters of Harley Drayton's Old Broad Street Group. When I got there I was shown into the boardroom where one of the directors was already at work. I introduced myself, saying I had only been at Stock Conversion a short while. Mr O welcomed me, saying I was working for a most remarkable company run by a Scotsman and a Jew. 'The Jewman makes the money and the Scotsman hangs onto it'.

At the time it was certainly one of the most successful property development companies in Britain and for many years after I left the group I followed its fortunes and remained good friends with some of its senior people. About 17 years later, after Clark and Levy had retired, the company was acquired by Jeffrey (later Lord) Sterling's Guarantee Trust and merged with P&O in 1985. I'm not sure who owns the properties nowadays but its most likely to be some Middle Eastern sovereign fund.

After two years in the property business, I eventually managed to find a job in publishing with George Rainbird who ran the book interests of the Thomson Organisation as well as being the founder of the International Wine and Food Society. I had to leave my little flat in Wigmore Street and found a much larger mansion flat in St. Mary's Mansions, Little Venice, but needed to find one or two mates to share with. As it happened a young Australian newly arrived in London was looking for accommodation and we were introduced through a mutual friend. Peter Cromer moved in and explained that he was about to start work with IBM in St John's Wood. He had a Czech background but had been born in Sydney, went to school there, obtained a Commerce degree from the University of New South Wales, qualified as an accountant and then joined IBM in Sydney. After a while, and like many young Aussies, he wanted to travel abroad and found he could best do this if based in London. I remember him returning rather shocked to the flat after experiencing his first day in the office. His shock was not caused by the pressure of work but on finding that his supervisor had been a classmate of his at school who, on leaving, had not gone to university or qualified as an accountant, but gone straight into IBM and risen through the ranks.

Later, Peter was telling me about his family history. His maternal grandfather had been a wealthy businessman in Prague from a Jewish background. In I think 1938 he was a widower with two daughters, one of whom was Peter's mother. One night there was a knock on the door and a neighbour had called to say that Jews were being rounded up. The daughters who were in bed should be woken up, they should pack suitcases and get a train from the railway station as quickly as possible, which is what they did. After much travelling they eventually ended up in Australia, having left their home with all its contents. Peter's grandfather had been an art collector and his collection had of course remained behind also. From Australia the family were in contact with the neighbours who said they had taken in the paintings and some furniture but the house had been taken over by the authorities.

When Peter told me the story he said he was hoping while he was in Europe to visit Prague, meet the neighbours and see where his family had lived. At the time it wasn't easy to travel behind the Iron Curtain, to bring gifts or to make any purchases whilst there. Eventually he and another Australian friend decided to go to Prague by car – rather bravely in a second-hand mini – and, I'm pleased to report, they arrived back safely. While there the neighbours showed Peter the pictures they had gathered up before the house was taken over and pointed out the difficulty in attempting to take any of the pictures to the UK. Eventually they hit on a plan. Firstly, remove the picture from its frame; secondly, visit the local flea-market and find a picture with a fairly similar content; and, thirdly, get a receipt for it. Then dispense with the flea-market item and see if the original painting and the new receipt would get past the customs officials at the border.

The plan went well and the picture duly arrived back in the UK. Peter then brought it to one of the leading auctioneers, Christie's or Sotheby's, and see if they could identify it. The expert said he believed it was by Maurice Vlaminck but that the world expert on this painter was in Paris – a certain Daniel Kahnweiler (1884-1979), rather elderly at the time – and he should be consulted. So Peter wrote to him. He replied saying he was sufficiently familiar with Vlaminck's work to be able to say from a good quality photograph if it was genuine. Peter sent a photo and the expert confirmed that it was indeed an original piece. After Peter returned to Australia, I heard from him now and again, and received an occasional card from Prague which indicated that he was probably collecting further pictures there, though of course after the collapse of the Soviet Union his task probably became a lot easier.

The 1960s were of course fabulous years to have been in London. Visitors came from everywhere to visit the King's Road, Carnaby Street, Portobello Road and the 20 or so department stores in London at that time – now reduced to about five or six. In addition, it was easy to get tickets for all the major sporting events such as Wimbledon, Henley, Twickenham and Ascot. Though I didn't have a car, I had friends who did and every year, for example, we would go to Arundel for the start of the cricket season which commenced with a one-day match between the Duke of Norfolk's XI and the visiting tourists.

As it was too far and too expensive for me to go home (to Cork) for weekends, friends very kindly invited me to their family homes for weekends or Sunday lunches. Grateful for the invitations, I was nevertheless envious that on these visits the mothers would attend to the laundry and usually gave their children a supply of goodies for the following week which might include half a pheasant, a cake and some marmalade, while I had to spend an hour or two in a launderette every fortnight.

In the main, the London pubs we frequented are still there: the City Barge at Strand-on-the-Green, the Chelsea Potter, the Cheshire Cheese at Fleet Street and the Bunch of Grapes on the Brompton Road which was our second home. A number have, of course, disappeared such as the Grenadier in Wilton Mews (where I once had a conversation with Lee Marvin without knowing who he was) and the Star Tavern in Belgrave Mews which was run by Paddy Kennedy, a rather disagreeable Irish ex-boxer who, if he took a dislike to you, would not allow you to go upstairs to watch football on the TV. That service was reserved for an honoured few who included Richard Harris, Christine Keeler and yours truly.

Before I arrived on the scene, the Star had originally catered for the servants who worked in the posh Belgravia houses nearby, but it wasn't until the 1960s that this tavern in a quiet mews became a pub with a history.

In 1963 the Great Train Robbery was planned by Bruce Reynolds and his friends in the upstairs room, where they met in groups of four to avoid arousing suspicion. The celebrity line-up in those days included Bing Crosby, Princess Margaret, Peter O'Toole and Diana Dors, as well as the wrong-doers "who all held a curious retro glamour".

Saturday afternoons were for strolling along the King's Road, preferably with a girl on your arm, and in my case AP fitted the bill admirably. She was a Southern Rhodesian, platinum blonde and wore a black bowler which certainly turned heads. I was in my element.

Saturday mornings were spent visiting art galleries and antiquarian bookshops. After the Times Bookshop had closed in Wigmore Street, I used to visit the second-hand department at Foyle's, run by Ronald Batty (husband of Christina Foyle who owned the eponymous store) and Bertram Rota's cramped but fascinating establishment in Vigo Street. I still have the books I bought then: Hours Press books from Mr Batty and copies of the stylish *Savoy* magazine with its Aubrey Beardsley illustrations from Mr Rota at ridiculously low prices. Then it was on to Victor Waddington's gallery in Cork Street for a chat and a glass of champagne. Prior to moving to London, he had created a gallery in Dublin before the War and had been a friend of my parents and Uncle Larry. In both cities he had introduced the public to many Irish artists but particularly to Jack Yeats and also to a number of continental artists including Georges Roualt.

As Victor had suffered heart problems, he said his doctor had prescribed a daily glass or two of bubbly as it would be good for his "ticker" and I was very happy to be of assistance in this health restorative process.

I was awe-struck by his contacts in the arts and his stories of their meetings: Henry Moore, Barbara Hepworth and Graham Sutherland, to name but a few, but then he was a leading dealer and I'm sure his list of collectors would have been equally impressive. He arranged for me to meet up with Tom Rosenthal, an eminent Director of Thames & Hudson and later MD of Secker & Warburg. As a result Tom wrote a scholarly essay on Jack Yeats which we were able to publish in the *Dublin Magazine* and which was very well received.

In the afternoons, when not on parade in the King's Road, there was usually a convenient (not convenience) stop at Bernard Stone's bookshop in Kensington Church Walk where literary types dropped in for a chat and a glass of Bernard's best wine. He specialised in poetry which he sold and also published in limited editions and welcomed me as the publisher of the *Dublin Magazine*, though I have to confess it was hardly his best seller. As a novice in the business it was fascinating to meet so many well-known authors. Laurence Durrell, Alan Sillitoe (who Bernard had known from their Nottingham links) and Christopher Logue dropped in from time to time, while Edward Lucie-Smith and Ralph Steadman appeared to be regulars. On one occasion Edward invited a number of us back to his place for supper and I recall his superb Spanish omelettes, while on another Ralph prepared cartoon sketches for me in two of his books.

Mentioning the City Barge reminds me that an Australian friend of Peter's came to stay at St. Mary's Mansions, where there was a spare bedroom that seemed to be constantly occupied by Australians. This was a rented flat and we had so many visitors I resolved that if I purchased a flat in the future, it would have only one bedroom so I could avoid running a guest-house and bumping into strange people going to or from the bathroom in the middle of the night.

Anyway, one of these visitors, Harold, ran a wine bar in Paddington, Sydney, called the City Barge and one of his objectives on the London trip was to steal the pub sign from outside the City Barge in Strand-on-the-Green and transport it to Sydney. A group of us went to visit the pub one evening to investigate the sign's removal but we soon discovered that it would not be possible without us being detected, so Harold settled on his plan B. This was to remove some of the street signs from Earls Court Square, which he considered would look just as good hanging in his wine bar, as Earls Court in London was known among the Australian ex-pat community as "Kangaroo Valley".

So off we went to investigate and ascertain how the signs were fixed to the railings. A couple of nights later we met up again armed with the appropriate tools – screwdrivers and the like – but as there were large numbers of people about we decided it would be best to first have a few pints in a nearby pub, the Hansom Cab. When it got to midnight there still seemed to be too many people around so, biding time and feeling hungry, we went to a nearby Indian restaurant for a curry and then, a little after 1a.m. we began to prepare for the dastardly deed.

There were about six of us altogether and it was agreed that it would take two people to remove each sign and the other four of us would be placed strategically on corners keeping a lookout for police.

However, when we got to our positions, we discovered that while we had been busy having our curries, some others had been busy removing all of the signs so there were none left to be shipped out to Sydney. I later mentioned our aborted plan to a friend who lived in Earls Court and he said he thought the signs were removed about every six months and he believed that the City of Westminster, who controlled such matters, must have had a large stockpile of them.

Another girlfriend, GL, had spent time as a lodger in the home of Prue Leith, the well-known restaurateur, and while around there one evening she told us a story about Cowes Week. She had received an invitation from Sir Max and Lady Aitken to be a guest in their home on the Isle of Wight. The invitation, however, came at a price: as Lady Aitken didn't cook, Prue would have to assist – and Edward Heath, then Prime Minister, was also to be one of the guests. They all gathered down there on a Friday afternoon and spoke about the catering arrangements. They didn't know what Mr Heath would want to eat until he arrived that evening and by that time all the local shops would be closed. Sir Max, however, said he knew a grocer who was a Conservative party supporter and he was sure to be happy to open up especially for the PM.

Eventually Mr Heath arrived and his chauffeur brought in his suitcase, followed by a collection of the usual "red boxes". Mr Heath said he wished to retire and not eat anything, so he was shown to his room. That still left the question of breakfast unanswered. So after a while Prue was asked to go upstairs and enquire what he wished to eat in the morning. She went upstairs and knocked on the door but there was no answer. She waited a little while and then knocked again. Eventually a voice from within shouted "come in", so she opened the door to find a grumpy PM sitting on the edge of the bed wrapped in a sheet. He said he would eat anything that was going but, because he looked so unhappy, Prue asked him if everything was alright. 'Some bloody fool has forgotten to pack my pyjamas' he replied. Doubting somewhat the veracity of the story, I happened to bump into a friend who actually worked in No. 10 Downing Street at the time and asked

EDINBURGH FESTIVAL 1957

At the age of about 15 I began to nag Mum and Dad to let me go to the Edinburgh Festival. On the one hand, they were impressed by my continuing interest in classical music; but on the other, I was too young to go away on my own (and there was also the question of the cost).

Dad spoke to family friend Gerald Goldberg, a local solicitor, supporter of the arts and later Lord Mayor of Cork, about his predicament. "Uncle Gerald" as I used to call him said my interest in music was to be encouraged and, in the months that followed, he obtained a copy of the programme for the following year. He selected a number of concerts for me to attend – actually far too many as it transpired – though his selection could not be faulted.

As there was not an adult to look after me, Mum and Dad, through Auntie Ethel in Glasgow, located a lady in Edinburgh who ran a guesthouse and she promised to supervise my every move. She would also ensure that her other Festival guests would keep an eye on me too.

So, in August 1957, aged 16, I set off for a city I had never been to before. In fact I had been to Scotland only once briefly to stay with Auntie Ethel and her family in Glasgow.

There were so many concerts to attend in Edinburgh, sometimes two a day, that I was left with very little time to do essential sightseeing in that most attractive of cities. The memory is somewhat hazy after more than 50 years but an early recollection was looking forward to hearing Maria Callas as Amina in "La Sonnambula", one of her most famous roles. Of course, she was an idol of mine and at that time was at the very top of her profession. I was due to hear her final performance.

Unfortunately Callas was (or claimed to be) unwell and at the last minute she was replaced by someone I had never heard of before – Renata Scotto. In the event the opera was a triumph and Scotto a revelation. Aged just 24, she had made her debut at La Scala in 1954 and was just at the start of what was to be a glittering career.

A few days ago (November 2011) I was at Covent Garden for a perfunctory performance of "Sonnambula", at the end of which some friends said 'wasn't that wonderful?' I told them I thought not, and that my first experience of the opera more than 50 years ago was with Renata Scotto singing the leading role at the Edinburgh Festival. 'Having started on a 'high', my attendance at this opera has been heading downhill ever since.'

The next memory at Edinburgh was a Sunday afternoon recital at the Usher Hall by another of my female idols: Victoria de los Angeles, then aged 34, accompanied by the incomparable Gerald Moore. The concert was remarkable not just for the beauty of the singing and the charm of the singer, but for the reception by the audience. At the end of the planned programme, the spellbound audience would not allow de los Angeles to leave the stage so that she and Moore gave more encores than I have ever heard since. So many in fact that the 'ad hoc' programme was longer than the planned one – and it only ended when the manager of the Hall went on stage pleading with the audience to leave as there were long queues outside of people waiting to enter for the evening concert by (I think) the Philharmonia Orchestra.

When de los Angeles died in January 2005, *The Times* printed a fulsome obituary of a very great artist and, as was becoming customary then, readers were invited to submit any anecdotes or stories which had been omitted from the obituary. A number of fans wrote in with their own particular memories and I wrote in with mine (published 15 February 2005). Fortunately the BBC had recorded the concert and a CD was produced, eventually, in 2002 to my surprise. It is a joyful reminder of a wonderful afternoon.

Another outstanding memory was of a concert featuring Dennis Brain, then the leading horn-player of the day, with the Philharmonia Orchestra. The concert received a rapturous reception and, as with all the other concerts I attended at Edinburgh, I went to the stage-door afterwards to collect the autographs in my programmes. Sometimes I was asked my name and, instead of a mere signature, got a full inscription "to David, etc."

Having got Dennis Brain's signature (or was it an inscription?), I heard the following day that after the concert he set off in his smart sports car to drive through the night from Edinburgh to his home in London. Nearing London, he was killed in a crash at Hatfield in the early hours of the following morning. He was only 34 and at his peak. Perhaps I was the last person to get his autograph.

While the Philharmonia Orchestra were very good, in my view the Concertgebouw Orchestra of Amsterdam were even better and I attended two of their concerts that year under their regular conductor, Eduard van Beinum. No histrionics here: his conducting was undemonstrative but obviously effective judging from the excellent reviews. He was clearly not in good health and was helped on and off the stage by an attendant. He died two years later aged 59.

Having waited for so long after the concerts to collect the autographs, it was a shock to discover some years later that Dad either lost or gave away my entire collection during one of our house-moves. I sometimes wonder if the collection was kept together or went off to some pulp mill.

Looking back on that fantastic festival, I can't understand what inward force made me want to visit Edinburgh so badly. The Festival has now gone past its 60th birthday, but in 1957 it had only been going for ten years or so and was barely established in the world of music festivals. Nor do I know to this day how Dad managed to pay for it. He never mentioned the cost to me and it wouldn't have been cheap even then. He gets top marks for allowing me to go, but none for "losing" my much-loved programmes.

ANECDOTES 1

When Dad became President of the Rotary Club in Cork in 1972, he had to find a guest speaker for his Presidential Dinner. He needed to look no further than Jack Lynch, a fellow Corkman, family friend and then Irish Taoiseach (Prime Minister) who was delighted to oblige.

The dinner took place at the Imperial Hotel on the South Mall and, after the dinner ended, Dad had arranged that the Committee and VIP guests would have a private room where they could continue their drinking.

After the select group had been in this room for some time – it must by now have been well past midnight – the manager appeared and enquired how long they would be there. Lynch, who by this time had consumed a large amount of booze, considered the question somewhat impudent and responded: 'what the hell has it got to do with you?'. 'Well, sir,' said the manager, 'let's say that while you are here we are unlikely to be raided by the Garda, who are sitting in their cars outside'.

It appears all the other bars in the hotel were full to bursting-point and the drinkers knew that the police would not enter until the Taoiseach had left.

It was the custom at the Rotary Club for the President to choose his own Christmas cards and it was fortuitous that Dad's year of office (1972) coincided with the 250th anniversary of the building of St. Annes church in Shandon in 1722. What could be more topical than to commission a picture of St. Annes by his old friend Marshall Hutson RHA, who was almost his exact contemporary, as the subject for the Christmas card? The church is without doubt Cork's most famous parish church and its tower in limestone and red sandstone can be seen for miles around. It also owes much of its fame to "The Bells of Shandon", memorable lines composed by Francis Sylvester Mahony (better known as Father Prout) that can be quoted by almost all Cork schoolchildren.

The Shandon Bells by Father Prout

St Anne's Shandon by Marshall Hutson RHA, 1972

ANECDOTES 2

I don't know why the Goldbergs were having such a big party in their lovely home on the Rochestown Road but my parents were there and so was Sean Collins a local solicitor, and nephew of Michael Collins, along with his wife. For some reason I was there too. It would have been about 1960.

My father was sitting on a sofa next to Sean Collins, who was boasting to Dad that he was such an expert on brandy he could tell VSOP from Three Star or Fine Champagne, and even identify the individual producer. My father was disbelieving, saying he couldn't possibly tell with such accuracy. They argued for quite some time until Mrs Collins entered the room saying 'Sean, taste this; there is something wrong with my whiskey'. (It would have been Irish, thus the spelling). She handed him her glass. He sipped the drink slowly, rolling it around in his mouth – and suddenly let out a loud bellow: 'Christ, woman, you've been drinking my brandy'.

He had in fact been drinking his wife's whiskey all the while he had been arguing with my father.

Footnote: Mum died on 22 August 2006 which happened to be the anniversary of the date on which Michael Collins was assassinated in 1922.

THE HIST

Having attended Trinity for four years – the normal BA course duration; it wasn't that I fluffed a year – I was a member of the College Historical Society (known as "The Hist") for almost all of that time. The Hist was and is the oldest surviving undergraduate debating society in the world and, from its earliest days, which began in 1770, it has concentrated on holding debates on all sorts of topics. Many famous people, from Edward Burke onwards, have been members of the Society.

I enjoyed the cut and thrust of the debates and, though (or because) I never stood for office, there were occasions when I was considered a "neutral" who didn't take sides between the executive and the opposition (such as it was) and, as a result, got invited to take the chair at the Private Business meetings that followed the formal debates and after the non-members ("strangers") had departed.

On a couple of occasions I was appointed an Honorary Steward for the inaugural meeting at the start of the new academic year when a number of celebrities would be invited to participate in the debate.

On one of the latter occasions my fellow Steward was Peter Hinchcliffe, a little older than I as he had done his National Service prior to attending university. Rather pretentiously, the gilt-edged invitations to the inaugural meetings each year requested "medals and decorations to be worn".

As I had gone to Trinity straight from Cork Grammar School, it was as much as I could do to produce a dinner jacket let alone a medal of any sort. Imagine my surprise then to discover that my colleague Hinchcliffe actually had both a dinner jacket and a medal to wear as, during his spell in the army, he had seen "active service" when he participated in the ill-fated Suez Campaign of 1956.

The inaugural debate itself was most memorable because the motion was about joining the European Community. Though I forget the actual wording of the proposition – it was something like "That this House would join the European Community" – the proposer was no less a figure than Paul-Henri Spaak, one of the founders of the EU, who spoke in French. The opposition to the motion was led by the veteran Labour politician Manny Shinwell who, in his quiet Scottish accent, made "mincemeat" of each of Spaak's arguments, one by one, to such an extent and with such wonderful oratory that the portly Spaak kept jumping to his feet on 'points of order' or 'points of fact'. Needless-to-say, the resolution was roundly defeated.

I understand from Ian Simons, who was Auditor (Chairman) of the Hist on that occasion, that Spaak refused to attend the celebratory dinner after the debate.

On another occasion at Private Business, a fellow undergraduate, Desmond Moloney (grandson of Sir Thomas Moloney Bt., who had been the Lord Chief Justice of Ireland) entered the debating chamber on his motorbike, interrupting the proceedings by making a great deal of noise as he revved up his engine to the consternation and amusement of those present, while leaving behind a lot of smoke and an awful smell in the chamber. At the same time the chairman of the meeting furiously banged his gavel as he tried to shout "order, order" above the din of the bike without any success.

I don't recall if Moloney was admonished by the authorities for his behaviour that evening but I was glad not to have been in the chair on that occasion.

There used to be an annual *Irish Times* debating competition for undergraduates of the Irish universities and the Hist representatives usually acquitted themselves well. The winning team were then invited to take part in *The Observer* competition for Britain and Ireland, and Trinity generally did well there too, though I remember there was very keen competition between Trinity and UCD.

CLUBLAND – DUBLIN-STYLE

After I began work in Dublin, I thought it would be useful if I were to join a gentleman's club. A number of my friends were already members of the University Club so it made sense for me to get proposed, seconded and elected to membership in 1965. It was essentially a club for TCD graduates and had been set up in 1850 during prosperous mid-Victorian times.

In 1976 it merged with the Kildare Street Club, which was very much home to the Anglo-Irish establishment, catering for rather more aristocratic country folk, and their members simply had to move around the corner into the impressive University Club premises on St. Stephen's Green – it then becoming the Kildare Street and University Club.

It was a convenient place for me to meet for a light lunch or a drink with friends after work. Then, when I moved to London at the beginning of 1966, I became an overseas member and was able to make use of the bedrooms on my fairly frequent visits to Dublin.

On a daily basis the Club posted a list of guests due to stay there that evening alongside the reception desk for all to see and, on one occasion, my visit coincided with a meeting of the Church of Ireland Synod in Dublin. Following the usual procedure, all of the out-of-town bishops who were members of the Club were named on the list. As I had booked sufficiently early, and managed to bag a room while they were still available, my name was also posted up. The names then read for all to see: Limerick, Armagh, Cork, Ferns, Waterford … and Elyan. I felt very proud to have been in such eminent and holy company.

As none of the bedrooms had en suite facilities, there were inevitable delays in carrying out ones morning ablutions and I remember one particular and frustrating delay when a fellow member's bath-time seemed to go on forever. I waited in my room for the sound of the door to be unbolted before then rushing out to be next to enter and avoid another long wait. However, on racing down the corridor and opening the bathroom door, the room was full of steam and the most disgusting smell of BO or something worse.

How, I wondered, could anybody who has just had a bath create such a stink. Still, I didn't have time to sit and wonder. I opened the window wide and got on with my business.

It was usual for guests at breakfast who were on their own to sit at the members' table. On arrival in the dining room, members would be found already seated there, reading one of the morning papers while waiting to be served and, according to custom, the newcomer would say a "good morning" to all and sundry. Without looking up, the seated members would mumble something from behind their newspapers that was intended to sound like a 'good morning' in response.

Similarly when members had finished their breakfasts and got up to leave, to go about their daily tasks in the city, the mumblings of good morning were again repeated.

One day I was seated next to an elderly gent who was bellowing his breakfast requirements to a timid young waitress of about 16 who had come to take his order:

"I'll have half a grapefruit and make sure that the pieces are cut up properly. Then I'll have the boiled egg – and make certain it's not runny. Have you got that?" The waitress replied "yes, sir" and rushed off to the kitchen.

What a crotchety old man I thought. Couldn't he see that the young girl was scared out of her wits?

When his breakfast arrived about 15 minutes later, his crotchety behaviour was explained: he had only one arm. As a retired army officer I guess he had been used to issuing orders to underlings all of his adult life and he wasn't now going to be put off his stride, so to speak, by a young slip of a girl who had probably only been working in the dining room for a week or two.

Going back to the morning of the smelly bathroom, when I got down for breakfast on that fateful day, I looked carefully around the breakfast table to see if I could identify "Mr Smelly" but there was no obvious culprit.

A short while later a member who was well below the average age got up from the table, left his newspaper on the back of a chair and took his leave, with all the repeated mumbled salutations.

When he was out of earshot, one of the remaining members said to another "I understand he is taking part in the Dublin marathon in a couple of weeks' time, and he runs all the way to the Club every day from Skerries". According to my elderly but trustworthy AA book for Ireland, that distance to Dublin was 19 miles. It was my misfortune to follow him to the bathroom, but I made sure it never happened again.

BOOKS AND BOATS

When in 1961 I raised some cash from friends in order to form a company, New Square Publications Limited, with the objective of creating a new literary magazine in Dublin, and perhaps publishing some contemporary poetry, it was not clear then how interesting the venture would turn out to be.

We put in just over £200 in total to get it started, managed to find a young American at Trinity, Donald Carroll, who was keen to edit it and settled on the title *The Dubliner*. The first issue came out in time for Christmas 1961, was distributed in Ireland by Easons, a number of bookshops in Britain such as Blackwells, Heffers and James Thin, and it sold tolerably well. Unfortunately, our costs were greater than our revenue so our initial capital was almost entirely gone. However, Mervyn Wall, secretary of the Irish Arts Council and an old friend of Uncle Larry, as well as a novelist himself, was very sympathetic towards our venture and promised me a grant equivalent to our losses up to a fixed amount. That was just what we needed because although we never expected to make big profits, we could not afford to suffer regular losses either. So over the next 13 years we had the reassurance that we would not end up in liquidation provided the losses did not exceed the amount agreed with the Arts Council.

Apart from the editor, who was unpaid, we found it difficult to find people willing to handle sales, marketing, selling adverts and subscriptions and any other jobs that needed doing. That we managed to find anybody to do these tasks was a minor miracle. Producing the accounts for each issue was down to me, as well as seeing that the costs did not exceed our estimated revenue and acting as overall company chairman.

Don Carroll left Trinity not long after the first issue and he was replaced by Bruce Arnold, then working as a sub-editor on *The Irish Times*. After a few years, Bruce had had enough and gave up, and in turn was replaced by Rivers Carew (who then worked at the Irish Tourist Board) and Tim Brownlow jointly. They kept the show on the road for quite a time and during this period Rivers and I jointly negotiated with Estella Solomons, widow of Dr James Starkey, founder and long-term editor of *The Dublin Magazine*, for us to take over the name of that title. Estella was in her 80s then, doubled up with arthritis but still very much "with it". I remember going to her house for discussions and tea on a regular basis where she was accompanied by her next door neighbour, Kathleen Goodfellow, who wrote in *The Dublin Magazine* under the pseudonym 'Michael Scott', and gave her considerable support in her later years. No doubt the fact that Uncle Larry was friendly with the Solomons family, and had founded the Dublin Jewish Progressive Congregation with Bethel Solomons, Estella's brother, helped just a little.

When Tim Brownlow wanted to leave Dublin and move to Canada, Rivers too decided that it was time to retire and John Ryan, who had edited *Envoy*, took their place. John was not a Trinity graduate but came from a staunchly Irish nationalistic home. His mother, Agnes, ran the family business Monument Creameries and the famous Bailey pub in Duke Street was also owned by the family. John's wife Patricia had founded the Irish National Ballet.

John wasn't much interested in book-keeping or the various admin tasks but he had excellent literary contacts in Dublin and elsewhere. He managed without much help to keep the magazine going for some years until a combination of ill-health and, I suspect, boredom got the better of him.

From London I was no longer in touch with the Dublin scene and unable to find a new editor to succeed John. A number of people expressed an interest in taking over completely, a course I would have preferred, but nobody was willing to devote the time or the resources to the venture. The magazine had run its course and in the ephemeral world of small literary magazines turned out to have been one of the most enduring in 20th century Ireland.

During its existence, New Square Publications published some slim volumes of poetry by Brendan Kennelly, Rivers Carew, Tim Brownlow and others with the authors paying the printer's bills. As the books were all printed by Colm O'Lochlainn's famous Three Candles Press, and though they were difficult to sell at the time, they have inevitably become collectors' items nowadays.

Of the various editors, the only one with whom I have remained friendly over the years is Rivers Carew. He came of a long line of Devon seafaring gents and inherited a baronetcy created in Charles II's restoration honours of 1661. One of his collateral ancestors, he told me, was Sir George Carew, admiral in charge of the Mary Rose, the pride and joy of Henry VIII's war fleet.

Before taking command of the ship, Sir George had served in several military roles including 'Lieutenant of the Horse' and had been taken prisoner by the French at the battle of Landrecy in 1544 .

A year later when the Mary Rose was to undergo sea trials off Portsmouth, before engaging the French in battle, the King decided to travel from his home at Hampton Court to preside at a great banquet at Southsea Castle. During the celebrations, Henry presented Sir George with a gold chain and whistle.

The following morning, on a bright clear day, the King, his courtiers and senior military personnel foregathered at Southsea to observe the Mary Rose performing her manoeuvres. The ship, overladen with guns and other equipment, took a sharp turn out at sea, keeled over and sank with the loss of all hands. Sir George, together with his gold chain and whistle were never found though the remains of the ship were raised in 1982 and partially restored in recent years. Many of Sir George's personal items were also recovered in almost perfect condition having been protected for more than 400 years by mud. All are now displayed in a splendid new museum in Portsmouth.

I have a sneaking suspicion that Sir George might have survived the calamity and, knowing his likely fate, such as having his head removed, he may have swum ashore slightly east of Southsea and hitched a lift on a boat heading for France while the navy were gathering up the corpses from the sea.

Sir George had two brothers: Peter who in his time achieved fame for launching an assault on Tréport, with Sir John Dudley, and was knighted; and Sir Philip who is covered briefly in the Dictionary of National Biography with the comment 'of whom nothing is known but that he was a Knight of Malta'.

In fact Sir Philip was a Knight before the Sovereign Order had landed and established itself in Malta in 1530. Shortly before this, Sir Philip and some fellow Knights decided to pay a visit to Nice where the Order was temporarily located having been booted out of Rhodes by the Ottomans and before being granted permission to settle in Malta. While there, Sir Philip became embroiled in a dispute with another Knight, it escalated and was resolved only when the other Knight was fatally stabbed. Sir Philip was put on trial and in the apocryphal account passed down by successive generations of Carews was found guilty of murder. The sentence was for him to be put in a sealed sack with a large stone and dropped in the Mediterranean. Rivers and I both laughed at such an implausible conclusion.

Some months later, however, while in Malta, I happened to read an article in the *Malta Sunday Times* by the eminent judge and historian Dr Giovanni Bonello about the English Knight, Sir Oliver Starkey, who had been secretary to Grand Master Jean de la Valette during the Great Siege of 1565 and after. In this article Bonello mentioned, en passant, that some other Knights, found guilty of serious offences, had been sentenced to death in the very manner of Sir Philip – so the Carew's story was almost certainly true after all.

In 2008, after he had retired from the European Court in Strasbourg, I was introduced to Dr Bonello by my good friend Nicholas de Piro, himself a Knight of fairly recent standing. On complimenting the judge about his fine articles on the subject of Starkey, and mentioning the story of Sir Philip, de Piro expressed amazement that even in the sixteenth century the so-called aristocratic Knights could have behaved in so beastly a fashion to their brethren. Bonello explained that this was the custom at the time, although it was usually a cannon ball rather than a stone that was placed in the sack. He added that some years later the Knights became somewhat more civilized and used to strangle the guilty party before putting them in the sack with the cannon ball.

I don't think it would have been very pleasant being a slave in Malta in those days. You would spend all day – weeks? months? – grinding stones so that they became cannon balls and then, when they were dropped in the sea in a sack with a body, you had to start all over again.

Sir Rivers Carew and Michael Calascione in Sliema, Malta. October 2003

VISCOUNT MONTGOMERY ET AL

After I had joined Rainbird's, I discovered one of the books we were working on was Montgomery's much-acclaimed "History of Warfare". He did the writing in his caravan in Hampshire, but the very considerable amount of background research was conducted by two history graduates working from our offices on the Edgware Road. One of them was Alan Howarth whose father, Tom, had been Monty's batman during the North Africa campaign and, after the War, he became a schoolmaster and worked his way up to the top of the education ladder becoming High Master of St. Paul's School in Hammersmith. It so happened that Alan had married Gill Chance, a Dublin lass and a contemporary of mine at TCD. We had friends in common and met occasionally at local race meetings.

Some years later, and long after I had moved on from Rainbird's, my parents were staying with me in Winchcombe and, one Saturday morning over breakfast, we were wondering what to do with ourselves that day when my mother came up with an idea: what about a trip to Stratford-upon-Avon, one of their favourite towns.

No problem. Half an hour later we were on our way through the Vale of Evesham where we always liked to stop at one of the many farm stalls and purchase some freshly-picked fruit and veg.

On arrival at Stratford we were strolling slowly about in the town centre when we bumped into the afore-mentioned Gill Chance who was surprised to see me so far away from our much-loved Dublin.

"What are you doing here?", she asked. "I've got a cottage nearby in Winchcombe. What about you?" "Well, my husband Alan is now the Conservative MP for Stratford", she replied.

(Later they divorced and he "jumped ship" and joined the Labour Party; and not too long afterwards was rewarded with a peerage from Tony Blair).

Now back to Monty. Every so often he would need to travel up to London to visit the editorial team working on his book and meet the two researchers at our offices, a mere stone's throw from Marble Arch.

As one might expect, his time-keeping was punctilious and I recall that on one occasion it was my turn to join two of our directors on the pavement to await the arrival of the great man for a two o'clock meeting, before accompanying him in the lift up to our offices on the fourth floor.

At about ten minutes beforehand, Monty's car would be spotted driving past and circling the block until the stroke of two when the car would pull up and the chauffeur would jump out to open his door.

The last time he visited us was to thank us for our efforts leading up to the book's publication. He was then rather frail though mentally alert and propped himself against a desk while delivering a short speech in gratitude for our efforts.

Below our offices, on the ground floor, was a large retail store of Swears & Wells, part of a chain of furriers with branches throughout the UK and Ireland. The intermediate floors were occupied by the head offices of the company which was chaired by the diminutive Mr Ross who was our landlord. In those days furs meant real furs, which were all the rage, and only later were they replaced by imitations as fashions changed and certain animals moved closer to extinction.

In the way that Marks & Spencer was known by Britain's shoppers as "Marks and Sparks", so Swears & Wells was popularly known as "Swears and Yells". Despite having been founded by Frederick Swears and Thomas Wells in Regent Street in 1816, a year after Waterloo and nine years before the street was completed, I imagine there must have been mountains of rubble for their customers to contend with before the pavements were laid down.

At the back of the building was a pub called the Carpenter's Arms where we used to go on most days for our "elevenses". When the telephone rang for any one of us, I can only assume that the receptionist said we were at a meeting and would be back before lunch.

One of our secretaries was Louise Philipps who lived in a family flat across the road in Connaught Place. She was always late for work whereas people who had a 60 minute journey were always on time or even early.

On one particular day she invited a number of us for drinks in the flat after work to celebrate her birthday. As I was taking off my coat in the somewhat dark hallway, I noticed a very nice, even familiar, painting which on closer examination looked like a Dufy copy.

Afterwards, when I got to know Louise better, I was to discover that her father, the Hon. Hanning Philipps, was the chairman of Schweppes (before it merged with Cadbury's) together with a number of other well-known companies. He was also the Lord Lieutenant of Pembrokeshire and a great friend of Graham Sutherland and his circle. Consequently I was left in no doubt that the Dufy "reproduction" – as well as many other paintings in the hallway and elsewhere in the flat – were, of course, originals. How could I possibly have thought otherwise?

As a postscript, I can't resist adding in a story told by John Julius Norwich on 'Desert Island Discs' in November 1997.

His mother, Lady Diana Cooper, was sitting next to Viscount Montgomery at a dinner one night and was surprised how well she was getting on with him. As their conversation progressed, he asked her not to address him so formally as Lord Montgomery. (She was after all herself Viscountess Norwich). "How should I address you?", she enquired. "Field Marshall will do", he replied.

George Rainbird, Viscount Montgomery of Alamein and Caroline Hill, October 1968.

MY TIME IN PUBLISHING

While at Trinity I developed an interest in publishing. Even at school in Cork I had begun to collect books, particularly those relating to the history of Cork, and I recall on my first visit to London with Dad, dragging him along to Sotheby's to inspect a copy of Smith's 'History of Cork' that was coming up for auction. I think that was 1954 and the book – still in my collection – cost £3:15 shillings. I later purchased the earlier and very much rarer two volume edition of 1750. At Trinity I worked on the college newspaper *Trinity News* and also on the literary magazine *Icarus* which printed the one and only poem of mine ever to appear in print. On graduating I would have liked to join one of the London publishing houses but I didn't possess any contacts and such connections were essential at that time. Instead I joined a property company, Stock Conversion, then based in Jermyn Street; and as they offered me a small flat at the top of one of their buildings, due for redevelopment, at 83 Wigmore Street, I had a most pleasant walk to and from work every day via Bond Street. I enjoyed my time there and made some friends with whom I remain in contact more than 50 years later. But I saw the position merely as a means to an end; as a way of earning a salary until such time as I could find a publishing position.

It wasn't too long before I joined George Rainbird, a publisher of big illustrated books such as Nancy Mitford's 'The Sun King' and J B Priestley's 'Prince of Pleasure'. My job was Budget Controller and I had to produce all the estimates – of sales, costs, book size and price, etc. – for consideration by the Board. If the budget was approved, I had then to monitor the costs to ensure they came out within budget and, if they didn't, I had to blow a whistle (not literally) and call a meeting to consider the cost over-runs.

After doing this job for some years, I spotted an opportunity at *The Observer* for a Commercial Manager of non-newspaper activities. I applied, got interviewed and was offered the post. I recall that my letter of engagement did not stipulate the hours to be worked and I thought it might be considered trivial to phone up to enquire about such minor details. Instead I thought I would simply turn up at 9 a.m. on the appointed day and if I were too early, then I would simply wait. Having got there at 9 a.m. I waited… and waited and waited. When it got to 11 a.m. I thought I had better enquire what was going on so I went down to reception – to be told that as the Ob (as it was called internally) was a Sunday paper, the working week was Tuesday to Saturday. The rest of the day was spent visiting art galleries in the West End.

In those days the Ob was located in Printing House Square, next door to *The Times* on whose presses it was printed, though the address was given as 160 Queen Victoria Street. The Mermaid Theatre, where we often went for a drink after work, was just across the road.

At the time I was living in a rented flat at St Mary's Mansions, Little Venice, and my nearest underground station was Edgware Road. The closest underground stop to *The Observer* was Blackfriars. As both stations were on the Circle Line, which was circular in those days, I counted out the stops going East via Kings Cross and Liverpool Street – 13. Then I counted out the stops going anti-clockwise – also 13. It would be fun, I thought, to go all the way around the Circle Line every day, one day clockwise, the next day anti-clockwise. Soon I discovered that it would be quicker to go just 5 stops to Farringdon and walk down Farringdon Street from there.

On my second day at Queen Victoria Street I arranged that, as it had never been mentioned to me that my working week was intended to start on a Tuesday, I would be permitted to work Monday to Friday.

The head of personnel enquired if I wanted him to find me a secretary. On saying that I did, for the first time in my life I came up against the strength of the trade unions. Bill Herd, the personnel manager, said the first step would be to enquire if anybody at *The Observer* would like to come and work for me; they had to be SOGAT members. If that enquiry drew no response, he would then contact the other Fleet

Street papers to see if they had anybody who was unhappy and wanted to move to work for me. Only when there was no response would I be free to look for somebody myself.

At that time the Ob was owned by the Astor family and the editor was the Hon. David Astor. I saw hardly anything of him as the running of the paper was left to TJ. (Tristan Jones) a very pleasant, plump individual, whose father, also known as TJ, had been head of the National Library of Wales and later David Lloyd George's private secretary.

Eventually, when I found a secretary, she had to be approved by Charles Vidler, 'father' of the SOGAT chapel at *The Observer* and join the Union. Mr Vidler appeared to have a rather menial job in the organisation, wrapping up parcels of newspapers to be distributed to newsagents, which belied his considerable power. This was apparent because all the staff were terrified of getting on the wrong side of him. Talking to Bill Herd one day I asked where he had come from. 'Don't you know?' he enquired. 'He had been Lord Astor's butler at Cliveden and no doubt would have been opening the bottles and serving the wine at the time of the "Profumo affair". However, he was sacked when he was found in Lord Astor's bed and, after that, he became David Astor's butler up in Elm Tree Road in St John's Wood, just behind Lord's cricket ground. When, later, David developed his great social conscience, he considered it inappropriate to be seen to have a butler. He had been a most obsequious and loyal servant of the family over many years, so he felt he could not make him redundant. Instead he found him a job on the newspaper where he steadily made his way up the trade union ladder to where he is now – a considerable 'thorn in the flesh' of everyone around him'.

He didn't cause me any problems, or me him any I hope.

COINCIDENCES

When Uncle Larry retired from the Irish Civil Service in 1960, he went first to South Africa for a prolonged stay and to recover from some 40 years in Governmental service, not that he ever seemed in any sort of stress whenever I visited him at Dublin Castle. After some months in Cape Town (principally), he then went to Israel where he was to remain for the rest of his life, a period of nearly 30 years.

On arriving in Jerusalem, he found a flat which was centrally located in Hamelech George that he rented and where I stayed when visiting Israel. After a while, he decided to go on an 'ulpan' – a crash course in learning the Israeli language Ivrit. Despite this, he was never able to converse in the language but used instead a mixture of Ivrit, English and Yiddish. When people got him down, usually petty bureaucrats in the bank or post office, he resorted to shouting in English only, liberally sprinkled with swear words. I was with him on a number of occasions in a long, noisy queue at the bank which moved only slowly in stifling heat. By the time Larry got to the counter he was in a right good mood. It didn't take long before he began shouting, to my embarrassment and to the amazement of the others in the queue who were suddenly silenced. Even if their knowledge of English was only rudimentary, they would have understood that the clerk was 'an incompetent arsehole' who needed 'the shit kicked out of him' because he couldn't find some document that Larry had given him and on which his life now depended.

Usually on the way home, with me trying to pretend to the others who had been in the bank that we had only just met, Larry would discover in his pocket the document that he had just accused the bureaucrat of having lost.

After some months, Geoffrey Wigoder, then head of English language broadcasting at Kol Yisrael, Israel Radio, found Larry a job which, for the first time in his life, he found fulfilling and enjoyable. He became a reporter and went out to interview in English well-known visitors to the city. I recall the names of Miriam Karlin and David Kossoff. Shortly afterwards he also presented a late-night radio music programme based on listeners' requests. It was called 'Happy as Larry' and to his amazement he received requests and, later, letters and cards of thanks from all around the world.

One day he was sent to interview three generations of a family newly arrived in Israel from Russia. He was fascinated by the grandmother who was in her 80s and blind. She did not speak any English and Larry of course did not speak any Russian but happily they were able to converse in Yiddish.

Despite her infirmities, the old lady was mentally alert and asked Larry as many questions as he asked her. She wanted to know where he came from; and when he told her Ireland, she said she had been there once herself in the early 1900s. He asked where she had gone; she replied Cork, to visit some cousins. He said he came from Cork; who were the cousins? 'A family named Elyan', she replied. Unfortunately she died not very long afterwards so Larry was not able to interview her a second time for his own purposes. It appears she was involved in the Russian Revolution and was later sent off to work in a salt-mine where she spent 17 years in one of those hellish labour camps.

Some years later on another visit to Israel, I stayed with Larry again, just after the Six Day War of 1967. For the first time Israelis were able to visit East Jerusalem, newly captured, and to experience the smells of the markets and the colourful dress worn by different races and religions: Russian and Greek Orthodox, Catholics and Armenians, Muslims and Chassidim.

One evening Geoffrey and his wife Devorah Wigoder took me out to a night club in East Jerusalem for a meal. While we had a drink at the bar awaiting a table, a young lady stepped backwards and trod on my foot. She turned and apologised in a broad Irish accent, so I had to ask her what part of Ireland she came from. 'The West of Ireland'. 'Where in the West?'

'County Roscommon'. I persevered. 'A small town called Boyle'.

'In Boyle itself?' 'No, just a little way outside; a place called Knockvicar'. 'By Knockvicar Lock?' I asked. 'Just so', she said. 'My mother is the lock-keeper'. So, from a dark and mysterious night club in East Jerusalem I could recall the very white-washed house which was her family home. I wonder what became of her and the Romanian boyfriend that she had met while working on a kibbutz. Perhaps I will find out next time I visit Knockvicar.

Moving on now some 20 years to Malta, I was at a dinner party one evening in Zebbug at the home of retired Rabbi Herbert Richer and his wife Dorien. Sitting next to me at the table was one of their neighbours, Juliet, a very attractive, widowed Englishwoman. Across the table one of the other guests asked Juliet when she would be returning to England. In order to keep the conversation going I asked her where she went in England. 'To my home in East Anglia', she replied. 'Where there? 'In Suffolk'. 'Which part?' I enquired. 'Near Aldeburgh', she replied, not giving much away. 'Where near Aldeburgh?' 'A little place you will hardly have heard of called Shingle Street'. I paused and asked: 'do you know the Ushers there?' 'Good Heavens', she exclaimed; 'they are my next door neighbours'. The other guests who must have been bored stiff by my line of questioning almost cheered. Both Juliet's late husband and Usher pére were retired naval commanders and good friends so it must have been sensible for them to retire to a terrace of coastguards' cottages on a real shingle beach bordering the North Sea. I remember the delicious asparagus they grew there and the bunches I left with to bring back to London. It was probably the sandy soil and the sea spray that gave it its particular flavour – almost certainly best eaten to a background of the Peter Grimes "Sea Interludes".

OFFICE LIFE

Having got to 70 without a computer or a mobile phone, people are amazed at how I have managed to cope with life without resorting to such technical contrivances.

From about 1970 onwards, that is for nearly 40 years, I was fortunate enough to have my own secretary. In the early days it was a manual typewriter (IBM, Olivetti or Olympia) that was used to bash out the letters after I had dictated them. There was nothing old-fashioned about such technology then. I remember that in the early days we had older secretaries, perhaps in their 50s or 60s who, in their younger days, had been called 'stenographers'.

After the manual typewriters, we moved on to electric typewriters and then word-processors. These devices had 'memories' and in turn were replaced in the 1980s by computers. Whatever the process used, all my letters, business or personal, were produced in splendid layout by my secretaries ready for me to sign. Seldom were any corrections necessary. If errors had occurred, they had been corrected and the letters retyped before I saw them.

Evelyn Berezin (1925-2018) who created and developed the word-processor said "if there is anything a man hates it is giving up his secretary". Many men will agree with this statement but it is interesting to note that her efforts over many years to advance the role of female office workers led to her creation having the opposite effect: the efficiency of the word-processor replaced many of these same ladies.

Photocopying was by Gestetner, Roneo machines or Ellam's duplicators which were somewhat messy and left ink stains on the paper as well as your fingers. After that came Rank Xerox and Canon machines which were far, far better.

When I joined the Board of Langton Software in 1987 – a joke to all my friends – there were any number of people there only too willing to produce my letters, create headed notepaper or business cards and attend to any hotel or travel arrangements that needed to be booked online. Perhaps, on reflection, if I had spent some time learning about computing then, I might be an IT wizard today. However, my role was to look after everything that was of a non-trading or technical nature and I believe my colleagues were very happy to be relieved of these (to them) boring tasks.

There are some office stories I should recall before they get forgotten about. Elsewhere I have written that my first job in London (1966) was working for a property company called Stock Conversion in Jermyn Street. My boss, the Company Secretary, was Terry McGee, a real eccentric. His family came from humble farming stock near Tralee, Co. Kerry. On leaving school, Terry attended night classes to become a Chartered Secretary and, after qualifying, immediately set about becoming a barrister, which he did.

At Stock Conversion his office was at the end of a long corridor and, as we all left our office doors open, the corridor carpet had alternate patches of sunlight and shade. Now Terry for some reason never liked walking on the sunny patches of carpet so when he returned to his office all I saw as he went past my door was him sailing through the air from one shaded piece of carpet to the next.

We had a young secretarial assistant called Rex Tester and Terry gave him one of the cleverest nicknames I have come across. He was known as Rexacles.

Later on I moved to Thomson Organisation's book company, Rainbird Publishing. The managing director George Rainbird was the co-founder of the International Wine & Food Society which published books and magazines on related subjects as well as holding themed dinners, wine and food tastings, etc. The IW&FS established branches throughout the world and, in London, a Young Members Society.

I had nothing to do with the IW&FS until I was summoned by George Rainbird one day and told there had been personnel problems with the Young Members committee and he was having to make some changes. His deputy MD was going to become the new chairman and an American cookery book editor was to be the new secretary. He would like me to be the new treasurer. As the function could largely be performed during office hours I readily agreed. Very soon afterwards I discovered that the previous chairman, a married man, had been having an affair with the previous secretary and they had both eloped to (I think) Hong Kong along with the slender resources of the Wine & Food Society Young Members.

My treasureship only lasted for 18 months or so during which time we rebuilt our funds and trust in the committee and I organised an outstanding 'blind' sausage tasting – won by a Cumberland sausage with M&S coming second.

Apart from me, we had an excellent committee. The chairman, Edmund Fisher was a son of James Fisher, the famous ornithologist, and Marjorie Fisher, an expert on children's books who wrote for the *Sunday Times*. Committee members included John Avery, son of Ronald, both distinguished wine merchants in Bristol, and Francis Sitwell, younger son of Sir Sacheverell and a nephew of Osbert and Edith.

I remember one day being invited to a party at the Rainbirds' country house at Whichford, near Shipston-on-Stour. In the afternoon there was a croquet tournament and, if you don't already know, there is nobody in this wide world who is a worse player of the game than me. In the first round I was drawn against Edmund Fisher's wife Elizabeth, herself the youngest daughter of Irving Berlin, and before long she had smashed my ball off the lawn and down the drive. The ball went through the entrance gates and gathered speed as it bounced down a hill. Following in hot pursuit, I saw that there was a couple in the distance talking to each other and pushing a pram up the hill. I shouted to them about the oncoming ball and they just managed to move the pram from its path in the nick of time. Thankfully the baby suffered no injury but my pride was badly hurt. Who said croquet is a gentle or gentlemanly game? Despite occasional invitations, I never played it again.

In my office, International Press Centre, April, 1984

GORDON & GOTCH

By late 1970, although my work at *The Observer* was full of interest, we were operating on a shoe string with little or no money to invest in new projects. Consequently my own prospects were not too bright either. We could wait until the Astor family sold out to somebody more able to finance the paper, or alternatively I could look elsewhere. As the paper might struggle on for a number of years yet, a move on my part looked to be a better bet.

Keeping an eye on the 'situations vacant' columns, one day I spotted an advert for a company secretary at Gordon & Gotch, a small but long-established public company. I submitted an application and after a couple of interviews the job was mine. I discovered later that as a qualified Chartered Secretary, and having gained first-hand experience on a national Fleet Street newspaper, I was uniquely qualified for the post advertised – and the managing director received letters of congratulation from far-flung parts of the British Commonwealth. The fact that I was Irish turned out, surprisingly, to be an added bonus because Chris Goodall, the managing director and his family, came from Ireland via Liverpool and all seemed to have been educated at Ampleforth.

Geographically, it was simply a move across Farringdon Street, from Seacoal Lane to Gordon House (now alas no more) on the corner of Stonecutter Street. The company was engaged in the distribution of books, magazines and newspapers to the English-speaking world and was effectively controlled by the Goodall and Berrill families, descendants of the original Gotch who flourished in the mid 1850s. The background of the company is rather interesting so I will digress for a while to tell the story.

Sailing ships travelled back and forth from England to Australia, carrying wool, tea and other commodities to England and returning with machinery of all sorts, engineering products and items such as English newspapers, magazines and books.

When I say 'back and forth' it was certainly not a speedy journey by today's standards: the trip took about four to six weeks in each direction.

Alexander Gordon, a Scot, realized there was a market for these newspapers among the British immigrants who had gone to Australia in search of gold, and who wanted to be kept informed of news back home. So in 1850 he opened a newspaper stall in a Melbourne market to provide for this demand. After a while he became friendly with John Gotch, a failed gold digger, and offered him a partnership if he could sell as many newspapers on the diggings as he sold from his market stand. At this time Gordon was 63 and Gotch 29. To economise, the two men slept under the counter on their stall.

The drive and energy of the younger man meant that he soon reached Gordon's sales and enquired whether a legal agreement should be drawn up to formalise their partnership. They decided against such formality because, in Gordon's words 'if we are honest men we do not need a lawyer and if we are dishonest men no lawyer can make us honest'. That was 1853.

By 1861 they had expanded to Sydney. The population of Victoria and New South Wales trebled in a decade and immigrants poured in from Europe, so that by 1867 business had increased so much that they needed to establish an operation in London to purchase goods and arrange the packing and the shipping for Australia. Later they expanded to Perth, New Zealand, Canada and Southern Africa; and by 1970 there were three public companies, led by family members, in England, South Africa and Australasia.

I soon discovered that one of management's main problems was dealing with a militant trade union at the company's packing warehouse in Plaistow, East London. Another difficulty was trying to stem the pilfering that occurred there, and I was glad that such responsibilities did not rest on my shoulders. It was amazing how annuals which arrived at Plaistow for packing and shipment to Melbourne or Wellington, on the other side of the world could be bought at knockdown prices on the street stalls in Leather Lane market before supplies were released to the UK book trade.

After a while, it became apparent that the company needed to raise some fresh capital for expansion and Chris Goodall, the managing director, gave me a dossier that he had compiled on the subject to read over a weekend. At the same time the Berrill and Goodall families were the shareholders in a private family trust that owned a portfolio of quoted securities as well as significant holdings in the South African retailer CNA and the separate Gordon and Gotch company (no ampersand) in Australia. Some of the shareholders in the trust were content to remain as shareholders, but there were others who had no interest or involvement in the business and wanted to get out for a variety of reasons. Unfortunately they could only sell their shares to existing holders and sometimes these existing shareholders did not wish to purchase extra shares and, even if they did, they might not have had the funds to do so.

Chris Goodall suggested that the Gordon & Gotch UK public company might make a bid for the family trust, offering its own publicly-quoted shares instead. Then those shareholders who wanted an exit could sell on the stock market and those who wanted to remain could simply retain their shares. When the transaction was completed, Gordon & Gotch could sell the portfolio of shares to provide the cash needed in the business.

The proposal seemed eminently sensible and provided a good solution for those family members who were 'locked in' to an investment that was not of their choosing. The directors of the public company and the family investors all supported the 'take over' idea.

The next stage was to find a merchant bank that could handle the transaction for us. Chris and I did not know anybody who could help, but our chairman, Sir Anthony Percival, knew somebody who might be able to assist. This was Jimmy Davis, a director of N M Rothschild & Sons, so one day the three of us went off to St. Swithin's Lane in the City for afternoon tea. Mr Davis liked our proposition and thought it should be handled by one of his senior managers, Bill Dacombe, who then joined us. Before we left Mr Dacombe had fixed the date for a follow-up meeting at which Rothschild's lawyers and ours could also be represented.

An interesting aside here is that our lawyers were Lovell, White & King; and Jimmy Burridge, the senior partner, had acted for Gordon & Gotch when the company went 'public'. Chris Goodall fixed up a meeting with him to explain our thinking but, when we got to his office at the appointed time, it was explained to us that Mr Burridge had been called away at short notice and had appointed his assistant to meet us instead. We thought that it must have been some extremely important business that prevented Mr Burridge from not honouring our appointment and so it turned out to be. Mr Burridge, as I later discovered, had gone to Cairo instead at the request of the British Government to commence negotiating compensation for the nationalisation of the Suez Canal by Col. Nasser. Some 20 years or so later, Mr Burridge was a headline on the sports pages when his horse "Desert Orchid" won the Grand National.

Now back to the Rothschilds. At the second meeting Mr Dacombe introduced us to Jock Green-Armytage, whom he thought would be best able to take our matter forward – the message received being that senior people in such an eminent bank were much too busy to deal with our piddling little transaction. Before we met for the third meeting, we had to brief our auditors and they, as well as Rothschild's nominated accountants, along with the lawyers described above, were all requested to attend meeting number three. At that meeting Mr Green-Armytage introduced his own assistant who henceforth would attend to most of the 'nuts and bolts'. At this meeting it was suggested that the shareholders in the family trust should be separately advised because the lawyers and accountants acting for the company would not be seen as independent.

As Chris and I were not on first-name terms with even one merchant bank, we were at a loss as to a second one but the Rothschilds saved the day by suggesting we might usefully consider Guinness Mahon. The latter firm were duly appointed by the directors of the family trust and, as you can imagine, they too had to appoint fresh accountants and lawyers to offer them advice.

At meeting number four, the original trio (or quartet if you include Mr Dacombe) had grown to 22; and Chris Goodall, aghast at such a large number of people sitting around one of Rothschild's many board tables and drinking tea, whispered in my ear 'do you realise that we are having to pay all these people?'

Anyway, Guinness Mahon turned out to be extremely diligent, so much so that they determined the proposals being offered to the trust's shareholders were not quite fair enough and the price per share should be increased. After lengthy discussions with Rothschilds, agreement was reached on a higher offer and of course everything was straightforward from then on.

This was my first, but not my last, experience of a City-style take-over and it provided me with a salutary lesson that made me very cynical of City of London shenanigans (or should I say procedures?) ever after.

AGB RESEARCH

AGB Research, a market research company, was founded in the early 1960s after a most inauspicious start.

Martin Maddan, Bernard Audley, Doug Brown and Dick Gapper all worked together at Attwood Statistics ("AS") in Berkhamsted where they were senior executives. Along with the American AC Nielsen company in Oxford, AS was a leading company in continuous (as opposed to ad hoc) market research; and by then Wallace Attwood, its founder, and another American, had passed the company to his son Bedford.

The above-mentioned individuals considered that they generated most of AS's revenue but were being treated as mere managers, whereas they felt they should have been made directors and shareholders in the company. In other words, their contributions were not being either appreciated or acknowledged.

They decided to confront Mr Attwood with a list of their grievances. He listened to what they had to say and told them he didn't need time to consider their proposals. In fact he could manage the business perfectly well without them and from that moment onwards they were all fired.

They had assumed that nothing would be lost by them making their requests known: after all they would still have their jobs and didn't remotely consider the possibility of being out of work with wives and young families to support.

Shocked by the reaction, they adjourned to a local hostelry to consider the situation and decided to attempt to stick together and form a new company of their own. This was to be called AGB Research and it would compete head-to-head with AS.

At the time Martin Maddan had political aspirations and did not wish to continue working full-time for the new company as he hoped to become an MP at the next general election (which he did) so he was appointed chairman.

Through the 1960s the company enjoyed spectacular growth and by 1970 could even contemplate 'going public'.

AGB, along with Nielsen and AS, realised early on, that to build a successful market research business, it was almost essential to concentrate on continuous research. That meant building consumer panels of 10,000 or 20,000 individuals and households with characteristics representing the British population as closely as possible. The panel members would report on their purchases or consumption on a regular basis – daily, weekly, monthly – and you could then charge customers annual fees to receive the market data produced. That information could be based on purchases of branded groceries, toiletries and cosmetics or even viewing figures for adverts on TV.

In many fields of business a company enters into a contract to perform a task, and on completion – all being well – it gets paid for its work but then has to seek a replacement order, which can take up a lot of time and effort. That of course was not the case with continuous research because once you had a signed contract, it was likely to continue in force for a number of years and you were then free to go out and seek new business, knowing that, as your costs were fixed, any additional revenue would come straight through to the 'bottom line'.

I remember Martin Sorrell, who at the time was Finance Director at Saatchi's, marvelling at AGB's financial performance and saying 'we tell the City institutions that we are just like AGB'. That wasn't quite true of course because an ad agency could never have such a high proportion of its revenue in continuous business as AGB had then. Still, I suspect Martin had the last laugh because after he left Saatchi's he went on to create and build the WPP giant into the world's largest marketing and advertising agency company.

Shortly after AGB was quoted on the London Stock Exchange, I was enlisted to create a company secretarial function and at that time, in 1974, there were some 300 employees in the UK, mostly located at Eastcote, Middlesex, with a small number at Hilversum in the Netherlands.

When eventually I left some 15 years later, following exponential growth, the company had become the leading UK market research company and the second or third largest worldwide with 4,300 employees and operations in more than 20 countries. In particular it had created a niche for itself as the expert in TV audience measurement. Before then we had acquired AS itself which had two subsidiary companies in Ireland: Irish TAM and Attwood Ireland. My reward was to be appointed a director of both companies which enabled me to visit Dublin on a monthly basis and meet up with my old friends there.

Not long after I joined AGB, the Conservatives lost a general election and went into opposition. The two events were not of course connected except that we had forecast such a result. It led to Sir Geoffrey Howe (later Lord Howe of Aberavon) joining our board as a non-executive director and he was allocated an office next door to mine. As we both tended to arrive at work early, we talked regularly and became good friends.

After the 1979 election which the Conservatives won – we forecast that result too – Geoffrey joined the cabinet as Chancellor of the Exchequer and we continued in touch. A decade or so later, when Sir Geoffrey delivered his resignation speech in the House of Commons on 1 November 1990, sending Mrs Thatcher up in smoke, I wrote offering him my congratulations and received a most pleasant reply in return.

During the two general elections in the 1980s, AGB came up with a novel idea to assist the Conservative party. We created a panel of 20/25 leading company chairmen and chief executives who agreed to be interviewed by telephone very early each morning when they were asked for their reactions to the previous day's speeches or other announcements made by the parties, the candidates and the media. The panel's comments were summarised and passed to Mrs Thatcher for consideration so that the good points could be re-emphasised and the bad points diluted or removed in speeches the following day.

While the company was growing so fast, it was an exciting time to be intimately involved and our reputation for performance was sky-high. Because we measured our clients' market shares, we tended to know what was happening in the various market places even before our clients themselves. We were, as they say, punching above our weight. As a result company chairmen and chief executives felt it was important to keep close to our top brass to find out what was going on. It followed that our chairman or a senior director were frequently seen "hob-knobbing" at Footsie 100 lunches or dinner parties, to the surprise of outsiders because we were such a small company by comparison with them. I was reminded of those little plover birds that are allowed to enter the mouths of crocodiles in order to clean their teeth.

In about 1980 two of our marketing people suggested at a board meeting that we should consider purchasing an apartment on the Med, adjacent to a good golf course, where important clients could be invited down for a weekend of golf. These clients would be the directors of the many regional TV companies then operating or the manufacturers of packaged groceries, etc., all of whom were known to enjoy 'the good life'. I have to say this life was very attractive and, if one was not too selective with the invitations received, it would have been possible to spend most of one's time at Ascot or Newbury, Lord's or Wimbledon during the day, with evenings at the opera, ballet or livery company dinners.

Being the company's admin director and a notable non-golfer, they all looked at me for my reaction as I would be the person expected to arrange the purchase and manage the property. They were delighted that my response was favourable and knew I wouldn't be spending too much of my time there playing golf with my friends.

I started by contacting the leading firms of estate agents in London to see what developments they represented and then drew up a short-list of the most interesting propositions with a view to visiting them with a keen golfer colleague. At about this point Doug Brown, who had his own polo team, announced that he had just paid a visit to Sotogrande in Andalusia and suggested that we could not do better than have a look. It was an estate of about 4,000 acres with two 18 hole golf courses and a hotel as well as adjoining villas and apartments. It also had a reputation for being well-managed: in fact a veritable Switzerland in Spain.

I duly arranged a visit and found that Doug was absolutely right. The development was only about six miles from Gibraltar "as the crow flies" and there were good views of the Rock and of the Rif mountains of Morocco beyond. Facilities included a good supermarket, some bars and beach clubs, a yacht marina, tennis courts and even a polo ground. It was just what we wanted. Furthermore it was all up and running.

A number of the other developments that I looked at seemed fine on paper but, when visited, the brochure illustrations turned out to be merely architects' impressions. Some of the buildings were only half-built and when I enquired when they would be finished, was told that depended on sales of the remaining apartments. It appeared that the developers were having cash-flow problems and if we'd gone ahead with a purchase, who knows when we might have been able to enter into occupation. It wouldn't have been much fun to have bought a fifth floor penthouse apartment in a block where the lifts had not been installed, and wouldn't be until the last flats were sold.

The apartment we were interested in was on the ground floor – I knew not to take too many things for granted in Spain – and had four double bedrooms all with en suite bathrooms. It was priced at £375,000 and during my time at AGB the price rose to well over £1million. My main worry at the time however was how to get it furnished; not an easy task from my base in London. When I mentioned my problem to the sales agent, she asked if we would be willing to go ahead if she let us have the show flat for the same price. Of course we would as that would save me a great deal of work.

Considering we bought the place to entertain (and, yes, to impress) clients and never really thought of its investment possibilities, it turned out to be a great success. Personally I was glad to be able to invite my own friends down there over the following years and, even if I didn't play any golf, I more than made up for it by using the tennis courts – and there was plenty of touring around to be done, visiting Gibraltar, Ronda, Marbella and Algeciras – at times when the property was not otherwise occupied.

By 1987 AGB had gone 'ex-growth' and I had begun to look for pastures new. I didn't wish to join another company on a full-time basis but instead fancied getting a portfolio of activities together which would enable me to devote a part of my time to charitable interests, possibly related to the arts. More of this elsewhere and in the meantime I managed to arrange matters in a satisfactory way. I joined a firm of pension consultants as a consultant (not on pensions but on bringing in new business); helped to start a successful vehicle leasing company in Newport Pagnell; and joined a computer software company in Twickenham where I had an office. The latter proved very useful in arranging visits to the nearby rugby ground, and our visits to the varsity match, with a buffet lunch beforehand, proved very popular.

When I left AGB I remained a pension scheme trustee for a year or two and during all of this time the scheme was solvent and fully funded (unlike so many other schemes nowadays). I made arrangements to transfer my own benefits into a private plan and about two years later Robert Maxwell arrived on the scene, offered a knock-out price for the company and made history by plundering the pension scheme. He directed that the underlying assets should be sold and used the proceeds for his own benefit. For a time it looked as if none of the pension scheme members would receive anything, but eventually a compensation scheme was put in place which met most, but not all, of the deficit. The pensioners of course received less than their entitlements.

It is amazing to note that more than 30 years later subsequent governments have not yet dealt adequately with the funding of pension schemes, nor have they introduced legislation to force companies to make up the shortfall in scheme deficits within a given limited period. As a result, if a company gets into difficulties, it is the pension scheme members who are likely to suffer by receiving less than their due, while the regulators and government ministers turn blind eyes to the enormous salaries and bonuses which company directors are allowed to pay themselves to the great annoyance of shareholders.

Although I was told when leaving AGB that I would be welcome to continue using the apartment at Sotogrande – 'if it weren't for you we wouldn't have it' – I thought it best to make a clean break and endeavour to find a place of my own albeit at a much lower price. As my language skills have never been more than rudimentary, everything pointed to somewhere in Europe where English was spoken. Largely that meant Cyprus or Malta, where English is an official language, as my destination. So, after the general election in 1987 in Malta, I went off there, having never visited it before, to scout around and, after seeing 14 properties in a week, settled on a three-story house in St. Julians. It has worked out very well and enabled me to make quite a few friends there while also providing a base for visitors to stay when visiting Malta and the next-door island of Gozo. My visitors book tells me I had more than 50 people to stay. However, by 2010, after being in St. Julians for some 23 years, I was being driven to distraction by building work going on all around me with the accompanying noise and dust everywhere. I sold out and moved to Floriana where I am five minutes' walk from the buses and the entrance to Valletta.

I remain there for now, but for how much longer? It depends on my health. Looking back, it was just as well I didn't rely on using the Sotogrande apartment for my holidays on leaving AGB. It was subsequently acquired by Robert Maxwell when he bought the company and I wouldn't have wanted to share any apartment with him.

CAPTAIN BOB

When I joined George Rainbird in 1968, one of my tasks was to become involved in preparing production quotations for other publishers both in the UK and abroad, for editions in English as well as in other languages.

At the time Robert Maxwell had been building his own publishing company, Pergamon Press.

He had discovered that academics worldwide were anxious to see their learned works appearing in print, regardless of whether any payment would be made, and he was usually able to acquire the publishing rights for a derisory £250 or £300. There seemed to be little or no competition for such works at the time, which in any event were most unlikely ever to become bestsellers.

At the same time he was aware that there were nearly 1,000 universities and other institutions in the United States alone, almost all of which had libraries, and large endowments to enable them to acquire new medical, scientific and technical works.

The Maxwell system was to have the books produced cheaply by letterpress (that is with no colour and only minimal illustrations) and in small quantities, so that he could charge correspondingly large prices. All of this helped to keep the costs down and the profits high.

At the end of the 1960s Maxwell acquired the 'New Caxton Cyclopaedia' which came in many volumes and he found himself immediately with a problem: that he would be in competition with the larger and extremely successful Encyclopaedia Britannica, which used students to sell its encyclopaedias from door-to-door.

Britannica was not just successful but also the market leader, while

Maxwell was very much the underdog. To enable him to compete, he hit on the idea of offering five annually updated year-books free of charge with every set of encyclopaedias sold. It was a very good idea, but who was going to produce the volumes for him? The answer was the Thomson Organisation, of which Rainbird was a part, and I in turn just happened to be a small part of Rainbird, whose duty it was to produce the costings and quotations.

I recall very well my first meeting with Maxwell around in his office, when we enjoyed a very nice afternoon tea on bone china, to discuss some of the information that we required with regard to the costings.

At that time he was Labour MP for Buckingham: tall, dark and quite presentable I thought, as well as being very agreeable. He also possessed a very deep voice. During the meeting I mentioned that I needed up-to-date sales figures, on which to base my costs, so he summoned an accountant to join us and told him "Mr Elyan needs the sales figures up to the end of last month".

"I'll have them for him by the end of the week" said the accountant, whereupon Maxwell exploded and thumped the tea-table so hard that all the cups and saucers jumped about six inches as he bellowed "Mr Elyan wants the figures today, RIGHT NOW". Of course it was not possible for the figures to appear so suddenly and I was perfectly happy to wait until the following Friday, even though I, too, was in fear of my life.

Later I understood that the shouting was intended to achieve two objectives: to terrify the accountant and to impress me.

On another occasion I was around at his office in Poland Street, at the HQ of the Maxwell Communications Corporation – MCC for short, and not related to an other rather better-known MCC. When I got there I was told he was late returning from a previous meeting. As I sat by his desk I noticed that his phone had buttons instead of the usual dial, and two of them were coloured red and marked 'Kevin' and 'Ian', presumably to enable him to thump the phone instead of dialing their numbers and waiting for his sons to answer.

In November 1986 Phillips and Drew, the stockbrokers, arranged a marketing seminar for their clients, at Whitbread's old 'Porter Tun" room in what had been for many years their brewery in Chiswell Street, where three companies – AGB Research, Reuters and MCC, – were to give presentations.

Coffee was served at 10.30 and the meeting was due to get going at 11, but at the appointed hour there was no sign of Captain Bob. The Phillips and Drew partners were seen whispering among themselves and wondering what had happened to him, and I understood he was again 'running late', as was his norm.

Shortly afterwards a message came back that he was on his way and he duly arrived at about 11.30. There then took place the ceremony of the introductions and the shaking of hands, followed by a quick cup of coffee.

Suddenly, while the throng stood around mumbling among themselves, Maxwell put down his cup, clapped his hands and shouted out: "OK boys and girls: it's time to get down to business", having kept everybody waiting for nearly an hour.

When I first met Bob, at a guess he would have weighed 12 or 13 stones. Over the next 15 years his weight must have doubled and I understood that on some days he had two lunches or two dinners.

As if in order to accentuate his figure, he took to wearing loosely fitting woollen suits and the ones that I recall were pale blue. Fortunately I don't possess any photos to accompany this chapter.

When in the late 80s AGB seemed to be losing its way, Clive Hollick's United News & Media Group decided to bid for us. That awakened Maxwell to the desirability of acquiring one of the world's leading market research companies, and he let it be known, furthermore, that he would not be outbid; notwithstanding the fact that he lacked the resources to complete the purchase – though none of us, of course, knew that at the time.

History tells us that, after he succeeded in the acquisition, some £400 million was "removed" from the AGB Pension Scheme as Maxwell ordered the sale of most of its underlying securities to pay for the company's purchase, in breach of all sorts of City and legal regulations.

I had retired from AGB some two years before that event but I had been a trustee of the Pension Scheme for a number of years and can confirm that it was then showing a good surplus. Yet within two years there was a massive deficit and the fund was unable to meet its pension commitments. That led to pensioners marching with banners outside Parliament, which got nationwide publicity, and was itself followed by a number of banks, which had received substantial fees in connection with

Maxwell's acquisitions, making contributions to the Pension Fund along with the British government. It didn't quite make up all of the shortfall so that some thousands of pensioners were left with much reduced pensions, while Maxwell was free to cruise about in his yacht, the Lady Ghislaine, or be seen wandering over Holborn in his helicopter.

When Maxwell took control of AGB he made no immediate changes to the Board and it continued under the chairmanship of Bernard Audley, who had been one of its founders.

As one board meeting was proceeding, Maxwell entered the room silently and sat at the far end of the board table from Audley: a little disconcerting, I'm sure, for any chairman. He never said a word until Audley's secretary entered the room and whispered in Bob's ear that there was a telephone call for him. He asked Audley if he might take it on the boardroom phone, which he did. The following one-sided conversation was heard: "Hello, hello, can you hear me? Hello, hello. Hello – is that the King of Jordan?"

Nobody did discover whether this was a put-up job or not. At the time it was thought to be true, but Maxwell's subsequent history makes one rather doubtful.

Another story is of a pretty young trainee journalist who happened to meet Maxwell while waiting for the lift in the Mirror building (which incidentally had a helipad on the roof). He invited her to his office-cum-flat where she was seduced, literally, with the promise of a journalistic promotion. A day or so later, not having heard anything from anybody, she decided to contact the personnel department to enquire and found herself out of a job (on Maxwell's instructions).

I have frequently been asked if I thought he had drowned or committed suicide, and of course I don't know for certain. His son Kevin said he was sure he had not committed suicide because "it was not in his character". But what was "in his character?"; and Kevin didn't exactly tell the truth in Court even though he was later cleared of fraud (before being declared bankrupt).

A friend of mine in Malta, who had worked as a stewardess on the yacht Lady Ghislaine, told me that hers were horrible duties as Maxwell used to defecate in bed, and she and a colleague were required to clear up the mess. He also had a predilection for urinating in the nude over the side of his boat; and when his body was recovered off the Gran

Canaria coast in November 1991, it was unclothed, which makes me think that it was unlikely to have been suicide.

With his warped mind, he probably would have been pleased that the mystery rumbles on some 30 years later.

The Story
of
School Prints

by

BRENDA RAWNSLEY

Edited with an introduction by

DAVID ELYAN

THE STORY OF SCHOOL PRINTS
by Brenda Rawnsley
Edited with an introduction by David Elyan

In 1970 my colleague at the *Observer*, Patrick Seale, suggested that we might consider publishing original graphics in larger-than-normal editions and at lower-than-usual prices. Those were the days of purchase tax, and artistic impressions (screenprints, etchings and the like) were subject to tax if the edition exceeded seventy-five copies. For that reason the well-known galleries in Bond Street and Cork Street limited editions to that number (or less) and, because of the scarcity value, were able to charge correspondingly higher prices.

It was well known that the *Observer* enjoyed a relatively large readership among students, undergraduates, academics, literati; whereas the *Sunday Times's* readership was among professionals and business people. We used to say at the *Observer* that our readers' taste 'was ahead of their pockets' and, consequently, if we could produce these larger editions of art, say 500 or 750 copies, we could reduce prices drastically – and the artist would receive no less than for the smaller art gallery editions. *The Observer* prints would be at prices our readers could afford but (and it was a very big 'but' indeed, because it had never been tried) would people buy them?

We commissioned and bought a number of prints by well known artists: Hamilton, Paolozzi, Frink, Hockney and Procktor. We offered them for sale in the colour magazine and they sold tolerably well. 'Observer Art' as it became known was up and running.

In the Spring of 1971 a letter was received by the then editor, David Astor, from a Mrs Brenda Rawnsley. I don't know what became of this letter but the gist of it was: 'Your newspaper is making valiant efforts to enter the art world; I'm trying to get out of it – would you be interested in buying my business in Belgravia?' The editor and most people in authority at the paper were not interested and, almost as an afterthought, the letter was sent to Patrick Seale. He and I discussed it, considered the suggestion to be somewhat unlikely, but we agreed I should contact Mrs Rawnsley as much out of politeness as of curiosity.

A week or so later I had arranged to visit Mrs Rawnsley's business and gallery in Motcomb Street. I knew as soon as I entered the premises that the business would not be of interest to us and, short of turning around and fleeing before Mrs Rawnsley came downstairs, I decided to go through with the expected charade. At the very least it would be interesting to hear how she had started a company called School Prints with the laudable objective of making prints available to schools and factories – and this just after the war when paper and artists' materials were in short supply, to say nothing of art itself.

Having walked around the premises and then down to the framing department in Kinnerton Mews, Mrs Rawnsley pointed out her stock in trade, some of which consisted of the remains of a series of prints which were produced as the result of a visit to France. These were works by Picasso, Braque, Dufy, Léger and Matisse. They had sold slowly at the princely sum of £1 each. Part of the stock had got water stained and been destroyed. The remainder was available for purchase as part of the business.

We went back upstairs again where, over a glass of whisky (or two), Mrs Rawnsley told me how she persuaded these famous artists to produce plates to enable prints to be produced for sale to schools and factories.

I arrived back at the *Observer* much heartened by the story – was it generally known in the art world? I wondered. Would it make a good story for the paper? We called a meeting. The response was uniformly favourable. There were enough prints still available to offer them to readers alongside an article in the colour magazine – but would Mrs Rawnsley be attracted to the idea? After all, her interest was to sell her business, not a part of the stock, which might then deplete the value of the business. And of course we did not know whether the prints would sell. We discussed at great length how best to put our proposal to Mrs

Rawnsley. We came to no definite conclusion.

While we deliberated about how to put our ideas to the owner of the prints, and who would best put our approach, the likelihood that Mrs Rawnsley might agree was, to my mind, substantially reduced by the fact that Patrick Seale came up with the crazy idea that the prints should be offered for sale at £15 each. That figure would allow £5 to cover purchase tax, packing and postage, £5 for Mrs Rawnsley and £5 for 'Observer Art'. Crazy when sales of the prints at £1 were not proving easy.

Somehow, I was entrusted with the task of speaking to Mrs Rawnsley about our ideas and, if not rejected out of hand, of mentioning rather gingerly the proposed selling price of £15. To my complete surprise (and relief) our plan was accepted, a writer was commissioned to write up the story and the artwork prepared for eventual publication.

During these preparations we received a visit in London from the art correspondent of *Die Zeit*, Petra Kipphoff. She was so enthusiastic about our plans that she asked if her paper might participate in the venture and have the opportunity to offer the same prints to German readers over the same weekend. As we were not at all assured of success, we decided to take the opportunity of lessening our risk by allocating a certain number of each print for sale to *Die Zeit* readers.

The articles appeared in the *Zeit* magazine on 7 May 1971 and in the *Observer* colour magazine on 9 May 1971. The entire stock of remaining prints was sold out within a week. We had all been vindicated – such is the influence of a powerful selling medium such as a national newspaper colour magazine. And Mrs Rawnsley's share of the proceeds came to slightly more than she was asking for the sale of her entire business.

David Elyan
1990

✱✱✱✱✱

DEREK RAWNSLEY was the grandson of Canon Rawnsley, who started the National Trust in November 1911. He went to Eton and Oxford. During his undergraduate course at Oxford, he made history by flying solo in a Tiger Moth from Australia to Oxford, saying, after putting off his departure for too long, it was the only way to arrive in Oxford in time for term. He was born with a mass of energy and a lot of original ideas. In 1935, he asked Sir Philip Sassoon to open a gallery called "Picture Hire" opposite Claridge's. The object of this gallery was to hire original pictures by contemporary artists. This helped the artists to get their work known and gave people a chance to hang fine pictures in their own homes. In 1937, he rented some rooms at 44 Gordon Square and started "School Prints" with a small amount of capital, well under £10,000, and with the object of hiring sets of reproductions to schools and changing them every term, so that children in the schools could learn about the world's great works of art.

In 1938, he founded the Federal Union Movement (for a United Europe) with Charles Kimber and Patrick Ramsden and he himself went around Europe giving lectures to see if there was some way of unification to avoid war. However, as the year went on, he realised that he was on a losing wicket and began then to think only of joining up with the RAF and, at the outbreak of war, this is what he did.

By 1940, I was working in the Ministry of Economic Warfare in Berkeley Square and we decided to get married in February 1941. Derek had a premonition that he was not going to live very long and he also knew that he was going to be posted overseas, but, to our great dismay, he was posted at midnight after the wedding. But I said that, whatever happened, I would try and get myself out to the Middle East as I had been brought up in Egypt and I could speak French and Arabic, so it seemed to me that someone with my qualifications would be needed. I also had some Greek. I had a hunch that if I gave up my lunch hours and walked up and down Whitehall, sooner or later I would meet somebody I knew and, in fact, this happened. I ran into a man who had been Air Attaché in Athens and was, by then, a Group Captain in charge of RAF Intelligence.

So, by the end of 1941, I had left Economic Warfare and become a WAAF Officer. Early in 1942, I was sent in a convoy in HMT Pastor to Freetown and eventually flew from Takaradi via Kano to Khartoum and Cairo and arrived at Heliopolis on 2 February.

On 10 March, Derek came into Cairo in a truck with his troops from the Western desert. He was working with David Stirling, of SAS fame. On 29 July, Derek was posted to RAF Healey outside Bulawayo in Southern Rhodesia and retrained to fly two-engined aeroplanes with a view to dropping people into Yugoslavia. By 1 September, I was posted to RAF Ramleh in Palestine, which put a great distance between us. I explained my desire to get some leave and get down to Bulawayo to my Commanding Officer, Group Captain Mungo Buxton, and said to him that I would hitch-hike my way down there, although I did realise it was forbidden for any WAAF officer to go further south than Egypt, but I assured Mungo that I would be coming back, even if I were one or two days late.

On 26 November, I left Ramleh as cargo in a Wimpey plane, bound for LG224 which was a landing ground on the Cairo-Alexandria route. On Friday 27th, I picked up a Beau-Fighter which was due to go to Khartoum via Luxor. There is not much room in a Beau-Fighter and I was alternately squatting and standing in the cockpit looking over the sergeant pilot's shoulder. We landed at Luxor and went in for lunch and then, unfortunately, on take-off, we went on past the runway and out into the sand, and for a moment I thought we were on fire, as the whole aircraft seemed full of fumes. Finally, we pulled up; and the pilot got out to inspect the trouble. The tail wheel had broken and the undercarriage was badly damaged. The fumes were, in fact, sand particles flying around at a furious rate. Of course this meant that I had to get into Luxor to a hotel for the night and think of some other way of moving south.

I met some South Africans and on Saturday 28th, I left with them in a Load-Star and went to Juba. Sunday 29th I was at Kasama and Monday 30th at Bulawayo. Derek did not get into Bulawayo, unfortunately, until Wednesday 2nd, as his leave got a bit delayed. However, he came straight in, found me at the Grand Hotel, Bulawayo and we both left for the Victoria Falls Hotel and arrived there on Friday 4 December.

On 6 December, we caught the night train and arrived back at

Bulawayo at 9 a.m. and I left with some other South Africans again in a Load-Star at 3.30 p.m. and headed off for Cairo via Lusaka, Nairobi and Wady Saidna. I arrived in Cairo on 11 December. I then got a lift in a car, driving the Sinai route to Jerusalem and was back at Ramleh on time on 14 December. My instinct told me that Derek would be killed fairly soon and I was right, for he was killed on 22 February 1943, at the age of thirty-one. *The Times* obituary on 12 March 1943 was lengthy and ended 'Derek Rawnsley was of the type essential to salvation which sets out to do things because they had never been done before and because they seem impossible. Unless after this war we have sufficient men of his type ripened by experience and judgement, the war may prove to have been fought in vain'. And the *Observer* said 'We owe such "fiery particles" one single and tremendous debt to keep all their torches burning and their causes from being lost'.

I thought my contribution would be to continue his work on art, for we had many times discussed the possibilities of publishing lithographs so that the primary schools which had no art of any kind could see original modern pictures at a very reasonable price. And we talked about these when we had leave and were sleeping out by the pyramids and we also talked about it whilst at the Victoria Falls.

In 1945, I applied for a special release from the forces because my work at School Prints was urgently calling and Victor Bonham-Carter and Raglan Squire, who were old friends of Derek and had already helped him with Picture Hire and School Prints, did the same thing. All three of us started up again, working from Gordon Square, where one secretary during the war had managed to keep the circulating scheme working and circulating amongst a few public schools. It was very necessary to enlarge the picture circulating scheme again and bring it into a hive of activity and at the same time I was very anxious to publish original lithographs for primary schools which Derek and I had been talking about in the Middle East. I had one difficulty in that I knew nothing about art and had seen very little in the way of art because I had been moving around the Middle East a lot, and in many places where there was little culture. However, people are very kind and very generous, particularly at that time, and I was able to get the help of many art experts, including Herbert Read, who suggested the English artists I should approach and also thought it would be wise to have between fifteen and twenty artists submitting sketches to a committee, and from these sketches four for each school term would be chosen. This was all organised and the first four artists were asked to go down to the Baynard Press and work on the stone under the supervision of the famous Mr Griffits of the Baynard Press.

Each lithograph had its own border as there was no timber available for frames at that time and sadly all of the pictures had to be printed on very poor quality paper because that was all we could get hold of. By December 1945, we had fixed up the twelve for the following year and worked out that we could send out four each term and that schools could own them provided they paid £3-10s for an annual subscription, including purchase tax.

We wondered how we would distribute these lithographs but luckily, whilst we were in Gordon Square, I spotted an advertisement by the Ministry of Supply for the sale of cartridge cases. These were just the right size. And so we ordered something like 12,000, but by that time we only had one room in Gordon Square and I can clearly see now the lorry arriving with all these cases. Finally we hauled them up on string over the balcony into the first floor room and stacked them all round the walls and in the end there was only just room for one small table in the middle. Obviously, to do any work it really was essential to move. Raglan Squire, an architect, was very able and found us a house at 13 Motcomb Street and we moved there during 1945.

The winter of 1945-46 was astonishingly cold. But on the ground floor there was a fireplace and I was living in Queen's Gate, so every morning, on my way to work, I collected some firewood from an old man. We lit the fire and four of us spent our time rolling the lithographs up and putting them into the cartridge cases ready for dispatch, and then we took it in turns to carry about twelve at a time round to the Knightsbridge Post Office to get them off to the schools. By then, as far as I recollect, we had something like 3,000 subscribers from the schools, and some large organisations subscribing as well.

One day I suddenly thought what a good idea it would be to advance slightly and widen the horizons of schools and go out and try to persuade six really great well-known artists of international acclaim to make original graphics for schools.

1947 and the beginning of 1948 was taken up with the complicated idea of getting the collaboration of the French artists. Firstly, of course, and most obviously, it was very necessary to find some form of plastic plates which were transportable for the artists to work on because it would be impossible with stone or zinc. I had been writing a lot to ICI Plastics Division because by then we had something like a hundred and fifty members of ICI using our Pictures for Industry circulating scheme and one of them was the Plastics Division. It's hard now to recollect exactly, but I know about the same time Cowell's of Ipswich were also trying to tackle the plastic plates problem and eventually, after a lot of correspondence in every direction, Geoffrey Smith of Cowell's of Ipswich came to see me in Motcomb Street to discuss our leaving the Baynard Press and moving to Cowell's with their new technique of printing from plates made from images drawn on granulated plastic sheets. They had just produced a series of Orlando books with this technique and this impressed me very much and so I got in touch with Henry Moore, who was to be one of our chosen important artists, to see whether he would come down with me to Cowell's and try out the plastic and see how good it was and what he thought of it. As far as I recollect, Henry came down with his sketchbook for I was very anxious to see whether it was possible just to print direct from the plastic plates. In Henry Moore's catalogue Part I, The Graphic Work, 1931-1972, item 6 and item 8 are two drawings from his sketchbook direct onto plastic, printed from the plastic and, of course, they came out with mirror writing. They were in black and white and were never really published although I have a proof of each and maybe Cowell's do as well. Certainly the Henry Moore Foundation have got copies.

Henry said that it was perfectly all right to draw on the plastic plates, but clearly Cowell's felt, and I think knew all along, that they would have to be photographed through onto zinc plates for printing. This raised doubts in the end as to whether my lithographs were really originals, but I claim they are, for the artist drew each colour on a separate plastic plate. In most cases, six colours were used, i.e. six plates were drawn on. Meanwhile, Henry Moore was agreeable to doing a large lithograph for us, but said that he had never really used colour and he was nervous and also slightly apprehensive of being included with the French masters. Henry was born diffident, like so many very great men. However, I reassured him and said I was certain that he could manage colour and so he said he would try strong colour, but before doing it, he would like to see what the French artists had done, so that he could get his own colours bright enough to compete with them.

Frank McEwan was working for the British Council in Paris and had a French-Algerian girlfriend called Denise Chesnay and I contacted Frank to see what possibility there would be of meeting the French artists and, on the whole, he was very pessimistic, but felt that Léger would probably see me as he was the least formal of the lot. But he didn't hold out any special chances and certainly thought that it would be quite impossible to plan it all ahead and the only thing to do was just arrive, when he would do everything he could to help us. So I thought a lot about this and being used to moving around in aeroplanes throughout the war, it seemed to me the only thing to do was to hire a small aeroplane and take it with us. Then, wherever the artists were, we could chase them up. We were very lucky in finding a very charming New Zealand pilot for our little plane and I set off with Raglan Squire who was Chairman of School Prints, and Geoffrey Smith who was Chairman of Cowell's and departed from Gatwick aerodrome for Le Bourget on Sunday 20 June 1948. That very day, in Paris, we met Herbert Read who was there for the International Art Critics Conference organised by Unesco, and Mr Bellew who was the director of the Arts & Letters section of Unesco, as well of course as Frank McEwan. Everybody seemed as gloomy as could be, but thought the idea interesting.

On Monday 21 June in the afternoon, having telephoned, we went round to see Braque in his studio in Montparnasse. He was interested and I think he liked us. Certainly we liked him, but his whole set up was rather formal with quite an expensive salon, so it was very obvious that he was no starving artist. Having talked things over with us, we only offered him £100 down and £100 when the first proof was produced, so he was very doubtful if he would do it for that money. He was most emphatic that Picasso would not take part and he also said that he would not join in unless Picasso said that he would. So, we left him in a very amiable way, knowing that if we succeeded with the others, we would actually get him to join in as well.

We had decided that on Tuesday 22 June we would set off and attack Léger. I was very keen on his work and decided to wear a bright yellow dress with a purple coat in his honour as I knew colour interested him very much indeed. He was to be found in his Montparnasse studio, high above dark, narrow winding stairs, where he had worked for years. It was a kind of a large modern box room with big dusty windows with the paint peeling off the walls. When I arrived, Léger was in a bright blue sports shirt outside his trousers and lining up rows of clean brushes on the steps of a folding ladder. It couldn't possibly have been more of a contrast with our visit to Braque.

He received us with great enthusiasm, and in an article written for *Vogue* in 1950 Rosamund Vernier said this about him: He said 'I didn't tell you about the English woman who came to see me – most unexpected – she was representing an organisation called School Prints. They print lithographs for English elementary schools. She managed to commission the colour lithograph from me and was going to print 3,000 copies to distribute amongst the schools. And she goes to Picasso too and Braque – can you imagine that happening here in France? I went round to see my old friend, Yvon Delbos, the French Minister for Education, with my lithograph under my arm. He asked me what I had there and I said: 'No, mon vieux, not for you.'

Léger greatly cheered us and so we left our plastic plates with him in his studio. That afternoon we visited Monsieur Maeght at the Gallery Maeght who was a very influential dealer and who was very encouraging and nice to us and we agreed that the following morning, Wednesday 23 June, we would take the plastics with us and show them to him. And this we did. After that, we had an interview with Monsieur Sabatez, the lifelong friend and adviser to Picasso, who also, in fact, looked after all the money side of Picasso's affairs and who was very commercially minded. He did, however, encourage us to go south and see Picasso at the earliest possible opportunity at Golfe Juan. He said Picasso would be coming to Paris, but really it would be almost impossible for us to see him as he would be too booked up.

We made contact with Peter Kapp, an English artist who knew Picasso and he agreed to come with us, as long as we took his white poodle, Annabella, with us. So we did. Denise Chesnay came with us, who helped with the general glamour side which we felt was necessary; she was a most beautiful and attractive French girl, and very intelligent and very knowledgeable about art, as well as being an artist herself. And she vaguely knew Piccasso, who had once painted her.

That afternoon, Geoffrey Smith, Rag Squire, Denise, Peter Kapp and myself started off in the aeroplane heading south. The starboard engine cowling flew off with a terrible clatter and very nearly came through my window while we were in mid-air, half an hour out of Paris. Of course we had to return for repairs and Denise very kindly said she would put us up for the night in her house at St Cloud. This turned out to be very amusing. Denise was a very good dancer and that evening, after dinner, she entertained us with her dancing.

The next morning we started off early from Paris on a most beautiful day, and when we were above the Alps and in sight of the Mediterranean, we opened a bottle of champagne. The pop from the cork at that height was phenomenal. The pilot imagined that we had guns and had started shooting each other. However, we arrived at Nice Airport at 12.30 in perfect weather and we hired a car to go to Golfe Juan and find ourselves a small pub to relax in and spend the night and also to find and meet Picasso's chauffeur, for we had been told that he was the key to everything. He told us the part of the beach which Picasso visited every day with Françoise Gilot and his small son Claude. So, on Friday 25 June, we all went down to swim early in the morning, occupying the exact spot on the beach that the chauffeur had told us to go to and then we started swimming and chatting to one another as if nothing was happening. We saw Picasso and Françoise arriving with Claude, as we anticipated. Denise and I splashed around in the water and looked with our goggles for fishes and things and gradually we bumped into Picasso. It's all really very simple, if you know what you are aiming at.

Since nobody else was about, this inevitably led to having chitter-chatter about this and that without letting on what we were doing or who we were. Eventually, Picasso said why don't we go and have lunch with him in his favourite little restaurant. And this we agreed to do. Lunch of course being French lasted from 1.30 till 4.30 and still we didn't quite say what we were up to. His favourite starter for lunch and for all of us was melon and this he has shown in the lithograph which he ultimately did for us. He seemed to find the whole thing rather a joke and said he was now working on pottery in Vallauris and would we like to go out and see his designs on pottery. This was very exciting for all of us and off we went with him. There he offered me a large pot but I said I really had no room in my small house in London for his large pot and anyway I wasn't mad about it. He also offered another one to Rag Squire who said he would like it very much and to this day he has it in his house in Chester Row.

After we'd looked round at the pots and things, we got down to our project and produced the plastic plates which amused him intensely. He's such a big man with such a good brain, he decided immediately that it was a good idea to show his work in a cheap way to children. Although we were not offering anything in the way of money as far as he was concerned, he would still do it for the love of les enfants du monde. So we left our plastic plates with him and a whole lot of photographs were taken and back we went to our hotel. Frightfully pleased with life, we opened another bottle of champagne to celebrate what appeared to have been from the start our most difficult person to track down. I offered him a trip in our aeroplane, but Picasso said he had never flown in his life, and his work and his own self were far too important to risk, and nothing would induce him to come up with me. Also, he said he might actually be scared – he wasn't sure – and was not prepared to try.

As Picasso wouldn't come up with us, on Saturday 26 June we left at dawn from Nice Airport and headed for Perpignan where we arrived at 11.30 a.m. and set off for the studio of Raoul Dufy. He was very crippled with arthritis and said he couldn't really do very much now with his right hand, but he had begun to use his left hand. He seemed to find our visit extremely interesting and was kind enough to show us many of his canvases and a very beautiful tapestry which he had made the design for. He was cautious about our new process and did a small doodle on the plastic and we said we would take it home and proof it for him and send it back to him so that he could see how simple it all was. He hummed and hawed as well as to whether he would be able to do the whole thing with his left hand but thought that he would.

In the end, out of the six artists, I feel that Dufy chose perhaps the most suitable subject for children, but also the most complicated to draw as a lithograph and to this day it is disputed whether he did it with his left hand or not. I am convinced that he did. He had integrity and when he said he was going to do something, no matter how painful or difficult, I personally feel quite convinced that he did every single bit of the work on the plates himself.

We left that day at 5.30 for Paris and arrived safely at 9 o'clock, and went back to Denise's house at St Cloud where we could telephone Monsieur Maeght who had promised to try and fix an appointment for us with Matisse, who was terribly ill, on the Sunday.

It all fitted in very well and we went back to Braque who again received us most cordially and once he heard what had happened on our trip, was delighted and said 'yes, of course', he would love to join in, and the fee was immaterial just as long as we paid a little something. Anything he could do to help les enfants du monde.

M. Maeght had been successful and we went over to see Matisse who was ill in bed and looking very, very white and shaky, but absolutely full of charm. His mistress, Lydia, kept a very good eye on him and was fairly firm with us not to stay too long. We left the plastic plates with Matisse and he said he was not sure if he would have the strength to draw on them, but if he possibly could, he would; but if not, he would make a papier déchiré (paper cut-out) and he would let us know. So that was as much as he could possibly do and we went off to the aeroplane, leaving Le Bourget at 4 o'clock for London and our own respective homes. I think all of us were very excited by what had happened and terribly grateful to all the French artists for receiving us so well and appearing to have so much time for us, when we had so little to offer them.

At that time, it was very difficult to get foreign currency of any kind and we had all sorts of forms to fill in to enable the artists to be paid in their own French currency by us. Well, all the artists drew their money most successfully, except Picasso. And I once had the most marvellous letter from Barclays Bank beginning, 'Dear Madam', and headed 'Your client, Monsieur Pablo Picasso', which continued along the following lines: 'We regret to inform you that your client Mr Pablo Picasso has not yet drawn his fees in French francs and the time limit for him to do this is just about coming to an end. Kindly inform your client of the position.' I did inform our client, but of course it was Monsieur Sabatez and he hung on until the rate changed in favour of the franc.

Geoffrey Smith has a story, which probably is true, that even on the trip we ourselves ran out of money because of the limitation on the number of francs we could take with us and, when we were invited to lunch by Picasso at Golfe Juan, the bill was left for us to pay and we had nothing to pay it with. However, Geoffrey knew a bank manager in

Marseilles who telephoned the money through to Nice to enable us to pay our bill at Golfe Juan. I am certain that things were not at all easy for any kind of luxury in a foreign country at that time.

The cartridge cases which I referred to before came in very useful as usual and enabled the French artists to post their plastic plates over to England. I had already arranged an import licence for these plates, but always had to go to Heathrow to collect them and then take them to Geoffrey Smith. Furthermore, they had to come back again and when the colour proofs were ready, they were posted off to the artists for their approval and then, as most of them didn't approve the first time, there was a lot of toing and froing of cartridge cases and comments, until at long last we got the 'Bon à tirer' from Picasso, Braque, Dufy and Léger. In the meantime, poor Matisse was feeling very frail and said that he couldn't manage to do anything except the papier déchiré and would I go over and see him, which I did. But I wondered how I was going to bring back a papier déchiré of vast value through the Customs until I remembered the British Customs are on the whole simple people and if you take ten sheets over with you, and they count ten sheets, and then you leave one sheet behind, and insert a Matisse instead, the Customs will count ten sheets in again, and that's exactly what they did do. Geoffrey Smith at Ipswich had to make the plates from the papier déchiré and Cowells had a lot of trouble proofing this particular picture, 'The Dancer'.

The reason for this is that Matisse, quite rightly, explained if the depth of colour of the red and the green was correctly contrasted and you ran your eyes down a straight centre line, the white dancers will actually dance; if there was any variation in the contrasting tones of the green and the red, they would not dance. This took a lot of time and produced quite a lot of difficulty until eventually we were able to get it right.

Picasso did really quite an amusing design, based on me and my trip to France. On the right hand side there is myself with three protruding front teeth, arriving in a small aeroplane, and on the left-hand side the melon that we all had for lunch that day on the table at the café.

The schools would not support this unsuitable modern art and our financial difficulties and our very heavy stocks of lithographs seemed to overwhelm us, for we had done 3,000 each of this international series of six pictures, quite certain that we would be sold out practically overnight.

By 1970, the stocks didn't seem to be doing very much in the way of moving and we felt there was only one thing to do which was to look around for some help. Something made me ring up Lord Thomson of *The Times* and see whether he could think of some method of making us solvent. In a funny way he did because he said he was not interested, but why not get in touch with David Astor of the *Observer* because the *Observer* was always short of cash and might be grateful for some method of collaborating with us so we could help each other financially.

School Prints gave the original plastic sheets on which the artists had drawn to the Tate Gallery for safe custody.

Finally, David Elyan of the *Observer* came to see me.

Brenda Rawnsley
1990

Brenda Rawnsley's original tape recording, on which the above article was based, has been presented to the National Museum of Fine Arts, Valletta, in 2001 together with a collection of original photographs, some related correspondence and a framed set of the French prints.
The material has subsequently been displayed at the Museum and in Gozo.

Picasso and Françoise Gilot on the beach at Golfe-Juan, June 1948

With Brenda Rawnsley at Pallant House Gallery, Chichester, March 2007

Henri Matisse   *The Dancer*

Raoul Dufy   *The Band*

Henry Moore   *Sculptural Objects*

George Braque   *The Bird*

Ferdinand Léger   *King of Hearts*

Pablo Picasso   *Composition*

WC HUMOUR

My father always seemed to have had a lavatorial sense of humour – something that I appear to have inherited. The most oblique reference to turds or constipation would have any Elyan, male or female, falling about with laughter.

I received my indoctrination at an early age, probably when I was less than two. It was the middle of the War and it was necessary for those with gardens to grow vegetables for home consumption. My father decided to grow a large crop of tomatoes and entered into this new activity with gusto. Friends advised him that they would thrive on a good diet of pig manure, so he obtained a couple of tons of the stuff from the Coughlans, farmer friends of the family. It came along on a cart and was piled high at the far end of the garden, or at least (because of the smell) as far from the house as possible. As a curious youngster, barely able to walk, I wandered outside to inspect this new garden landmark, tripped over a rake and fell headlong into the mound, to the consternation of both parents. I understand it took more than one wash of me and my clothes to get rid of the stains and the smell.

Some years later, on a seashore walk in Youghal with my father, a large seagull dropped its excrement on my head from a great height. Did I get any sympathy or help to clean up the mess? Not a bit of it. After Dad had recovered from laughing he exclaimed 'you're lucky that cows don't fly' and resumed his laughing. (More recently, I told this story at a dinner party in Malta where one of the guests quite spontaneously added 'that indeed was a pat on the head from your father)'.

There is a family joke that once when Dad was not feeling well and consulted John Kiely, our family doctor, he was advised to produce a urine sample and take it to the hospital for analysis. Not being able to locate a suitable plastic bottle at home, he washed and used instead an empty whiskey bottle with its label still on which he then delivered to the hospital. Some days later he phoned the doctor to enquire if he had yet received the results of the test. On contacting the hospital to enquire about the delay, Dr Kiely was told that the whiskey bottle had been stolen from the laboratory.

Jon Pertwee, the actor, told a story about when he was beginning his career in repertory theatre in the North of England and appeared on the same bill as Arthur Askey, who was then at the end of his career and told him about an amusing incident many years before. When Askey was starting off he once stayed in digs in a Lancashire cotton town and bought a bottle of sherry which he kept in his bedroom wardrobe. Every evening he used to pour himself a glass of the stuff before going downstairs for his supper and on to the theatre. After a few days, however, he noticed that the sherry in the bottle was going down at a faster rate than he was drinking it. So he decided to transfer the sherry to another bottle which he kept hidden in his suitcase and peed in the original bottle which he then placed back in the wardrobe. To his surprise he saw that the level of the bottle in the wardrobe went down just the same as before. Eventually his run in the town ended and he prepared to return home. Whilst paying the landlady and saying his goodbyes, she said 'I hope you didn't mind me taking a little bit of your sherry every day, Mr Askey. It wasn't for myself, of course, only to put a glass or so in your trifle'.

Auntie Sadie and Dad, Castletown c.1990

FRUGALITY

My father, coming from an impoverished background, had to work hard all his life and didn't let up until he was past 70. At the same time he enjoyed his life and was most generous to his family and his friends but not to himself. Though there was never any money in the bank – in fact he had an overdraft right up to the time he sold his business – we never wanted for anything. We had wonderful holidays every year when we were young at Youghal or Tramore, and later further afield in counties Galway or Mayo or in Northern Ireland. I was encouraged to buy books and classical long-playing records and would not have known of the precarious financial position or how, at the end of the war, Dad borrowed money not just from the bank but from close family and a friend to start his own business.

Later on I found that without really thinking about it I, too, disliked spending money on myself though I was happy to do so on family or friends. I detest waste in any form. For me money is only to be spent on a taxi when absolutely necessary and it is better to walk than to use public transport if at all possible. My own meals, like my clothes, are usually cheap and I enjoy finding 'bargains' wherever I go.

When Lord Goodman, on the radio programme 'Desert Island Discs' in 1971, was asked a question about the best advice he had received, he said that it had come from his employer, the solicitor Royalton Kisch, who said 'you should not be so thrifty as people notice it.' That advice might also have been given to me, but it wasn't and I hope therefore that not too many people have noticed.

Only when he died in June 2006 did I realise that Lord (Kenneth) Thomson of Fleet had a reputation for his meanness. Considering that he had been ranked as the world's 10th wealthiest man, he always travelled economy and had his wife cut his hair. Clearly he inherited this trait from his father Roy who had grown up in Canada in penury. I had some dealings with Roy, the first Lord Thomson, in the 1960s when I worked for George Rainbird, a part of the Thomson Organisation. Roy lived in a rather nice house in Uxbridge and he couldn't bear the time it took him to get up to London in his chauffeur-driven car so he used to get his gardener to drive him to the local underground station. There he would catch an underground train, along with all the other commuters (some of whom were no doubt his employees), where his two-toned Rolls Royce – dark brown and beige – registration number RHT 1, would collect him at Chancery Lane underground station and drive him the last few hundred yards up the Gray's Inn Road to his office at Thomson House.

One day I was going to Thomson House myself for a meeting and arrived just before 2.30 p.m. As I got there I noticed the familiar Rolls pulling up at the same time. It was the day of Roy Thomson's 75th birthday and Sir Dennis Hamilton and his fellow directors at Times Newspapers (owned by Thomson) had been holding a lunch in his honour at the Savoy Hotel. Thomson had left early to return to work leaving his colleagues behind to continue roistering for the rest of the afternoon. We travelled up in the lift together.

I like to think that in our very different ways Roy Thomson and I both learned the value of money and appreciated that it was harder to accumulate than to spend. He, after all, had been bankrupt in Canada before his arrival in Britain and it must have taught him a salutary lesson. On my part, the independence that some modest wealth has provided and the fact that I have been able to devote significant sums to charities involved with art and education, particularly, has given me a good deal of satisfaction. My father, too, believed in charity and made donations out of all proportion to his income or his assets. As a result people thought he was much wealthier than was the case.

Nicolo Machiavelli, writing almost 500 years ago:

> With time he will be considered more generous, once it is evident that as a result of his parsimony, his income is sufficient to defend himself or undertake enterprises without overburdening his people. In this way he appears generous to those from whom he takes

nothing, who are many, and miserly to those to whom he gives nothing, who are few. Only the spending of your own resources is what does you harm. There is nothing that uses itself up faster than generosity; for as you use it you lose the means of employing it, and you become either poor or despised. So it is wiser to live with the reputation of a miser than be forced to incur the reputation of rapacity because you want to be considered generous.

What a sensible fellow he was.

MEMORIES OF JANET BAKER, DBE

While there are many fine opera singers in the world at any one time, there is only a handful or so that have voices which are instantly recognisable. Among these are Kathleen Ferrier, John McCormack, Maria Callas, Luciano Pavarotti and Janet Baker.

I almost heard Callas sing at the Edinburgh Festival, except that she was indisposed and cancelled at the last minute, but I have heard Pavarotti on a number of occasions and Janet Baker in recitals, oratorio and opera on many.

My most vivid memories of Janet began on 26 April 1976 when, following the centenary concert of the Bach Choir at the Royal Albert Hall, she and a couple of hundred others attended the Choir's centenary party at the nearby Royal College of Music. This had been organised by the Choir's long-standing musical director, Sir David Willcocks, who went on to hold this position for 38 years until 1998.

As an entertainment, Sir David had arranged for David McKenna (1911-2013), a leading light of the Choir and of British Rail, to sing "Rule Britannia" clothed in a sheet and holding something resembling a harpoon. Next he invited Janet Baker to sing the Beatles' song "Yesterday". She was speechless and went a little pink so he gave her ten minutes to familiarise herself with the words, while somebody distributed copies of the score to enable the assembled crowd to become the choir. Ten minutes later Janet sang the song splendidly as we knew she would.

A little more than five years later, on 15 December 1981, I just happened to be at the Royal Opera House for a performance of Gluck's "Alceste", which was to be Janet's swansong and her last operatic performance. Her retirement was quite a surprise to me, and I dare say to her many other fans, as at the time she was aged 48 – not at all old for an opera singer.

At the end of the performance there was of course a wonderful response from the audience and a mass gathering of the great and the good on stage to witness Sir John Tooley, the Opera House's director, present Janet with a framed set of costume designs for the opera by Michael Stennett.

Some years after that I attended an outstanding performance of Elgar's "Dream of Gerontius" at Worcester Cathedral as part of the Three Choirs Festival (which I attended every year more than 25 times consecutively). Janet as the Angel was superb. Later, the BBC broadcast the performance on TV, which also included Robert Tear as "Gerontius", so that the music was accompanied by camera-work showing the cathedral's wonderful architecture which was a joy to behold.

Now we fast-forward some ten or fifteen years to a party at the Royal Academy of Music to celebrate something long forgotten where I was reintroduced to Dame Janet.

She was pleased to hear that I had attended her last "Alceste", the title role of this opera having been described elsewhere as one of the most arduous roles in all of opera.

Then I recalled that enjoyable Bach Choir centenary concert and party. 'Wasn't it fun?' she said. 'Did you get a copy of the score that was distributed at the time?' I assured her that I had a tendency to keep everything. 'Is it too much to ask if you have kept your copy?' 'No, it is not too much to ask. Didn't you keep yours?' 'Yes, but it got lost over time'. Needless-to-say I sent Janet a copy for her records.

Finally, I reminded her about "Gerontius" at Worcester and her performance which brought tears to my eyes. 'I can't remember when it was, but you never sang better and I will remember it always'. 'It was 1984' she said without hesitation. 'Wasn't it hot.' Later I checked on the date and found she was absolutely right: 18 August 1984.

Goodness knows how many times she had performed the role but it was amazing she could still recall that particular performance so readily.

A truly outstanding artist.

THE BACH CHOIR CENTENARY
1876-1976

The Chairman and Committee of the Bach Choir
invite you to a party
to celebrate the Centenary of the Choir.
Monday April 26th at 10 pm
at the Royal College of Music.

RSVP
A D C Rau
c o The Secretary
The Royal College of Music
Prince Consort Road SW7

Black tie

"Yesterday" arranged by Sir David Willcocks, 1976

TALES OF THE UNEXPECTED 1

In about 1985, my excellent secretary Rita decided to leave in order to pursue a career in personnel management. Before she left she promised to locate her successor but, because of our fastidious standards, she had not found anybody she could recommend at the date of her departure. Thus she did what I was dreading; she recruited a temp.

The temp as it happened could not have been better. She was 40ish, a bit bossy (just what I needed) and seemed both knowledgeable and well-travelled. I remember driving off to work one morning, from my underground garage to the office underground car park, while listening to a test match on the radio from Perth while the London rain bucketed down. When I reached the office Gina was already there, drying out after the downpour. On mentioning the lovely weather in Perth, she replied 'Do you know it? It's a really nice place'. Some days later a letter arrived from my parents in South Africa. 'Do you mind if I keep the stamps?' she enquired. 'A lovely place Cape Town' she added. Gina Bourdé had worked in both cities. She was also able to correct my grammar and spelling. I had considered offering her a full-time position. She clearly needed the money but I anticipated she would turn me down because the work was unvaried and particularly unexciting to somebody who had travelled the world.

One day she was typing a particularly boring pension fund document which contained my (then) Winchcombe address. She put her head around the door and asked 'Do you live in Winchcombe?' 'At weekends' I said, 'do you know the place?' 'Yes' she said, 'my parents live near there'. 'Where exactly?' 'At a little place called Postlip'. As far as I knew Postlip had only a handful of cottages and a couple of much larger houses. 'Postlip Hall or Postlip House?' I ventured. 'Postlip House' she replied. 'In that case you must be Georgina Christie-Smith' I announced firmly. She went very red. 'How could you possibly know that?' 'Because I live next door to Frank Lawrence'.

Frank had worked as a gardener for Lord Dulverton at Batsford Park where Major Christie-Smith, Gina's father, was land steward; and when the Major retired and bought Postlip House, Frank went to work there as a market gardener. In our over-the-fence conversations many years before, he had told me that the Major had two daughters and the elder girl had been 'a bit of a handful'. She had run away from school at Malvern and was found in London. Later she ran away again, to France, with a man called Bourdé, and from there they went to Costa Rica where they bought and ran a saffron farm.

The Christmas just before she came to work for me, they both returned to Gloucestershire to spend the festive season with her parents. On travelling up to London to do some shopping before returning to Costa Rica, they appear to have had an almighty row that was so serious Gina refused to return to Central America. He went back and she stayed in London. As she had no money, she turned to her only skill apart from growing saffron – as a secretary as a means of survival. Her parents knew nothing of the row or their separation and I was sworn to secrecy. Eventually after some weeks she plucked up the courage to phone her parents and tell them what had happened. After that I visited her and her parents at Postlip from time to time but she really preferred France and the French to England. She left England some time later and I expect she is still living somewhere in France.

The second half of the story, if there is one, will relate to what happened after she moved abroad, but for this I must bump into her in some French café-bar.

TALE OF THE UNEXPECTED 2

When I was a boy growing up in Cork, in the early 1950s, my mother announced one evening that my father was unable to go to the opera and she proposed taking me instead. My heart sank. The thought of listening to all that shouting and screaming filled me with fear. I'd much rather have stayed at home reading the *Beano* or my then current book. Anyway, mother prevailed, as mothers usually do, and with a mild bribe. I could bring my autograph book and at the end of the opera we would go back-stage and get the singers' autographs. She was herself a good violinist who had played in the local Cork Symphony Orchestra and knew her way around the Opera House. That settled it. The opera was "Il Trovatore" sung by an ad hoc collection of young professional singers, who were performing in five or six different venues in Britain and Ireland. Until then my autograph book was filled with signatures of footballers and cricketers; people like Stanley Matthews, Tom Finney, Billy Wright or Raich Carter, so some new names would not go amiss.

I was surprised that I enjoyed the occasion so much and at the end we went behind the scenes where, as Mum promised, I met the soloists. The men were very much matter-of-fact and simply put their names or "sincerely" in my book, followed by their signatures, which they then handed to my mother. The ladies on the other hand seemed much more interested and asked me my name, to which I squeaked "David", so they then put "to David", or drew a little flower, while one lady put a bar of music which I didn't understand as my Italian was not very good – it said "stride la vampa".

Now we jump ahead by 50 years or more to 16 March 2002, the eve of St. Patrick's Day, obviously a good omen, and I am going to attend a performance of "La Traviata" at Valletta's lovely Manoel Theatre; and to hear for the first time the young Maltese tenor, Joseph Calleja, who had received such good reviews a year or so previously at the Wexford Festival. He was to sing Alfredo in my father's favourite opera. It was a joy and I was certainly not disappointed. During the interval Tony Cassar Darien, manager of the Manoel, introduced me to Joseph's vocal coach, a certain Paul Asciak, then aged 83.

When I asked if he was the person I had heard singing Manrico in "Trovatore" at the Cork Opera House all those years before, he was amazed. When I told him he had given me his autograph, and I also collected those of the other soloists in my autograph album, he was astounded – even though I was unable to pronounce his surname for all of that time. He said he later sang again in the Opera House in the late 50s – which was the last performance before it burnt down. He said he would love to see my autograph book if I ever returned to Malta. When Tony told him that I had a house in St. Julians and returned regularly, it was agreed that on my next visit from the UK we would meet up, and I promised I would not forget to be accompanied by my autograph book. Some months later the meeting took place in Tony's office at the Manoel. Paul was delighted and said he hadn't seen some of the other soloists since that original trip around the British and Irish theatres. He asked if he could have copies of the relevant pages as a reminder of the people he had toured with, at a time when he himself was a young singer making his name in the world of opera, and only a little older than Joseph was then.

After those initial encounters, Paul and I bumped into each other in Valletta fairly frequently at artistic or musical events over the subsequent years; and I have to confess that it was usually he who spotted me before I noticed him – which said much for his eyesight. I also marvelled that he walked so erectly and without a stick until well into his 90s. Such happy memories of a remarkable man and I'm so glad that I got to know him albeit in our latter years.

MEMORIES OF THE OWS CLUB

One Saturday morning in 1968 I wandered into the Times bookshop (owned by *The Times* newspaper) in Wigmore Street, ostensibly to have a look around their second-hand book department. While there I noticed that they had on display five pieces of original artwork by Donald McGill, painted in his usual bright colours as designs for his often naughty seaside postcards which were extremely popular for about fifty years until his death in 1962.

The pieces were priced at £6 each and I loved them. However at the time my salary was less than £1,500 per annum and I could only afford to purchase two. Pleased with my purchases, I had them framed and they were given pride of place in my flat for many years thereafter.

In those days I greatly admired early English watercolours but the problem was that I could not of course afford them. I still can't afford them and have had to make do with original cartoons in pencil or pen and ink – and, dare I say, later English watercolours. About a year after my original McGill purchases I received a postcard from the Times bookshop announcing that they were closing down as a result of their lease coming to an end and having a sale with most of the stock reduced by 25%. Along I went on the following Saturday to see what was still available and, to my surprise, they still had one piece of the McGill artwork left – now reduced to £4-10s (that being before decimalisation). Of course I had to buy it. Now some 50 years later I have some 20 McGills and am pleased to report that they have more than kept up with inflation, although they were bought because I liked them and they amused me and not as an investment. Some years ago Chris Beetles

Gallery had a sale of Michael Winner's collection which amounted to some 200 works. That put me in my place.

Also, in the late 1960s I used to visit some of the West End galleries on a Saturday morning. Looking back (as I frequently do), these visits performed an important part of my art education though I didn't know that at the time. One gallery I particularly liked was the Fine Art Society in Bond Street, still there to this day. Over time I got to know the man in charge, a Mr Naimaster; and as my circumstances improved I began to make some purchases from him. Nothing spectacular, but works by Frank Brangwyn and Edward Hayes, cartoons by Tom Browne, George du Maurier and Harry Furness as well as pencil drawings by Sir John Tenniel and other artists who drew for *Punch* in Victorian and pre-War times.

I remember Mr Naimaster as being rather portly with a goatee beard, rather like some of the Paris gallery owners as depicted by the impressionists. One day he suggested that I might like to pay a visit to the Old Watercolour Society's Club, then located at 26 Conduit Street, where there was to be an RWS exhibition and a "soirée" – that is an evening entertainment provided by music students from one of the London conservatoires and organised by the Secretary, Malcolm Fry.

I agreed to meet Mr Naimaster there the following week but when I got there he hadn't yet arrived. I didn't have to wait long; only a few minutes later a taxi pulled up and he jumped out. As his gallery was only around the corner from Conduit Street I assumed he must have been travelling from somewhere else. He shook my hand vigorously (perhaps not expecting me to have turned up) and said 'Have you seen Willie?' As I didn't know who Willie was, I shook my head. Later I discovered that Willie was no less a person than Sir William Russell-Flint; and he together with Mr J. L. Naimaster, Robert Austin (then President of the RWS) and the Hon. Arnold Palmer (presumably the watercolourist and descendant of Samuel Palmer, and not a famous US golfer) comprised the Committee of the Club.

I never did meet Willie. He didn't attend that evening as he was unwell and died shortly afterwards aged 89. That soirée would have taken place in November 1969 and I note from my records that I joined the Club in January 1970 when I received a letter of welcome from Malcolm Fry. Though I didn't know any of the RWS members in those days, I did enjoy the exhibitions with their pleasant musical interludes.

In August 1980 the Club's lease came to an end and the landlords, Sotheby's, required the premises back for their own purposes so it became necessary to move somewhere else. Unfortunately other alternative locations were not as convenient as Conduit Street, or proved too expensive, and after a search it was decided to move to Bankside (along with the Royal Society of Painter-Engravers, known as the REs). Any mention of Bankside then always elicited the question 'where's that?' The available space was originally intended to be a supermarket for Sainsbury's whose head office was nearby but they considered it to be too small and so it was fitted out for the RWS and the REs. Meanwhile the OWS Club became the 'Friends of the RWS' and a little while later changed again to the 'Friends of Bankside'.

Malcolm Fry retired in May 1983 having been Secretary of the two societies for some 25 years and Director of the Bankside Gallery for three. I recall him always being very smartly dressed with a flower in his buttonhole. Michael Spender, his successor, introduced me to the Friends Committee and a little while later I became Hon. Treasurer under the Chairmanship of Bill Blackshaw, who came from an educational background having been a master at Repton and Head of Brighton College. Perhaps a year after that Bill and I were appointed Directors of Bankside Gallery and Bill became its Chairman. When eventually Michael Spender decided to move on, and before Judy Dixey his replacement arrived, I was asked if I would take over as Company Secretary of the Gallery for a short while. Being a qualified Chartered Secretary I was only too happy to oblige, believing that my "standing in" would last for maybe three months or so. Though I was familiar with the saying that nothing is as permanent as the temporary, I hadn't realised quite how true it was. In the event my secretaryship of Bankside lasted for more than 17 years until October 2009 when I eventually retired and it completed a period of about 40 years since my involvement commenced with Mr Naimaster's introduction to the OWS Club.

However, my involvement did not quite finish then. Shortly afterwards I was elected an honorary member of the RWS – and since then there has been an exciting development in that the RWS has been offered the space for an entirely new gallery in Whitcomb Street, literally just across the road from the National Gallery on the North side of

Trafalgar Square. It will not be cheap to run but will be helped enormously by the grant of a 250 year lease without reviews at a peppercorn rent. I don't know the price of peppercorns these days but am told you can buy a bag of them for £1.

I'm looking forward to the opening very much and, who knows, I may even be able to play a part in it.

THE ROYAL WATERCOLOUR SOCIETY

In the late 1980s, Leslie Agius, who was then the Director of the Malta Tourist Office in London, invited me to the opening of an exhibition of watercolours of Malta by Hugh Buchanan at the Francis Kyle Gallery in London. The exhibition was good but terribly crowded and it was almost impossible to view the pictures and hold a glass of wine without being jostled by other guests. At the time I was involved with the Bankside Gallery, home of the Royal Watercolour Society, and wondered if it might be possible to arrange for RWS members to be invited to Malta to sketch and paint and then hold an exhibition or two to show the resultant works back in the UK.

My first step was to mention the idea to Michael Spender, Secretary of the RWS, who said it sounded interesting. Though he had never been to Malta, his parents were stationed there before he was born and he was, he believed, Maltese by conception. Next I spoke to Leslie Worth, at the time President of the RWS, who was also receptive to the idea but he wondered if we would get a good enough response from his members. We decided we required at least eight painters as a minimum in order to be able to go ahead as this would mean we could put on a group exhibition with a number of different styles. Some years before, the Society had paid a visit to Venice and produced 'Venice in Peril', an exhibition which proved a great selling success. But, we concluded, Malta did not have quite the allure of Venice even though the views of Grand Harbour from the Upper Barrakka Gardens are, in my opinion, the equal of any painted by Canaletto or Guardi.

When I contacted Leslie Agius with a certain amount of support, he also expressed his interest but pointed out some clouds on the horizon:

there would be a general election in the near future in Malta following which, even if the Nationalists were returned to power, a reshuffle of ministers was likely. This could lead to delays in the decision-making process. However, he did urge me to set down my ideas on paper and my two-page outline was faxed through to his minister in Malta. A few days later I was phoned to say that there was considerable interest on the part of Dr Michael Refalo, Parliamentary Secretary for Tourism. Dr Refalo would be visiting London shortly and he would like to meet me and also visit the Bankside Gallery on his trip. We met up, got on well then and have remained good friends for some 20 years since that first meeting.

A committee was set up in London to progress the arrangements. This included Brian Sewell, the well-known and outspoken art critic in print and on TV, who was the personification of politeness at our meetings even though his dress for such occasions – a black T-shirt – didn't quite coincide with our more formal attire. A letter was sent to all 75 RWS members notifying them of the proposed trip and to our pleasant surprise some 16 of them signed up. A visit to Malta followed so that with spouses, gallery staff and other riff-raff including yours truly, we were just short of 50 travellers in all. The group stayed at the Grand Verdala Hotel in Rabat which meant they could wander around Mdina and Rabat with their sketch pads, pencils and cameras. Some hired cars or took buses to Valletta or the southern fishing harbours of Marsascala or Marsaxlokk. There were escorted trips by coach and harbour cruises, as well as a reception hosted by the President, Dr Censu Tabone, at the Palace in Valletta. Apart from much late night noise emanating from the disco club at the hotel, inconveniently located below the bedrooms, the trip was a great success. Some people loved, and others hated, a special Sunday visit to Mystic, Marquis Joe Scicluna's strange castellated creation in Madliena, very well captured in some of Clifford Bayly's and Olwen Jones's paintings. In the way of things, some asked if they could return again on the following day to continue while others could not get away fast enough.

Another memory I have is of Elizabeth Scott-Moore who went on the trip aged 90 and produced some amazingly firm and confident pictures. Sadly she died a year later and before the exhibitions took place.

Before the group left Malta to return to the UK, they arranged a surprise dinner for me at the Birdcage restaurant in Rabat, now no longer there. During the evening they decided that the painters present would do cartoons of me but there was one problem; nobody had any paper. After a detailed search of the premises they came up with some brown corrugated paper and the sketching was done on that. The work of art so produced was presented to me with all due ceremony. I later had it framed and, despite the inferior nature of the material used, it is a nice reminder of a very happy evening.

Moving on some two years to 1994, we come to the first of two exhibitions celebrating the visit to Malta of the RWS at the Bankside Gallery in London. Some weeks before the opening, Michael Refalo called me to say that he had been asked to write a brief introduction for the exhibition catalogue. As I knew a lot about the RWS and something about Malta, whereas he knew a lot about Malta but nothing about the RWS, could I possibly help him out? Agreeing, I wrote some text and sent it to his office in Valletta. He called me to say it was fine and he wouldn't want to change a word of it.

A day or so before the exhibition was due to open, Dr Refalo began to suffer from chest pains and, though he was due to go to London to open the exhibition, his doctor said he was not well enough to travel. So at short notice the Malta High Commissioner in London at the time was asked to deputize for him. In opening the exhibition the HC apologised for Dr Refalo's absence and said 'I can do no better than quote Dr Refalo's words in his introduction to the catalogue' and he went on with a short reading. I'm glad to report that my text was very well received, to judge by the applause.

During the reception that followed, I was talking to some guests when Clifford Bayly, a Vice President of the RWS, came up to me in a somewhat agitated state and asked if he could speak to me privately. His problem, he said, was that the High Commissioner, the VIP guest, wanted to buy one of his pictures and although it was listed at £1,500, the HC only wanted to pay £750 on the basis that it would hang in his office and lots of important people would see it there. What was he to do? He wanted to hold firm on his price which he considered to be fair, but at the same time he did not wish to create an international incident with Malta breaking off diplomatic relations with the UK. 'You must hold firm', I said. 'The exhibition has only been open for some 30 minutes and after some weeks here it will then be travelling out to Malta for some further weeks. There is every likelihood that somebody else will purchase the picture at the full price'.

He did as I said but, to my concern (and no doubt his), at the closure of the exhibition at Bankside, Cliff's painting remained unsold. What if it did not sell at all? How would my advice be perceived then? Maybe Cliff would expect me to buy it as even £750 would have been better than nothing.

Fortunately the work did sell at the Auberge de Province in Valletta before the exhibition there ended, and at the full price.

Overall more than 80% of all the pictures on show at the two exhibitions were sold, making it one of the most successful RWS exhibitions for many a year.

The bright Mediterranean light had posed unusual problems for our painters not familiar with such conditions; and the Maltese, used to seeing the works of their own local artists, were delighted to see unfamiliar scenes by professionals who had not seen Malta before.

Sketches done of David Elyan
at a Dinner in his honour at
Rabat, Malta, on 25 May 1992

by
Tom Coates RWS
Jenny Wheatley RWS
Charles Bartlett RWS (Past President)
Leslie Worth RWS (President)
Olwen Jones RWS
Clifford Bayly RWS (Vice President)

142

WORK THAT REMAINED IN PROGRESS

Over the years, when I mentioned to people that I was having a book printed at the Stanbrook Abbey Press in Worcestershire, the home of some Benedictine nuns, the question was invariably asked – why there? It is a long story, and I shall tell it as briefly as I can.

By way of background, I was an undergraduate at Trinity College, Dublin, in the early 1960s – a most exciting time to have been there – and, as I had some literary aspirations, fulfilled various managerial roles on the College newspaper *Trinity News* as well as on the literary magazine *Icarus*. Subsequent events however led me away from the literary life.

In 1961 I helped to create a new Irish magazine *The Dubliner* which later, after the death of Seumas O'Sullivan and by arrangement with his widow, the painter Estella Solomons, assumed the title of the longest-established of all Irish literary magazines, *The Dublin Magazine*. I was chairman of the company that owned the magazine, New Square Publications Limited, and we produced it with a fair measure of success until 1974. Beginning in 1963, New Square Publications published a small number of limited editions of poetry, invariably the work of undergraduates or graduates of Trinity College, and all of them printed at Colm O'Lochlainn's 'Sign of the Three Candles' Press in Dublin. It is rather pleasing to note, some thirty years later, that these slim volumes have become highly-prized collectors' items. And to think we had difficulty selling them at two guineas a time. At the beginning of 1966 I moved to London. Although in full-time employment, and continuing to be responsible for New Square Publications and the business side of *The Dublin Magazine*, I had a hankering to publish some further poetry, to be printed at leading UK 'hand' presses.

Having for some time been familiar with and admired the work of Stanbrook Abbey Press, I decided to write to Dame Hildelith Cumming – we did not know each other – and ask, ever so politely, if she might contemplate printing a slim volume (for that was all I could afford) of poetry by the Irish poet James Clarence Mangan (1803-49). After all, I thought, if she was too busy or did not reply there were plenty of other printers who might be interested.

Dame Hildelith replied promptly, on 19 December 1966: 'hoping we can come to some arrangement that will make it possible for us to print for you', while pointing out '... another consideration is our method of working and the short hours at our disposal which makes production a slow process. Limited editions on hand-made paper are printed damp two pages up, and this takes a very long time. This is essential if the press work is to be of a high standard.' Having accepted that time was not important, I nevertheless noticed that there appeared to be a dragging of heels at the Stanbrook end. Later on, when I got to know Dame Hildelith, I asked her the reason for this delay. Had she gone cool on the idea, or was it pressure of work, I enquired. No, she said, it was simply that having agreed to go ahead with the book, we realised that nobody at Stanbrook had ever heard of this poet Mangan. Some time after this an Irish nun arrived for a brief stay at the Abbey and one of the printers, remembering Mangan, asked her if she had ever heard of him. 'Of course I have', replied the visitor, 'sure isn't he the Irish Tennyson?' Any doubts that may have existed disappeared at that moment.

By September 1967 Dame Hildelith was planning a book to sell at ten to fifteen guineas. The letter that suggested those prices bore a Rev. Keble Martin 4d. 'British Flora' stamp, so if postage increases over the intervening period are an indicator of what the price would be today, an increase of something like fifteen times, we would be talking of a book selling for £150 to £225 at current 1993 values. A quarto book was visualised, 'with the text set in Lutetia: roman for the introduction, italic for the poems.'

My first visit to Stanbrook was in October 1967 and that in itself was quite an experience as anybody who visited the Abbey parlour will be able to testify. All communication took place through a grille below which was a counter containing a drawer. The various materials to be inspected by either of us had to be passed backwards and forwards in this drawer, and the drawer locked after each movement. Despite all that, we got on well from the first moment of our meeting. Although I had no wish to be rude, when I did get around to commenting on this strange procedural need to conduct business via the grille and drawer, Dame Hildelith told me what an 'advance' this had been as, not long before, outsiders would not have been allowed to enter the parlour under normal circumstances. She recounted the story, amid great mirth, of the day the plumbing failed and the steps that had to be taken to enable a plumber from Worcester to enter the premises and attend to the repairs.

Our correspondence and my visits to Stanbrook continued. By March 1969 I was hearing how the design 'has given me endless trouble'. 'The source of the trouble has been the twin principles which hitherto I have kept to absolutely: (i) never to turn over a line, however long, and (ii) never to turn the page in the middle of a stanza. For short poems this is not too difficult but for Mangan's which present one with 4, 5, 6, 8, 10 and 12 line stanzas, it challenges all the findings of arithmetic. However, now at last I think I have done it; and it will be a challenge to the experts to find me out in all my little deceptions. I have achieved now the two principles and what is "giving way" is the page length. I did this in "Patriarch Tree" and had a basic page length with a white line at [the] bottom that would be used if necessary. The immense variety of stanza lengths in Mangan means that I have to have three possible lengths instead of two. (I have not heard that anyone has found out the PT deception – and I hope the JCM one will not show either.)

'The worst offenders are the stanzas with multiples of 5 instead of 4 – i.e. 10 lines and 15 lines. In the 15 line ones .... I think I shall have to resort to $\frac{1}{2}$-point difference in leading, and I think I can also solve the backing up problems.'

At the end of 1969 Dame Hildelith was appointed director of the monastic choir, another cause of delay, but by the end of 1970 she was able to send me a pull of the first poem 'My Dark Rosaleen' – 'not laid out as the book will be of course, but just to send you as a Christmas Greeting.'

Although completion was now – cautiously, we thought – moved forward to summer 1971, that season came and went, almost without being noticed. At the time I was up to my eyes working on other projects, particularly helping to commission and market works of art for *The*

Observer (as described in Matrix 10), so that little or no thought was given to Mangan until June 1973 when Dame Hildelith emerged from her own problems to state that the past two years had been very difficult and that she had been dogged with ill health. ' ... Either myself or my secretary – there is not much to choose between us. When she is off I have to do her work and can't do my own. Then my main keeper (compositor for my books) died and another member of staff was removed and replaced. So that everything has slowed down.

'The book, I am sure, would have been finished and sold by now, had I been able to find an opaque white hand-made paper. I held up for several months at one stage awaiting a promised sample from Italy – it still has not come. Would you consider the use of a toned paper? It takes gold beautifully and would make a really handsome book.'

By November (1973) the text paper was in place, well, more or less. 'I have heard from Wookey Mill. They are practically closing down hand-mades, but very fortunately they are continuing the buff parchment we decided on. However, none in stock and they will not be making until the new year. I am putting in a large order and hope that all the oddments, like cover paper, will be settled by the time the paper is ready to receive print.' Needless to say Wookey Mill decided not to make up the paper at the time promised for all sorts of reasons, though we were still able to anticipate publication by 1975. Margaret Adams, who had agreed to prepare the initials at the commencement of each poem, and who had begun to experiment with designs and with colours, was suggested by Dame Hildelith to design and pattern the cover paper. From the preliminary work which I had seen, this was something with which I was very happy to agree.

March 1974 saw the Wookey Mill paper in progress and the making paid for. 'No VAT on books in the Budget. I hope the proofs will be on their way to you by the middle or end of April'. That was not to happen of course. There were soon thoughts other than Mangan on the mind of the printer and this time the delay was caused by my own somewhat injudicious suggestion.

'I have followed up your suggestion of a centenary exhibition at the V&A – so far hopeful. The idea now has to be "sold" to the powers that be – the underlings are enthusiastic so that is hopeful.' After some consideration a senior official at the V&A suggested that an exhibition linking Stanbrook with Sir Sydney Cockerell might find favour with the Director and, if Dame Hildelith approved, perhaps she could write formally so that her letter might be put before that gentleman. She did approve and wrote a letter as suggested, commenting to me, 'one can't expect a place like that to move quickly. If nothing happens in the next fortnight or so, may I write and ask your help? (P.S. I also send two copies of a little thing I ran off two years ago in two days. Maud Sumner is S. Africa's leading artist, I think – a cousin of our Lady Abbess).'

At about this time I acquired a weekend cottage just outside Winchcombe in Gloucestershire, where I have lived happily ever since. It prompted a letter from Stanbrook as the move evidently found favour there: 'I am delighted to hear that you will be a "neighbour" if at a certain distance. I think the SAP most certainly needs an "eye" kept on it.'

Regarding the V&A: 'Not a word except a letter from Mr H saying he'd so far not been able to get the necessary people together. So I would be most grateful for a nudge from another direction. I've almost given up hope'.

After pondering this new problem, I decided to write not just to the V&A but to the British Museum as well, where I had some useful contacts, just in case the V&A decision turned out to be negative. It seemed to do the trick, because shortly afterwards I received a letter from Mr H at the V&A saying that the Director had given his approval for an exhibition in the autumn of 1976. This was followed almost immediately by a letter from Stanbrook: 'Now a big thank you to you. By the same post as your letter I received one from the V&A. I am most grateful to you for bringing this to a head. Now we know where we are. It was very kind of you too, to write to the BM. What happens now if they say 'yes'? Is it 'done' to have shows at both places? Of course the SCC attachment makes the V&A quite unique, so I would think that if the BM agreed to have books there need be no overlapping.

But, of course, they may not say yes..'

As was always likely to happen, and indeed as I had correctly anticipated, the BM and the V&A discussed the possibilities between themselves and decided, as the V&A Director had approved the project, that there would be no point in the BM proceeding with another albeit different exhibition to commemorate the same centenary.

Although I had my own private doubts that Mangan would make any progress before the closure of the V&A exhibition, because, to be realistic, the exhibition was so very much more exciting than dull old Mangan, it did not prevent Dame Hildelith being her usual optimistic self: 'Please don't think that I have put Mangan aside for exhibition plans: I mean Mangan to be in the Exhibition and he must get finished, if our planned bibliography is to come out at all. But I am sorry to try your patience so sorely. Margaret Adams has started a campaign on behalf of 'the Irish poems' and every letter ends with an enquiry about how it is getting on'.

Nothing much did happen over the next eighteen months except that shortly before the exhibition opened I had a letter (now typed for the first time): 'The situation is this. The book is entered in the catalogue and I have undertaken to get a few sheets completed so that they can show the book as 'work in progress'. There is one tiny thing to complete, when our own centenary book is finished which should be by the end of next week. This means that I fully intend to begin the actual printing of Mangan in the New Year. But I have meant to do it before, and it hasn't come to anything...'

The years went by and were accompanied by much illness. The onset of a coronary meant that Dame Hildelith could not any longer undertake the heavy work associated with hand-printing, such as lifting the formes, and there were not many others at the Press on whom she could rely. 1982 saw her off work for almost a complete year. 'When I really did get ill, I felt I was beyond thinking about things like that and the staff were not efficient enough to do it. So please forgive these years of just hanging on. I am determined now that the book shall go on to a proper finish. I have procured the services of a very good young printer to undertake the machining for me, as I can't consistently lift formes of the size needed alone.'

The years again passed by with nothing much to show in the way of progress, so that by 1990 discussions were opened with John Randle of the Whittington Press to ascertain if he would be willing to take over the project and see it through to completion as Stanbrook could no longer cope with so large a task. Dame Hildelith was by this time over eighty years of age and in poor health. For my part, if Dame Hildelith could no longer complete the task, then John Randle, whom I had known for many years and whose work I collected, would be a worthy successor.

Although John was interested in the task and indeed agreed to undertake the printing, we agreed subsequently that despite the quarter of a century of work in progress, there was no longer any enthusiasm for the book as originally envisaged and planned. The momentum had gone so we decided to let the whole idea fall quietly away.

Looking back on it now, in 1993, while it was clearly disappointing that the book never saw the light of day – either in 1969 as originally anticipated or at any of the subsequently revised publication dates – the disappointment was so gradual that there was never any particular moment when I felt let down or disheartened about it. Indeed, I suppose that if I am honest I had long before given up any idea that the book might appear. Despite the optimism conveyed in her letters, and all the obstacles that appeared in the path of progress, I expect that Dame Hildelith in her heart of hearts will have felt the same, though it did not prevent her from writing and indicating some progress, no matter how slight, which gave me some hope and led me to believe that the book might, somehow, miraculously, appear one day.

I am sure that had Mangan appeared in 1969 as envisaged it is most unlikely that circumstances would have permitted a further publishing venture on my part, either at Stanbrook or at another press, because I did not have the time any longer to devote to such activities. As a young man in London then there were more pressing demands on my time, such as a full-time job, and on my needs – more's the pity – such as saving for a first car or for the deposit on a first flat as well as all the other things one requires.

It would also be true to say that if Mangan had appeared at the anticipated time, the twenty-five years of correspondence and friendship with Dame Hildelith would not have occurred. It is doubtful if the sense of satisfaction in having been involved with the successful publication of the book, albeit in a fine limited edition, would have produced as much enjoyment as the subsequent correspondence has provided. After all, Mangan's poems had all appeared previously in print and were accessible to those of sufficient determination in the copyright and other major libraries of Britain and Ireland.

My initial objective in embarking on the project was to create a fine edition of a selection of Mangan's poetry. Could it be that the real creativity in the project was not the book itself but the correspondence on which this article has been based and the story of the book's failure to appear?

Dame Hildelith Cumming, OSB (1909-1991) trained as a concert pianist at the Royal Academy of Music in London and later joined the Benedictine community of nuns at Stanbrook Abbey, Worcestershire. She took charge of the press there in 1956 and continued in this role until her death, establishing its reputation as 'one of the great private presses'. Stanbrook Abbey itself had moved to Worcestershire in 1838 but closed in 2009 when the remaining nuns moved to a new monastery in North Yorkshire. The old abbey buildings have now been converted into a luxury hotel.

"Selected Poems of Clarence Mangan" is described and illustrated on pp. 204-5 of David Butcher's "The Stanbrook Abbey Press 1956-1990", published by the Whittington Press in 1992. Dame Hildelith's letters are quoted with permission of the Abbess of Stanbrook.

VICTORIA
AND
ALBERT
MUSEUM

You are invited to the Private View of the

Stanbrook Abbey Press & Sir Sidney Cockerell:
A Centenary Exhibition

*to be held in the Library Book Production Gallery, Room 74
on Wednesday 10th November 1976
from 16.00 to 17.30
Admit two*

ASVP
Ser Keeper's
Press Office,
Victoria and
Albert Museum
London SW7 2RL

TALL STORIES

Uncle Larry wasn't just a talented actor. He also knew how to tell a good story. A number of his stories, no doubt with a good deal of embellishment, were told to his friend Frank O'Connor, the noted Irish writer, who was described somewhere as the finest short story writer since Chekhov. O'Connor in turn will have polished the stories till they shone and in due course they were published or broadcast on the radio.

With regard to one of them, there is a postcard in the Elyan Collection (at the University of Malta) which says – I quote from memory: 'For God's sake don't let your brother-in-law listen to my short story on Radio Éireann next week. He'll kill me.' Most of the stories had a sting in the tail and were reminiscent of O'Henry or Roald Dahl's 'Tales of the Unexpected'. I can no longer remember most of them but two I can remember refer to a renowned family of antique dealers who had a shop, somewhat akin to Aladdin's cave, in Grafton Street, Dublin, for about 100 years. The head of the business used to travel frequently to England to attend auctions and visit country houses that had entire contents or single items for sale. Often he was accompanied on these visits by Joseph (later Lord) Duveen.

On one occasion they were visiting a country house in the Cotswolds and, after viewing the contents, decided to have lunch at a small, nearby pub. Having ordered their food, one of them went to the Gents and, on the way back, spotted what looked like a Ming urn from about 1600 AD in a dark corner which was being used as an umbrella stand. He mentioned this to his companion who, surprised as he might be, then also went to the Gents to have a closer inspection. On his return he confirmed that the urn was indeed a rare item. But what to do about it?

The pub was virtually empty and soon their food arrived. The landlady, not having seen them before, enquired if they had business in the area to which they replied that they were actually looking for a country pub to purchase for their retirement. They loved the local scenery and were looking for somewhere with lots of character.

'That's a coincidence' said the landlady 'because I have been trying to sell this place since my husband died a couple of years ago'.

The antique hunters said they had one very specific requirement, which was that to be of interest to them the sale should include all the contents. That, she said, was not a problem.

After further discussion they agreed on a price and the visitors said they would consult a local solicitor.

Later, after the parties had exchanged contracts and a deposit had been paid, but before completion, the purchasers removed the urn and announced they would not be able to complete the purchase owing to a change of circumstances. They were happy for the landlady to retain the deposit and, in addition, were willing to pay an additional sum as compensation for the inconvenience caused. The landlady was not unhappy with this and a few months later she found a new buyer and at a higher price.

We don't know how much our intrepid travellers paid her, or how much they received when they sold the urn, but apparently it produced handsome profits all round – and of course it made for a good story.

The second tale related to the Dublin antiques dealer alone. He was visiting Sotheby's in London one day and was looking at items to be auctioned later in the afternoon when his eye alighted on an unusual, elaborately jewelled Turkish candlestick which would have been one of a pair. The auction estimate was low because the chance of finding its companion was very slim.

He duly bid for the item and was pleased to be able to acquire it for less than the estimate. He brought it back to Dublin and placed it in his strong-room for safekeeping.

Three or four years later, he was studying a newly-arrived catalogue in his office one day and nearly fell off his chair with surprise when he saw that the companion candlestick had appeared and was due to be sold at a provincial English auction house shortly afterwards. In due course he went to the auction to bid for the item and, although it cost him a good deal more than the original stick, he didn't mind because the value of the two together was substantially in excess of his two one-off payments and, in time, would yield him a useful profit.

He returned to Dublin with his booty and could hardly wait to open his strong-room door to compare the two items and put them back together once more.

Horror of horrors. On looking for the original candlestick he found that it was missing. He was soon to discover that his son, who had recently joined the firm, unknown to his father, had a penchant for gambling and had clocked up some sizeable debts locally. On looking in the safe in the strong-room for something he could sell and that wouldn't be missed, he had discovered the perfect way of repaying his creditors.

North Gate Bridge, Cork. c.1950 (since replaced). Oil by Sidney Smith (1912-1982)

THE TCD DINING CLUB

Having moved from Dublin to London at the beginning of 1966, I attended my first Dining Club dinner in London on 6 April 1967 – when to my surprise I was also "elected" to the Committee. Not long afterwards, when Michael Knott (son of General Sir Harold Knott, head of the RAMC) failed to turn up at an Annual General Meeting, having agreed, according to Dr Gerry Little, the Secretary, to take on the Treasurership, I was asked if I would take it on "for a little while", defined as being up to a year until Mr Knott could take over. This was the first of two examples I experienced of nothing being as permanent as the temporary – the other being at Bankside Gallery nearly 20 years later.

Mike never did take over as he moved shortly afterwards from London to Southampton and as a result I found myself acting as Treasurer for some 26 years: from age 26 to 52. Gerry Little was a GP in Ilford and by common consent the nicest and gentlest of men, though he had some very strange ideas about business. He presumed, for example, that Dining Club members would turn up at dinners (of which there were three or four a year) unless they indicated otherwise. As the Secretary had to confirm numbers to the venue concerned – all our dinners were held in London clubs; usually the National Liberal, Royal Overseas League, Irish or the Savile – 48 hours before the dinner, the attendance was usually much below expectations.

The gaps at the table were faithfully reflected by gaps in our finances as most clubs insisted on being paid for the number booked as opposed to the number sitting down to dinner. However, as Gerry had operated in this way for many years, and was very good at locating speakers, the youngest member of the executive was not going to change him. No matter how hard I tried in fixing the price of the dinner to take into account the "no shows", Gerry always seemed to be one step ahead.

The previous Treasurer had been David Gwynn, a civil engineer who had been sent to Nigeria to head up a large project on behalf of Balfour Beatty. Gwynn's father had been Provost of Trinity and his brother John was Permanent Secretary at the Home Office. As David Gwynn had to leave London at fairly short notice, John Goode had assumed the task temporarily. Goode was a very wealthy bachelor who had attended Sligo Grammar School before reading engineering at Trinity. He made his fortune by inventing a method of producing "liquid cement" for the building industry.

Chairman of the Club then was Sir John Craig, a former Deputy Master of the Mint, when the Mint had been near the Tower of London and the Master was and I think remains the Chancellor of the Exchequer. When Sir John retired, he was succeeded by John Goode. Other prominent members of the Club in those days were Col. Kidd, Col. Gilmour, Dr "Paddy" Warriner, Dr Robert Press CB, CBE, Dr Dick Sandys and Desmond Fitzgerald. The two colonels, along with Craig and Goode were then well into their 80s. I remember Kidd telling me that he had been a very good hockey player in his young days – which must have been about 1905 or thereabouts and he later became a leading administrator in the game. At that first dinner in April 1967 I was introduced to Paddy Warriner who was a GP in Sussex. Like me he was born in Cork and had also attended Cork Grammar School. With those links, and as he seemed to be the next youngest person present in the room, I thought I would sit next to him. Only later when he pulled out photographs of his grown-up grandchildren did I realise he must have been a lot older than he looked. He used to organise the annual dinners, held then at the Connaught Rooms or the Café Royale and rather quaintly called "ladies nights". We usually had an attendance of about 120 -150 members and guests.

At one of those annual dinners in the Connaught Rooms – my first visit to that venue – I asked on arrival where the Trinity College event would be held. 'Third floor', said the attendant. Up I went in the lift with a number of others in dinner jackets and followed them into a very grand room where I joined a small queue to be received by some big wigs. I was surprised to find the then Archbishop of Canterbury (Ramsey) shaking hands with the guests, as there had been no mention of his attendance in the circulated publicity material. I dutifully shook hands with him and then some others, one of whom asked when I had been 'in the school'. 'School' I echoed, sipping my glass of sherry, 'you mean the University?' 'No, Cranleigh School', he said. I apologised and nearly choked on the sherry. There were in fact two dinners on the third floor and I left that room as quickly as I could.

One evening, sitting at dinner in the Irish Club, opposite Col. Gilmour, while talking to one of my neighbours, there was a loud tinkle as made by a heavy soup spoon hitting a soup dish. I looked across and Col. Gilmour had slid under the table. He was having a heart attack but fortunately there were a number of TCD doctors to unbutton his collar, take his pulse, etc. He spent the night in one of the London hospitals and was released after a couple of days. Sadly he died not long afterwards from a further attack.

Dick Sandys, another medical doctor, had represented Trinity, Leinster and Ireland (in the Davis Cup) at tennis. I vaguely remember that he represented Trinity at another three sports for which he obtained his university colours. He later became a distinguished Chairman of the Queen's Club and a member of the All-England Club committee at Wimbledon.

Dr Robert Press, from Belfast, had studied science at Queen's University, Belfast, and then chemistry at Trinity. He later entered the civil service in London, becoming Deputy Scientific Advisor to the Government – Sir Solly Zuckerman was Chief – and operating out of the Cabinet Office. Succeeding John Goode as Chairman, Bob died some years later following a swim at Hope Cove in Cornwall. He was in the chair for one of our dinners when there were only four members present. I was there so you'll have to take my word for it. At the end of the meal he stood up, raised his glass for a toast and announced 'Gentlemen, what we lack in quantity we more than make up for in quality'.

Desmond Fitzgerald, another engineer, was Managing Director of George Wimpey, at that time Britain's leading firm of civil engineering contractors. Through his good offices, all our mailings and printing of programmes were produced and paid for by Wimpey at no cost to the

Club. This was a great help in significantly counteracting the cost over-runs on the dinners.

During the 1970s a number of approaches were made to the Club by Trinity requesting that we should admit ladies as members. I was against the move because alongside the Dining Club there existed a ladies club that did not admit men: the Dublin University Women Graduates Association (DUWGA), and many of us failed to see why we should be expected to allow ladies to join as it would change the character of the Club. Eventually Trinity did approach the ladies who said they would be prepared to become the TCD Association (London branch) if some of us men were prepared to serve on their committee. Despite the fact that I was Treasurer of the TCD Bridge Club in London as well as of the Dining Club, I agreed in 1975 to become their first Treasurer. The other men recruited were a mixture of active and inactive members of the Dining Club: Bob Press, Roy Stokes, Joe Tunstead and Rex Monaghan.

Of our three or four dinners a year, there was a time in the 1970s and 80s when we used to hold one of them at the Irish Club on the corner of Eaton Square and Lisle Street. The food was never very good but there was a feeling that as we were an Irish club ourselves, we should give it support and one redeeming feature was that the barmen knew how to pull a good pint of Guinness.

We went there until there were so many complaints about the food that we were forced to move, but where to? Two of our members were also members of the Savile Club (Prince and Hooberman) and they arranged for us to go there at least on a temporary basis. More than 40 years later we still hold one or two of our dinners there each year. Another example of the temporary becoming the permanent.

However, before leaving the Irish Club there was a period when the IRA were very active in London. At our dinners my procedure was to collect the dinner charges while members were having coffee and just before the toasts and speeches commenced. We didn't require that members should send in cheques in advance. What a trusting lot we were.

On one occasion the Irish Club received a bomb scare phone call just before the main course was served (appropriately it was duck), so we all had to troop out of the premises and remain on the pavement for ages until we were given the "all clear". When we were allowed back in again I was dismayed to find that more than half of those previously present had not returned but had headed off to catch their trains home instead, leaving the newly served food on the table. It took me many months to recover the unpaid dinner charges.

Before I took over as Treasurer, John Goode had made an extremely generous donation to the Club in the form of £1,500 in shares, principally to put us on a sound financial footing. There was discussion at the time as to how the income, which amounted to about £50 a year, might be utilised. One plan was to have money available with which to entertain a TCD graduate, newly arrived in London, to a free meal on his first visit to the Club.

The second plan was to have some funds available for the entertainment of guest speakers. You have to remember that these figures amounted to quite a lot in the 1960s: ten shillings bought a good dinner. Up to that time, apart from the ladies nights, all the speakers were Club members who were encouraged to speak about some aspect of their lives and experiences. At one such evening our member-speaker failed to turn up, so Gerry Little turned to me, just as we were sitting down to dinner, and asked me to give an impromptu talk about my hobby collecting first editions.

On taking over as Treasurer, I was a little concerned that the shares held were not what could be called growth stocks. They had in fact declined in value over a number of years while the stock market had actually risen. However, as the new boy on the block, I didn't feel able to change the investments and risk possible offence to our most generous donor. In due course, after some years of what fund managers would call "negative growth", I was invited to make changes and it is very satisfying to be able to say that by the time I stood down as Treasurer the value of our small portfolio had increased to more than £10,000 — and that was after deductions which were paid over to Trinity in connection with the quatercentenary celebrations in 1992. I must emphasise that this increase in value was achieved at a time of good stock market conditions, coupled with better stock selection, rather than the Treasurer's sagacity.

Although I had been against the admission of ladies to membership at the time when the issue was first raised, it was clear that as time went by more members were becoming reconciled to the idea and eventually it was agreed that they should be allowed to join the men – a move which I supported. Lady graduates have joined in increasing numbers over the years and now play as important a part in the running of the Club as the men, if not more so, and to date we have had two lady Chairmen as well as some 20 female committee members.

A MALTESE GOOSE CHASE

At the end of a meeting of the Cartoon Art Trust (now the Cartoon Museum) in London in the Spring of 1988, I was approached by Diana Willis, one of the founders of the Trust. 'I have heard' she said 'that you have recently acquired a house in Malta'. On confirming that this was in fact correct, she added that her father had died on the next-door island of Gozo in 1970.

Her father was none other than H. M. Bateman, the famous Australian-born cartoonist, who drew for *Punch* and many other publications, and was probably best known for his "The Man Who" series which provided an insight into a pre-war British society obsessed with manners and observing conventions. In many of his cartoons he had displayed his distaste for income tax inspectors by making fun of them, so it was not surprising that when Malta introduced the sixpence-in-the-pound tax scheme after the War, Bateman became one of the early 'sixpenny settlers' as they were called and moved from England to Malta to benefit from the arrangement.

'When he died in 1970' said Diana Willis, 'the Malta-Gozo ferry refused to allow his remains to be transported to Malta on their vessel for burial. However, a very kind Father Hili offered to convey the coffin on his boat and we were very grateful to him. 'I remember it being a very rough crossing in very bad weather, and only my sister and I, together with the priest, attended the burial.'

'Every year since then I have sent a Christmas card together with a small cheque to the man who looks after the cemetery but I have not heard from him over the years. We haven't been back to Malta since and I keep wondering if the grave is being looked after properly.'

'I wonder if you could pay a visit to the cemetery and have a look for us. I will give you the address even though I can't pronounce the name of the place.'

The name Ta' Braxia meant nothing to me even though I had driven past it any number of times on my way to Valletta; and I couldn't pronounce it either.

Having discovered its whereabouts, I drove there one morning only to find the gates firmly shut. I noticed that it wasn't open every day so I decided to call back again on the next 'open' day.

Arriving on the next open day I found the gates were again firmly locked and, on paying greater attention to the notice outside, saw that the cemetery was only open for a few hours on certain mornings.

At the third attempt the gates were wide open and after wandering around inside I eventually located the caretaker. To my consternation he had never heard of H. M. Bateman and, just as bad, had no idea where he might be buried. My heart sank as the cemetery seemed to go on forever (which I am sure was the intention when it was first opened).

He decided, however, that if Bateman was an Englishman (much the same as an Australian to him), he must be buried 'over there'. So over there I went in search of the grave. Walking up and down the rows for ages I eventually came across 'Henry Mayo Bateman 1887-1970'. The grave was so difficult to find because, as I discovered when I found it, the stone was not upright but flat and therefore much harder to spot.

The grave was well tended, so Diana Willis had no cause for concern, and I took some photographs for which she was most grateful on my return to England.

Some years later, Alan Keighley produced for Din l'Art Helwa, Malta's leading heritage society, an excellent and most useful booklet about the cemetery and made reference to the many well-known people buried there, but largely from a Maltese perspective, and he seemed to ignore Bateman.

A short while after the booklet's publication I met Alan at Andy and Jenny Welsh's home in Qrendi and said how sad I was that Bateman's name had been omitted. He expressed surprise. As he had drawn up a detailed plan of the cemetery, he did not believe Bateman's remains resided there – and he should know. Too true, but then didn't I have a photo of his grave?

We agreed to meet up at Ta' Braxia the following week and, when I arrived at the little office there, Alan was waiting to greet me. 'I owe you an apology' he said. 'I hadn't realised that Henry Mayo Bateman on my plan was the same as HM Bateman, the famous cartoonist'.

It is pleasing to be able to report that a new edition of the Visitor's Guide produced in 2010 made amends with a suitable entry for Bateman.

While the Guide contains a number of the worthies well-known in Sweden (Gollcher) or in Russia (Princess Nathalie Poutiatine Tabone), it is my belief that the 'unknown' H. M. Bateman who was renowned internationally is probably the most famous person there. And to think that I wouldn't have known had Diana Willis not asked me to do her a favour.

Diana died in the summer of 2010 and I wrote to her husband Dick to express my sympathy on the loss of a good friend and a founder and benefactor of the Cartoon Museum. Enclosed with my letter was the above unpublished piece about my "discovery" of HMB's grave.

Later, Diana's elder daughter Lucy, a well-known watercolourist, acknowledged my letter and said that the following May (2011) she hoped to pay her first visit to Malta while leading a group of amateur artists on a painting holiday and wondered if I would be there then.

Well, I was there and we did meet up. Lucy hoped during her trip to be able to visit some of the places that her grandfather had frequented and painted, and to obtain some local assistance in identifying the locations painted during his retirement years in Gozo.

Fortunately I was able to introduce Lucy to Marie Benoit who interviewed her in *The Malta Independent* on Sunday and was able to give her the names of some of the painted locations. Her brother, Joe Said, then Chairman of Malta Heritage, was able to supply the locations of the remainder.

In September 2013 Heritage Malta organised a splendid exhibition of Bateman's Gozo and Malta pictures, accompanied by an excellent catalogue. Simultaneously, the Cartoon Museum in London displayed Bateman's famous cartoons, most of which came from their permanent collection, and the Curwen Gallery put on a show of Lucy's watercolours, resulting from her visit to Gozo. Not to be outdone, Malta Post produced a set of five stamps depicting three of Bateman's Gozo scenes and two of Edward Lear's from the Maltese national collections. At last Bateman had received the credit he was long overdue.

MISS MARY SMALL

In August 1999 I purchased a small watercolour from Abbott & Holder by Daniel Maclise.

When I went to collect it, John Holder mentioned that a descendant of Mary Small had contacted him to offer information about her and her family to the purchaser should it be of interest. Of course I was interested and so was put in touch with Peter Currie at Sherborne.

Mr Currie wrote to me on 29 August, saying that Mary was born in 1812, the second of five daughters of Robert Small (1779-1850), a successful London merchant who had a home in London's Regent's Park as well as an estate near Hastings. Mary's elder sister was Mr Currie's great grandmother and Mary was god-mother of his great-aunt. (I hope you are with me so far). Robert outlived three of his five daughters, including Mary who died at 31 and who was 17 when painted by Maclise.

Robert's father (that is Mary's grandfather) was the Rev. Alexander Small, Minister of Newtyle, Perthshire and later of Kilconquhar, Fife. The Rev. Alexander had married a Jane Stewart whose cousin was a friend of Sir Walter Scott and the inspiration for one of the characters in "Waverley". Mary had never married and Mr Currie was curious as to how Robert Small had managed to commission Maclise to paint no less than four family portraits, albeit in watercolour – one of them of Mary – only 18 months or so after the young Maclise had arrived in London from Cork and who would hardly have been well-known at the time.

Now, while I knew nothing about the Small family until I received Mr Currie's letter, I did know something of Maclise. His father had been a soldier in a Highland regiment which had been stationed in Cork. He had settled there, married at the Presbyterian church in 1797 and worked as a leather cutter.

Daniel was born in 1806 and aged 14 went to work at Newenham's bank where he spent two years before entering the newly-founded Cork Academy of Art. In the meantime he had obtained permission from the owner of Bolster's bookshop (then at 70 Patrick Street) to sketch the customers. In the autumn of 1825 he attracted some local fame by making a surreptitious sketch of Sir Walter Scott in the bookshop while Scott was visiting Cork to give a lecture. The following day the sketch was displayed in the bookshop's window. Scott was so impressed by the young artist's likeness that he signed it at its foot and was introduced to the artist. He is reputed to have said to Maclise that if he ever wished to go to London, he would endeavour to help him. On the strength of this sketch, and a letter of introduction to Crofton Croker, the distinguished writer then resident in London, he was enabled to enter the Royal Academy Schools and while there won the highest prizes available.

It is almost certain therefore that Scott not only helped Maclise to move to London but also introduced him to the Small family enabling the set of four pictures to be produced in 1829.

Maclise went on to establish a considerable reputation as one of the foremost painters of his generation. Also in 1829 he exhibited at the Royal Academy of Arts for the first time. He became an associate member in 1835 and a full member in 1840. Between 1858 and 1864 he produced the paintings for which he is probably most famous: "The Marriage of Strongbow and Eva"; and "The Meeting of Wellington and Blücher" and "The Death of Nelson" for the Palace of Westminster. He produced mostly historical works but also illustrated many books, in particular Thomas Moore's "Irish Melodies" and Father Prout's "Reliques".

Towards the end of his life he suffered from ill-health and this was probably the reason he declined the presidency of the Royal Academy which he had been offered and also turned down a knighthood.

He died on 25 April 1870 and as the day of his funeral coincided with the Royal Academy's annual banquet his friend Charles Dickens delivered "a most impressive eulogy".

Sadly Dickens himself passed away little more than a month later.

Miss Mary Small, watercolour by Daniel Maclise RA, 1829

A WALK IN BAVARIA

With a few friends, I took off for Munich in April 1998, primarily to attend a performance of "Nabucco" (by Verdi) at the Bavarian State Opera. None of us had been there before.

Before going I had been put in touch with Peter Lurie, who had been a successful architect in Johannesburg but whose ambition was to be an opera singer. After studying singing in his home city he was offered an engagement with the Bayerische Staatsoper (Bavarian State Opera) in Munich. He would be there at the time of our visit and, yes, he would be able to join us for lunch.

On our arrival at the hotel, the Platzl, in the historic old town, and getting to my room, I looked out of the window. The room was at the back of the hotel overlooking a narrow street and there on the other side from the room – horror of horrors – was the Hofbrau House, the best-known and probably the largest beer hall in Munich if not in Germany. At the best of times I am a light sleeper. Would I get any sleep at all during my stay, I wondered.

I need not have worried. They ceased serving drinks at about 11pm, the music stopped 30 minutes later and the beer drinkers had dispersed from the street quietly by midnight. All so well organised and so unlike Britain.

By coincidence, I discovered that Malta's leading soprano, Miriam Gauci, would be in Munich at the same time and singing "Madama Butterfly" on the night after "Nabucco". Whereas we had planned to go out for dinner on that second (Saturday) night, we now arranged matters so that we could go to "Madama Butterfly" and have dinner afterwards at the nearby Spatenhaus restaurant. The prima donna of the opera would be happy to come along too.

While we were entering the opera house for "Madama Butterfly", one of the finest theatres in Germany, I saw some notices that the conductor named in the programme had been replaced by another, but as I had not heard of either of them before, thought the matter was of no consequence.

At the end of the performance, which was a very good one incidentally, my friends made their way to the restaurant with instructions that they should proceed to order and eat and not wait for my arrival. I knew that waiting while Miriam turning herself from a fifteen year old Japanese girl to a rather older Maltese lady would not be a quick process.

However, when I left my friends and made my way to the rear of the opera house, I found Peter Lurie awaiting me with a message from Miriam. I was to go straight up to her dressing room and not wait downstairs with the usual autograph hunters and well-wishers. When I got to her floor and found her room, she was there with two dressers (or were they undressers?) and in floods of tears. There was a problem.

Apparently on the previous Thursday there was due to be a rehearsal, but the conductor (the original conductor named in the programme) had cancelled it as he was travelling to Vienna to conduct a concert there that night. When he returned to Munich the following day, he was summoned to the office of the Director, Peter Jonas (previously of the English National Opera in London) and dismissed, because he had been in breach of his contract by going to Vienna. That was all very well but the Bayerische Staatsoper now had no conductor for the following night's performance.

There followed much frantic toing and froing, probably wringing of hands and certainly telephoning all around Eastern Europe before, eventually, a conductor was found – in Budapest – but he would not arrive in Munich until lunchtime on Saturday. With no time for a rehearsal, there could only be a brief chat with the principals beforehand.

Miriam had been distraught at this turn of events and had phoned her own agent in Vienna, Dr Rudolf Raab, for solace and advice. As it happened, he said, he was free on Saturday night and would travel to Munich for the performance and, in any event, he would welcome an opportunity to talk to her afterwards about future engagements before taking a plane back to Vienna.

I could see where all this was leading. Miriam would not be able to join us for dinner, I would return to the restaurant alone, and my friends would consider me a name-dropper who didn't really know the star of the opera. We kissed, said we would catch up in Malta, and I left. On arriving at the restaurant my friends were already enjoying their meal. I explained the position as I waited for the menu and some food. It was now almost midnight and the restaurant was nearly empty.

Half an hour or so later, Julie, who was facing the entrance, suddenly exclaimed 'I think your friend is here after all.' I turned around in my seat and there was Miriam, smiling and carrying a gigantic bouquet, followed by Dr Raab, approaching our table. I was relieved and not such a name-dropper after all.

That, however, is not the end of the story. The following morning after breakfast, I was at the reception desk paying my bill when one of the receptionists said 'Mr Elyan, there is a telephone call for you.' My heart sank. Who knew my number? My sister Doreen did and all I could think at the time was that there was some bad news about Mum or Dad in the Isle of Man. 'Please go to box number four' said the receptionist. I did as she said, moving slowly and fearing the worst.

'Hello' I said. 'This is Miriam' said the voice at the other end. 'You mentioned last night that you and your friends were going for a walk this morning. Would it be possible for me to join you? Just say if it is too difficult'. Boy, was I relieved. 'Of course you can join us. We'll be going in about an hour'. 'Can you tell me how to find your hotel?' 'No need to, I'll call to collect you at your apartment as it is on our way to the Englische Garten'.

When I got to the apartment, there was a short wait while Miriam came down. It was unseasonably warm in Munich for that time of the year – late April. When the lift door opened, Miriam appeared wearing high-heels, a fur coat and underneath a chunky-knit scarlet pullover. My jaw dropped. 'I'm not sure those shoes are suitable for walking in the Englische Garten'. 'They are nice shoes, are they not?' 'They are lovely shoes, very attractive, but hardly suitable for a long walk. They will get very scuffed and that would be a great pity. Also, it is very warm outside. You will hardly need a coat'. 'Are you sure it will not be cold later?' 'Ok,

I will go back upstairs and change'. Ten minutes or so later we were off and had a really good long walk in the park which was supposed to be Bavaria's idea of an English Garden although in truth I've never seen a garden in England quite that size – or with nearly so many topless girls sunbathing.

It's a strange life being an opera star. We see them performing and, at the end, savouring the curtain-calls and receiving their bouquets and acknowledging the applause. But then, when the curtain finally falls and the audience leaves the theatre, it is back to a normal life that can often be very lonely, particularly in a foreign city, without friends, filling in time before the next performance perhaps some days away.

At the end of the walk Miriam asked me if I would take her photograph outside a record shop near the opera house. The windows were filled with posters of her and "Madama Butterfly" CDs. It made a very good subject for a photograph.

Recently I spotted the following piece in *The Times*, dated 8 August 2019. 'For nearly a century bare bottoms have been as inescapable a fixture of the German summer as barbecues and beer. Yet nudist societies say the pastime is beginning to wane in the age of smartphones. In Munich so few naturists strip off in the English Garden – once celebrated for its cheerfully lax approach to clothing – that a Frenchman has launched a campaign to revive the custom'.

Perhaps it's time for me to pay another visit to Munich.

Miriam Gauchi, Munich, April 1998

With Miriam Gauchi
in the Englische Garten, Munich

NO TRUMPS AND FEW POINTS

Not many people, when they wish to learn to play bridge begin by helping to create a new bridge club for the purpose, which is exactly what I and some friends did in 1967. I had never played bridge before, my parents didn't play any card games, but I thought it was something that I should learn to do; so helped by Russell Telfer as my guide, he having played regularly at Trinity and for Trinity, we enquired if any of our London friends were interested in a new venture catering for TCD graduates in London. We received some definite support, not a lot perhaps, but enough to occupy 3 or 4 tables on a regular basis.

As I was then on the committee of the TCD Dining Club, the matter was raised at one of their meetings and it was agreed that they would lend us £50 to enable us to get off the ground. This meant we could hold a reception at the Irish Club in Eaton Square, form a committee and decide how often to meet (and in case anybody is interested, the loan was repaid within a year). We decided we would meet every Monday because that was the evening when young people in London recovered from their hectic weekends of party-going (and, I'm told, when the young ladies washed their hair).

Russell was elected Chairman, Andrew Fox-Robinson became Secretary and I was appointed Treasurer. The evenings would usually commence with Russell giving a talk about some aspect of bridge, after which three of the four tables would play duplicate while Russell would act as supervisor and teach rubber bridge to a table of beginners.

Not long after we got going, Russell was invited to a game of "social" bridge one evening but one of the participants dropped out at short notice. The hostess phoned Russell to ask if he could suggest a replacement. 'You could ask David Elyan' he said; 'but isn't he much too good?', 'what do you mean too good?'. 'Isn't he treasurer of a bridge club?'. 'Yes' said Russell, 'he's a good treasurer but not much of a bridge player'. I didn't know of this conversation until much later, though Russell now claims he has forgotten this, if it happened.

In order to get some experience of duplicate bridge, Russell suggested he and I should go along to the Young Chelsea Bridge Club. On our first occasion there we were very surprised to finish joint second and, when the results were announced, we were approached by Warwick Pitch, who ran the club, and a couple of the team captains enquiring if we would be available to play for the club in matches the following week. We couldn't manage any of the dates suggested following our "beginners luck", and it may have been just as well because we went along again a few weeks later and finished well down the field. No further invitations to join any of the teams were received.

Meanwhile, back at the Irish Club, before long our numbers built up to 30/40 each evening and we were ourselves able to enter teams in the London Business Leagues. Clearly the standard couldn't have been too high because I was able to play on one of the teams and cannot have covered myself in glory. In fact all I can remember of the matches was that I particularly enjoyed playing against the John Lewis Partnership in Oxford Street and at Truman's Brewery in Brick Lane because when play ended the hosts provided a veritable banquet and there was no shortage of wine.

One of the pleasant activities of the Club was our going away once or twice a year on what were called "bridge weekends" at some hotel where we did almost anything except play bridge apart from a few hours after lunch on the Sunday afternoons. Tennis, walking, shopping and even squash were especially popular.

It was obvious early on that we could not exist with Trinity graduates alone, so we decided to open our doors to Oxbridge people and, not long afterwards, to members of the Irish Club which gave their members an opportunity to participate also. This arrangement continued for many years until the Irish Club got into financial difficulties and we were required to seek a new home.

Before this Russell and Andrew had left London and owing to pressure of work I too had to stand down, but we were very fortunate that by this time Richard Waterbury had arrived on the scene and was more than happy to take charge, encouraging a new raft of his friends to join in.

One particular bridge evening sticks in my memory and it was arranged by the Worshipful Company of Makers of Playing Cards at one of the City of London livery company halls. Attendance was restricted to livery company members and as a founder-liveryman of the Chartered Secretaries Company I was eligible to play. I contacted our Clerk and told him I was available for the CIS team but in the event nobody else showed any interest and the advice received was that I could take part if I could find another liveryman. After some enquiries I located Ian Bray, who was a member of the Grocers Company and we duly took our place. It was a splendid evening full of big names such as well-known judges, MPs and members of the House of Lords.

At the halfway stage when we adjourned for dinner, Ian and I were placed 6th out of 36 pairs. However, the food and the wine took their toll and we slipped down the rankings in the second half to finish closer to the bottom than the top, but a creditable performance nonetheless.

Although I still enjoy my bridge, I don't nowadays take it too seriously and my peripatetic lifestyle leads me towards playing socially, which means accompanied by a nice meal and a lot of conversation. Some of these occasional fours have now been in existence for more than 30 years.

In general while I consider myself to have had a good and lucky life, my bridge cards have always been below par. More experienced players have often reassured me – and indeed I believed myself – that a run of bad cards would always be followed by a run of good cards, but having been a player for more than 50 years I am still waiting for my luck to change.

It has been pointed out that if I played bridge twice a week for 40 weeks a year, and if I played an average of 20 hands each evening, after 40 years, if my arithmetic is correct, I would have played some 64,000 hands with a point count of 10 which is average.

THE ACADEMY

Though I had lived no more than ten minutes walk from the Royal Academy of Music (RAM) on the Marylebone Road for more than 10 years, it was only when Jennifer Scott (Scottie) invited me to have supper with her then boss, who lived nearby, that I made a discovery: that the Academy produced a vast range of music which was open to the public, often free of charge. The plan for that evening was to attend one of their concerts after we had eaten but we then discovered that the concert had been cancelled.

However, my interest had been aroused and so I got the RAM diary of events, went to some concerts myself and then joined the fairly-new Friends organisation. That would have been in about 1991. Not long afterwards I was invited to join the Friends' committee and about a year after that I received a phone call from Sheila Lumsden, President and founder of the Friends, whose husband Sir David was Principal of the Academy, asking me if I would pop in to have tea with her. A strange request I thought but I nevertheless accepted. When we met she told me that Philip Feakin, the then Chairman, who worked for British Gas, was being transferred to the Far East and had been forced to resign and, as a result, she would like me to take over. But, I said, there's the Treasurer and the Secretary, both more senior to me; and most of the other committee members were far more knowledgeable about music than I. Wouldn't one of them be a better bet? Sheila replied that she had 'taken soundings' and they were unanimous that I would be the best person to take on the task. Suitably flattered, I accepted.

Though she was President of the Friends, Sheila didn't mind rolling her sleeves up and often was to be found, along with Daphne Regan, wife of Christopher, the Registrar, making sandwiches for an evening event. Daphne and Christopher became good friends and after he retired we used to meet up at their new home opposite Tewkesbury Abbey, where Christopher often played the organ at the Abbey, not at his home. He was a third generation at the Academy, a link that went back some 90 years.

In the way that the Isle of Wight is frequently confused with the Isle of Man – others often confuse the Academy with the Royal College of Music. Worse than that, they also confuse the Royal Academy of Arts at Burlington House in Piccadilly with the Royal Academy of Music, but I learnt to live with these difficulties. In actual fact the Academy is recognised (at least within the Academy) as the senior British conservatoire having been established in 1822, and in Europe only the Paris Conservatoire is older.

I saw that one of my first tasks as Chairman would be to build up the membership from about 400 and make ourselves much more widely known. One way of doing that, particularly within our part of London, would be to link up with other non-competing organisations. We started with an approach to the Friends of Regent's Park, whom we invited along to a concert and a supper afterwards. They accepted gratefully and in good numbers but we made a fatal mistake in our costings. We quoted a price which included wine, expecting them to drink an average of a glass each, but the actual consumption turned out to be three times that. We had ignored the fact that as they lived nearby, and nobody was driving, they didn't need to worry about alcohol levels and we lost some hundreds of pounds on the evening. We had learnt a salutary lesson and from then onwards we always operated a cash bar.

Later functions took place with a number of other friends organisations: the Marylebone Society, the Friends of Holland Park, the Friends of Bankside and the Royal Academy (of Arts); and our membership climbed slowly to the 500/600 level. A notable joint event with the RWS at Bankside combined their latest watercolour exhibition of British scenery with a recital of English song given by Christopher Maltman, then an Academy student but now an international star.

When we joined up with the Royal Academy Friends, as their membership was something like 70,000 with a full-time staff of 12, they had to ballot for the 100 or so tickets made available to them as the

Duke's Hall could only accommodate about 400. And when, later, we went to Burlington House with the RAM Jazz Band, and a background there of the latest Roy Lichtenstein exhibition, we had a most enjoyable occasion – and again their members had to take part in a ballot. We also brought chamber music to the nearby headquarters of John Lewis and Marks and Spencer for the benefit of their staff.

One day out of the blue I received a call from the Southend-on-Sea Music Society, one of the largest in the UK, asking if they could join us for a concert at the Academy. I hadn't realised quite how big they were (with 10,000 members) but we managed to allocate 150 tickets to them and they arrived in three coaches after two or three hours travelling – each coach following a different route into London and picking up passengers on the way. By the time they got to the Academy, after so long on the coach, and bearing in mind that most of them were rather elderly, there were long queues for the toilets to the annoyance of students and staff alike. I'm not sure that they all got to the concert before it started.

Not strictly relating to the Academy, but in 1994 I was at home listening to a Prom concert from the Albert Hall and, during the interval, there was a broadcast of a conversation between Daniel Snowman, a senior commentator on Radio Three, and Sir Thomas Armstrong, Principal of the Royal Academy of Music between 1955 and 1968, who was then aged 96 and father of Robert Armstrong, Lady Thatcher's "fixer".

His recall even at that venerable age was remarkable. He had been particularly friendly with Holst, Vaughan Williams and Lord Berners, and could remember his dealings with them as well as with Elgar before World War One. One of his stories went back to the time when he was organist at Christ Church cathedral in Oxford and also acted as Secretary of the Oxford Symphony Orchestra, mostly comprising talented students and retired professionals from the London orchestras who lived in the vicinity. Sir Thomas Beecham always had a 'soft spot' for this orchestra which found it difficult to survive financially, and he knew that whenever he was their conductor they were assured of a full-house at the Sheldonian Theatre.

One day Armstrong received a phone call from Beecham in London. 'Is that you, Thomas?' Beecham enquired. 'Yes, Sir Thomas', Armstrong replied. 'I'm looking in my diary and find that I have a free day in a couple of months' time – say 12 March. Is it any good to you?' 'Yes, Sir Thomas, it would suit us very well'. 'OK then, usual form – I'll see you at the rehearsal'. "Usual form" was that Beecham would take a late morning train from Paddington to Oxford, then walk to the Mitre Hotel and have lunch, after which he would stroll over to the Sheldonian, where all the players would be in position for a rehearsal. After the usual greetings and shaking of hands, Beecham would step on to the podium.

On this occasion he turned to the leader of the orchestra saying 'we're not playing any symphonies today, are we McCallum?' 'Yes, sir, we're doing Brahms number two'. Clearly that was not what Beecham wanted to hear. 'But, McCallum, you and I have played that work many, many times before so there is no need to rehearse it.' 'Yes sir' – whereupon a student towards the back of the second violins raised his hand. Beecham bellowed: 'yes, boy?' Whereupon the "boy" said 'excuse me, Sir Thomas, but I have never played Brahms second symphony before' to which Beecham replied 'my dear boy, it is adorable, you will simply love it' and began to conduct all the other works on the programme.

The conversation between Snowman and Armstrong took place at Armstrong's home at Olney, Bucks, in April 1994. Clearly it took place out of doors because a blackbird could be heard singing in the background. Sadly Armstrong died some six weeks afterwards, and before the interview was broadcast about three months later.

My chairmanship of the Friends lasted for seven years and I stood down in 2000 as my residency in the Isle of Man had commenced and it wouldn't be quite so easy to get to meetings. It would no longer be a ten minute walk away.

I have been to so many wonderful concerts and opera performances over the years that I can strongly recommend any of you to support the Academy or one of the other London conservatoires. In particular, they each produce an opera a term performed by outstanding students – who will be the stars of tomorrow – and at a fraction of the price you'd pay at a commercial opera house at home or abroad.

SOME MEMORIES OF PRINCESS DIANA

Dublin in 1961 was a most exciting place, particularly for an impecunious student from Cork at Trinity College aged 20. There were cocktail parties every night, and two or three to be attended on some evenings. Horse racing was in close proximity to the city centre, polo in the Phoenix Park and other sociable activities such as beagling and point-to-pointing were not too far distant.

The pinnacle of the year was the Royal Dublin Society Horse Show each August attended by the Anglo-Irish in great numbers from County Sligo to Sloane Square, peers of the realm, baronets, continental counts and barons; and people without titles but double or even treble-barrelled names abounded.

There was a hunt ball every night for a week at one of the major hotels: the Shelbourne, the Gresham or the Royal Hibernian. The names of the hunts I can recall: the Galway Blazers, the Meath, the Kildare, the Scarteen Black and Tans, and the Ward Union. "The Horse Show" was part of the London "deb" scene just as it was part of the County Limerick scene, and revelry went on until breakfast time the following day or even later.

I had two problems: a lack of money and an inability to dance more than a few steps without crippling my partner by stamping on her toes. That meant I spent more time drinking than dancing and so got to meet more people than most of the guests. I cannot quite remember how or where I met Edmund (Lord) Fermoy but I imagine it was at the bar at one of these events. Though he was a highly accomplished horseman, and I was not, we had a common interest in books. In my case this interest manifested itself in collecting antiquarian books and first editions, whereas in his case his interest was bookbinding.

Lady Diana Spencer was born on 1 July 1961 so she would have been in her cot when I was carousing at these drunken Irish hooleys.

Somehow my friendship with Edmund Fermoy continued despite our different backgrounds and the fact that he was in Berkshire while I worked in Dublin. In 1966 I moved to London and by this time Edmund had set up a book bindery at his home near Hungerford. I visited him there occasionally and was invited to stay for Sunday lunch.

On one of these visits his sister's "Spencer" daughters were also present, staying for the weekend and playing with the Fermoy's children. The girls individually were most attractive and quiet but together could act like a pack of wild dogs. I did not particularly know which Spencer girl was which but on one occasion they were making such a racket that I couldn't hear myself speak. In desperation I picked up a newspaper and belted the nearest child with it. The child was Diana and it stopped the noise immediately.

At this time she would have been about nine, and I did not see her again until after her marriage in 1981. As HRH Princess of Wales she told me she remembered being whacked on the head and blamed me for her lack of a brain. She thought, however, it might improve it if she were to learn to play bridge and I was drafted in a few times to make up the numbers. She really had no aptitude for card games and soon retired to seek an alternative interest. As she did not fancy equine pursuits as her husband did, I think the attempt at bridge was her early effort to find an alternative identity for herself away from the restricting confines of the Royal family. Creating her own identity was something she was to accomplish subsequently with astonishing success.

On another occasion I was recruited to make up a four at tennis, fearful though I was of newspaper reports about her smash, powerful forehand and lessons from no less than Martina Navratilova. I expected to be thrashed but surprisingly acquitted myself rather well by playing whenever possible on her backhand. To my disappointment, I was never invited again.

At a performance at the Royal Opera House I was hosting some guests in our company box to the left of the stage when, just before the curtain rose, I noticed Charles, Diana and some friends appearing in the Royal box directly opposite. So engrossed was she with the opera and her other guests that I assumed she had not seen me. When, eventually, we met some months later she said that, of course, she had spotted me and wanted to wave during the interval but 'I would not be allowed to do that sort of thing in the Royal box'.

In the 1990s when I joined the Friends of the Royal Academy of Music, I discovered that Diana was the Academy's President, though I heard many complaints that she hardly ever appeared there. This compared badly with Charles who, as President of the Royal College of Music, attended many college concerts as well as the annual graduation ceremonies. He was much more musical (in the classical sense) and sang with the Bach Choir. I offered (or was asked) to see if I could persuade HRH to take a more active interest in the Academy. I received a courteous response and the promise that she would attend a concert now and again if I thought she really would like the music. In truth I think that by this time she had already begun to put the hundred plus organisations of which she was patron into one of two categories: those in whose work she was greatly interested and those in whose work she was not. Unfortunately, the RAM fell into the latter grouping.

In October 1994 1 found a concert that she would like, featuring the Elgar Cello concerto, conducted by Yehudi (Lord) Menuhin and featuring Lynn Harrell, then Principal of the Academy. She agreed to attend. We had a little reception on her arrival at which she was surprised to find that the wine labels on the bottles bore the Royal crest. She questioned, jokingly, whether we had received "Royal" permission. None of us knew so I asked whether she might not give us permission herself there and then as our President. Oh no, she said, these decisions were reached at Buckingham Palace much higher up than at her level. On the night, Yehudi Menuhin was wearing a patterned blue silk shirt and crumpled suede shoes that looked like bedroom slippers. Before the concert began I whispered that Lord Menuhin liked to conduct wearing the top half of his pyjamas. He did so for luck. She looked at me seriously in case I meant what I had said before a lengthy chortle. "Yes, it does look a bit like that, doesn't it?" she said.

Later she came to the Academy for a "working visit", informally, with no advance publicity, to watch the students practising. During the lunch break we went down to the restaurant to meet more of the students. There I introduced her to the President of the Students' Union.

Early on in their conversation he asked her who her favourite composer was. She replied Mozart and added that she also liked Beethoven. The SU President quickly enquired: 'If you like them, how could you possibly go to Dire Straits' concerts?' 'I like them too', she replied, laughing.

I remember particularly Diana's visit to the Academy in October 1995. Jennifer Micallef and fellow student Glen Inanga will also remember it because they were chosen to play a piece for two pianos before a select audience consisting of the Princess, the Principal of the Academy Dr (later Sir) Curtis Price, their professor Frank Wibaut, and yours truly. Before the other visitors arrived the pianists rehearsed some Brazilian dances by Villa-Lobos, the final one of which was a lively Latin-American number. When they had finished, I mentioned that I thought the Princess would prefer the final jazzy number to the relatively sombre earlier dances.

'Do you think so?' enquired the two pianists rather anxiously. 'No: you will stick to the plan' said their professor sternly. Seconds later the Principal arrived with the VIP guest and after introductions and handshakes all round we settled down for the short performance. You can guess which piece they played. The Princess was enthralled; and of course as Jennifer was Maltese, the little recital was given extensive coverage in the Maltese press.

A month later Diana's famous interview on TV with Martin Bashir took place and I don't think I was alone in my amazement at such a well kept secret.

When eventually she announced that she was giving up most of her public appointments, more than a hundred of them, to concentrate on five or six, the Royal Academy of Music was one of those from which she resigned. Although I contacted her to see if there was any possibility of a change of heart, I was told that there was not, though she would be pleased to be invited back for the odd concert. She never did return.

Having known her slightly for more than 25 years, I found her great fun to be with, kind, with a good sense of humour and, of course, strikingly good-looking. I was always impressed when accompanying her how, when we approached a crowd of people, the crowd would somehow melt away so that a passage always appeared in the middle for us to walk through.

Over the past few years I noticed she was relying more and more on her own judgement and on her "gut feel" rather than on court advisors who had all but disappeared. She also turned increasingly to friends but, unfortunately, some of those she trusted most let her down badly, and the advice she received was sometimes neither well-meaning nor helpful. These experiences led in turn to an increasing sense of isolation, loneliness and unhappiness. They also led to uncertainty particularly with regard to her future.

Speculation in the press can only have magnified these difficulties.

I shall remember the charming and boisterous young girl quietened by a smack with a newspaper and, later, the kind and considerate adult who was the greatest fun to be with and who was so sadly cut down before her time. She had so much more to do and so much happiness to dispense just as she was finding such a satisfying role for herself.

September 1998

Guy Whalley, Princess Diana and (on right) Sir David and Lady Lumsden at the Royal Academy of Music

With Princess Diana and Sir Curtis Price at a Royal Academy of Music concert

Meeting students at the Royal Academy of Music, October 1995

SOME DIARY ENTRIES

5 October 1990

Reaching 50 yesterday turned out to be nothing special, apart from an enjoyable party at Lord's Cricket Ground and all that it involved. It was a dry evening and the floodlights were switched on so that guests were able to walk on the hallowed turf – a unique experience for ladies in those days – and then visit the museum, which had been especially opened, prior to supper and drinks.

40, even without a party, was quite alright: life beginning then and all that; and with a fair wind, there might still be at least another half of my life to look forward to.

50, however, means that one is well into the second half and it comes at a time when I have just got used to being in my 40s. Still, it is always better than being older, no matter what the age. My father, who will be 83 in a matter of days, says he is in 'injury time' and that the good Lord, who appears to him to be a referee, is looking at his watch and about to blow his whistle.

It is a time to look back and see how little I have achieved. It isn't so much that I don't have a wife or a family. Is that an achievement? Most men of my age have a wife – or two – and children, if not also grandchildren, but in many other respects they, too, have achieved nothing of significance.

I have always wanted to be creative: to leave something behind as a lasting memorial to my having been here; and all there is to show so far are some ephemeral publications like *The Dubliner* and *The Dublin Magazine* and some slim volumes of verse. They will be collectors items one day, even though the poetry and criticism we published would probably have appeared in other journals if we had not existed.

Though I consider myself, and am considered by my peer group to be, an astute businessman, it hasn't taken me to the top of any ladders in the business world or to any significant fortune. The fact that I am comfortably off is more the result of not having married and not having to send children to expensive public schools, as many of my contemporaries have done. Being comfortably off does provide a measure of well-being and a certain degree of independence which means that I can do what I like when I like and am not totally dependent on a job, or being an employee, for a living. At the same time I have to watch that I don't become too selfish and self-centred – qualities that I hope my friends will not be too afraid to point out.

My degree of independence has enabled me to work only part-time and spend a goodly amount of time doing unpaid voluntary work – 'helping others' – in the arts, which I particularly enjoy, and which hopefully will lead in time to an even bigger contribution in this area. If life is about helping others, then I am fortunate in that I can spend my time indulging in that activity and doing the things I like doing. How I wish that I had more money, not to spend on myself but to enable me to play a bigger part in helping others less fortunate – and above all to do something of significance.

Good health is quite a blessing. Jogging, playing squash, hill walking are all things that I enjoy and while contemporaries do perhaps some of these things, fewer and fewer as the years go by seem to indulge in them as much as I do. That gives me a quiet satisfaction and the hope that continuing good health will enable me to carry on for some time to come, whether I am 50 or 60.

Having started life in lower middle class circles, the son of a cabinet maker who left school at 14, I have progressed as far as middle class through my own endeavours as evidenced by my membership of Lloyd's, the MCC, the Kildare Street Club in Dublin, becoming a founding liveryman of the Charted Secretaries Company and a Freeman of the City of London. Hardly a world shattering performance. A London flat, a weekend cottage in the Cotswolds and a holiday home in Malta are the envy of friends but, if truth be known, selling the lot would only purchase a not-very-large home in London or a more substantial residence in Cheltenham or Malvern.

My future plans will involve taking a bigger role in the arts through the Royal Watercolour Society – despite the fact that I can hardly paint – and in the Royal Academy of Music – though I cannot play an instrument. Time will tell if I can make progress in these directions. Artists and musicians are not usually good administrators or business people; and administrators and business people are seldom very creative. We should be able to help each other and I have the time, and the inclination, to make my contribution if allowed to do so.

Despite turning 50 it is just possible that the next decade will allow me to play a role of significance in one or other of these artistic areas. That would be very satisfying if I can achieve it and provide some compensation for advancing through middle age.

19 October 1993

Returned home after playing squash at Hurlingham. Couldn't help thinking of Hilly: she had been a member there. I last saw her on Wednesday at Richards Place, the house she had moved to in order to spend her last days at home in preference to the Cromwell Hospital or a hospice. She was very frail and managed to get downstairs with difficulty, to open the door and let me in, while all the time shouting to me outside not to go away and that she was on her way. I helped her back upstairs and to bed before getting her a coffee with 'half cold water'. She had cancer of the liver and had not long to live: we all knew that; but Hilly carried on as if she expected to make a full recovery. A few days previously I had been asked to buy screw-in bulbs: 'no not twelve, make it eighteen', she said, 'and could you get some round plugs as well – for the standard lamps'. I did as directed. She was amused when I pointed out that the recessed ceiling lights were a mixture of 100 and 60 watt, which just happened to be what I had bought, because it was only when I entered the shop at Twickenham not far from my office that I realized that the instructions did not include the wattage.

Her mind was as clear and she as sensible as she had ever been, though there had been times some months before when we wondered about her sanity. She made plans then only to change them once people had been committed to her course of action. It was infuriating at the time though, months later, it seems hardly to have mattered. She realized now she would need a nurse in case she had another shivering attack in the middle of the night, though she was concerned that she should like the person appointed; and, at the same time, resented that there should be somebody in the house who was not a friend or of her family. It was unlikely, she thought, that a nurse could be on the same 'wave-length'.

'Jacky has volunteered you', she said, 'to clear out the spare room for the nurse'. Clearing out the room, I thought, was not a problem so long as there was somewhere to put all the clobber. That was Wednesday. I could not help on Thursday or Friday and would be away in Gloucestershire for the weekend. So unless another friend could do the job in the meantime, it was left that I would do it the following week. I resolved to telephone her the following Monday to check on the position.

It was only six months previously, at Easter, that I got to know Hilly well. She had invited me to join her and some friends at her house in Brittany, largely to make up a bridge four. I demurred for some time and then agreed following persuasion from mutual friends. The whole venture was a recipe for disaster. Our hostess was not in the best of health and was awaiting the result of tests which she expected as soon as she returned to London. The weather was awful – it rained every day for most of every day; and the others, it transpired, were severely addicted to walking come what may regardless of the rain; and the slippery, muddy tracks all conspired to create maximum discomfort. The immediate countryside was unattractive. Granted that Hilly had bought some cottages from French cousins, knocked them into one fine house – but it was in the middle of nowhere and a very long drive from Fulham. Why, I wondered, did she want to be there instead of Gloucestershire or Dorset or somewhere more accessible. Despite all these unpromising ingredients, the trip went well and I enjoyed it. Do I overstate the faults or possess some hitherto unnoticed quality of affability? Perhaps it was Hilly herself whose personality made it enjoyable.

When I left that Wednesday and kissed her, there were tears on her cheeks. She was going to the Cromwell in the afternoon for a check-up and hoping they would not want to keep her in. Acceptance of a live-in nurse would be her compromise to be allowed to return home.

As I went out into the South Kensington October sunshine I believed that – despite her frailty – the soundness of her mind, her determination, her interest in living and in the activities of her close friends would keep her going for some months to come. 'I'm sorry', she said, 'but I don't think I'll be able to go to your recital at the Bankside

Gallery tomorrow. I don't think I could sit for that long even if I could get somebody to drive me there'. 'Did you hear that the people at Swansea say I don't exist? They have lost any record of my driving licence – and I need one to be able to get a residents' parking permit'.

I hope the check-up goes well, I thought, and they allow her back to Richards Place, so that she is there when I phone her on Monday next to arrange to call around.

However when I got back to London from Gloucestershire on Sunday night, there was a message to say that she had died that morning. She was only 46. How, I thought, can a life be so fragile. How unlucky she was.

Note: Hilary Mallinson was the daughter of Sir Paul Mallinson Bt. and sister of Sir William Mallinson Bt., who died shortly after her, also of cancer.

Hilary had been married to Michael Gooley and together they founded 'Trailfinders' the well-known long-distance travel firm.

21 May 1994

I was just about to write a note on my recent experiences of bladder blockages – a subject on which I am now something of an expert; so much so that I am consulted in confidence by my friends who have problems in that very private area – when news came through on the radio that Jackie Kennedy (the name by which we all knew her), who had been receiving treatment for cancer in hospital in New York, had discharged herself and returned to her New York penthouse apartment because the doctors could do no more for her. She died early the following morning.

The obituaries today have majored on the way she protected her own and her children's privacy after Jack's assassination; her grace and her intelligence and the way in which she returned to work as an editor at Doubleday; and the 'normalness' of her two children, both lawyers. There were photographs of Jackie walking in Central Park with her companion, Maurice Tempelsman, only last week. There was a report of the children being with their mother when she died, and how John Jr later set off alone on his bicycle to return home.

My mind inevitably turned back to Jack's assassination in

November 1963 and the oft-quoted words: that everybody knows where they were when they heard the news. For my part, I remember waiting in a pub in Dublin after work – the Bailey – for Robin Willcox to turn up, and when she did she asked agitatedly if I had heard the news. I hadn't and made some inane comment about Kruschev because what she had said couldn't be true. People – certainly not world leaders – did not get killed in that way at that time. Now, more than thirty years later, not just Jack but Bobbie, Martin Luther King, John Lennon, Ranjit Ghandi, his mother and many other well-known people have followed. How sad it is that the more seemingly civilized we become, the more we develop selfish, callous and cynical qualities. People protest – quite rightly – about food additives, air and sea pollution, but there seem to be more stabbings and certainly more shootings, muggings and robberies. Where is it all going to lead? Hands up all those who want to be in the next generation. Prince Philip, in a lecture at the Royal Society of Arts last year, marking his 40 years as president, remarked: 'I sometimes think I'm glad I'm as old as I am'. I know what he feels and means.

Jackie Kennedy led a life which was often sad and troubled but she led it with dignity. She gave no interviews and, indeed, decreed that her memories which were recorded should not be published until 50 years after her last surviving child had died.

Most people would rush into print immediately to collect the enormous cash advances. It is facile to say that Jackie did not do so because she was already rich, and had no need of the money. But there are rich people, most of whom are also greedy, who could not wait to cash in. It is the latter who are more representative of our age, unfortunately.

What, I wonder has become of Robin Willcox. I hope she is a happy grandmother by now.

I wanted to include the following anecdote somewhere but couldn't find an obvious place. The nearest I could get, as it refers to John F. Kennedy, was to tag it onto my piece about his wife Jackie.

Pierre Salinger (1925-2004), White House Press Secretary under Kennedy, was guest of honour at a dinner in Goodwood House, Sussex, sponsored by one of my favourite magazines, *Institutional Investor*. It was 23 October 1988 and I was a guest of the publication. After dinner a few of us were chatting to Salinger when he told us what later was to become a piece of history.

He was working in his (White House) office late one evening when his direct line phone rang. The voice at the other end said 'Is that you Pierre?' 'Yes, Mr President'. 'Can you come over as there is something I wish to speak to you about'. He went straight over to the Oval Office and was shown in, where President Kennedy was sitting alone. 'Thanks, Pierre', and after some pleasantries Kennedy said 'I would like you to get me 1000 Petit Upmann Cuban cigars by tomorrow morning. Do you think that'll be a problem?' 'I'll do my best, sir'. He returned to his office, sat down and racked his brain. It was already very late and all the usual cigar suppliers would have closed for the night. The only way was to call in some favours from Democratic party supporters. After some ringing around, he was off in his chauffeur driven car, doing the rounds of Washington, and eventually acquired the requested quantity. On the following morning he wasn't long in his office when the phone rang. It was the President, asking how he had got on and to come over and give him a report. He went over to Kennedy's office to tell him about the previous evening's activities. The President was evidently pleased. While Salinger sat there, he watched as the President unlocked a drawer in his desk, withdrew a document and signed it. It turned out to be the embargo on the importation of Cuban goods into the United States, dated 7 September 1962. All in a night's work at the White House.

Later I met Salinger again at a US embassy drinks party in Regent's Park and asked him about Nikita Khruschev's appearance at the United Nations and his famous "shoe banging" episode in October 1960. When he arrived in New York, Kennedy and various senior United Nations personnel met him at the airport. He was seen stepping down from the Ilyushin plane wearing a long, heavy coat and a Russian fur hat: it was very cold at the time. Standing on the "tarmac" below, as a piece of public relations, Kennedy appeared in a two-piece suit with his tie waving in the breeze, giving the world's media the impression that a young, virile American President was meeting an elderly decrepit Russian leader. This was the impression that was successfully flashed all around the globe: and the 23 year age gap between them seemed more like 46.

Khruschev was later removed from power in 1964 and what the

Russians considered a "shameful episode" was presented by Khruschev himself as "an act of valor".

10 January 2006

Christmas 2005 has come and gone and it is interesting to look back – not just at the year past but also on my achievement in reaching age 65 in October without too many mishaps along the way.

Age 65 brought with it the 'old age' pension and a monthly amount which exceeded my expectations. Bearing in mind that my employers and I have been contributing towards it for nigh on 40 years, it remains a fact that I would not be able to survive on it alone. Thankfully, I still have my personal pension plan, which I haven't yet begun to draw and which has been increasing in value satisfactorily each year since moving to the Isle of Man in 2000. Obviously stock market conditions have been good to me and my own hand-picked investments over the period have done well, so let's hope the success continues.

What sort of a year has it been? Apart from an eye irritation and a tendency to irritable bowel now and again, not at all bad on the health front. On other fronts I have seen a number of enjoyable operas and been on some pleasant trips abroad; for example, in recent months to Austria with the Gustav Mahler Society and to Boston, Cape Cod and Martha's Vinyard with friends.

The political scene at home and abroad is quite worrying. A Labour government in Britain which promised so much has delivered so little and the situation in Iraq does not improve. Car bombs and suicide bombers explode with awful consequences, mostly killing ordinary Iraqi citizens going about their business. It is bordering on civil war without any obvious end-plan other than to cause as much chaos as possible.

Then there are the military or despotic regimes in many countries such as Iran, Syria, Belarus, Burma and most of Africa whose rulers salt money away in secret bank accounts abroad while their populations die of aids or starvation and are tortured if they have the strength to protest. The so-called civilized West tends to ignore such goings on, sends aid which more often than not falls into the wrong hands – those of the ruler's family and supporters – who might only get a mild rebuke via diplomatic channels. If the country concerned produces oil, gas or precious metals, there is no rebuke at all.

Back to personal matters and the fact that the number of good friends has diminished somewhat during the year; not due to any falling out or parting of the ways, but rather to them leaving this world before their time. In all some 10 friends have departed – people with whom I played bridge or went to the opera. Among them was Dudley Staunton, a retired general surgeon who was Chairman of the Trinity Dining Club while I was Treasurer, and who lived not far away in Regent's Park Road. Apart from the Club dinners, we had lunch or dinner from time to time, and there were other occasions when I would stroll over to the Stauntons and enjoy Dudley's generous portions of Scotch. It was lucky that he lived so near and that I was able to get there on foot.

One evening Dudley was telling me about his last trip to Cheltenham Races when he and his wife Rena drove there and back in the day, and it took him something like 90 minutes to get out of the car park and onto the main road. I said that next year they must borrow my flat in Cheltenham as it was only a short walk from the racecourse and stay for the duration of the March national hunt festival. I never attended and it was such a pity to leave the flat empty when the regular racegoers booked their accommodation from one year to the next. He said he would mention the possibility to Rena when he got home.

At about 11pm that night my phone rang. A phone call at that late hour usually meant bad news so I answered it with some trepidation. It turned out to be Rena who said 'Dudley has just told me of your very kind offer. Of course we'd love to accept'. While Dudley came from Mayo, Rena hailed from Fethard in Co. Tipperary, the heart of the 'horsy' country. She had been a regular rider in her young days and in fact exercised Dr Bethel Solomons' hunter on her days off from nursing in Dublin – he then being the Master of the Rotunda Hospital. More recently she continued to follow the form and had her weekly flutters.

Nearer the time of the visit to Cheltenham, I called around to see the Stauntons and deliver the flat keys. Over a possibly larger glass of whisky than usual I said to Rena that the flat was so close to the racecourse entrance, that if she wished to go to the Ladies, as there would inevitably be a long queue – there were long queues for everything at Cheltenham – it would be quicker to go to the entry gate, obtain a

Dudley Staunton at a TCD dinner

readmission pass and go back 'home' to do her business there. We laughed and I left.

Some weeks later I called around again to collect the keys. Rena said 'Oh, and by the way, I took you at your word. You were quite right'. I looked puzzled and it showed because I had clean forgotten what my 'word' had been. She reminded me that I had advised her to do her business at the flat. 'I hope you don't mind', she said 'but I brought three lady friends with me'.

To my great regret, Dudley was diagnosed with secondary cancer last March and he passed away some six months later. In the intervening period he reached his 50th wedding anniversary but failed by a matter of days to reach his 80th birthday. He was buried on his birthday instead and I think he would have appreciated the perversity. I miss our wide-ranging conversations about Trinity, our fellow graduates and the state of Irish rugby.

4 October 2010

Told at my 70th birthday party at the Royal Academy of Music: A couple of months ago I needed to go down to the local supermarket to purchase a few items. For those who don't know, my house in Douglas is located in an area which the estate agents call Upper Douglas; and the supermarket is located in an area that I call Lower Douglas. Between the two is a very steep hill called Crellin's Hill. It takes me about 15 minutes to get down to the supermarket, and nearly double that time to get back up again. Of course it takes longer still if I am carrying something awkward like a chest of drawers.

Anyway, on the particular day I am describing, it was raining. Nothing unusual about that; it is often raining in the Isle of Man – so I dressed appropriately for the trip and set off.

On reaching the store I collected a wire basket and, being a gentleman, took off my cap and placed it in the basket. After a wander around the aisles my shopping was complete so I proceeded to the checkout where a lady scanned my items and passed them to me so I could put them in my shopping bag.

Having paid and set off on the journey home, I was near the top of Crellin's Hill when I suddenly remembered my cap. Surely the checkout lady must have seen it at the bottom of the basket? Was she blind? And by now she will have served another ten customers and placed their baskets in a pile on top of my cap. What a bore. There was nothing for it but to go back down the hill again.

When I arrived at the supermarket, I went straight to the customer service desk, ostensibly to complain about the blind checkout lady, but on seeing a jolly smiling young lady there thought the better of it.

'Can I help you?' she asked in a rather bored voice. She probably asked the same question ten or twenty times in every hour.

'Yes. I left my cap in a supermarket basket about half an hour ago and I wonder if it is still here'.

'What did it look like?' she enquired. That sounded hopeful, I thought.

'Well, it was waterproof and dark green' I replied.

'Oh.' she said brightly, 'was it like the one you are wearing?' If I could have disappeared in a puff of smoke at that instant I would willingly have done so. Such is the advent of old age – and there is undoubtedly worse around the corner.

Not told at my birthday party, because it occurred some years later, but one day I set off to go to a meeting from my flat in Albany Street and after I had been walking towards the underground station for five minutes or so I became aware that my left foot was making a different sound from my other foot when it hit the pavement. It puzzled me and I wondered if a part of a shoe was about to fall off. Not so. I discovered that I was wearing two odd shoes. Fortunately they were both brown so, rather than returning home to make a change, and causing me to be late for the meeting, I continued on my way and was glad that nobody noticed my odd footwear.

Talking of shoes, which I do only infrequently, reminds me that in 1997 I received an invitation to Chris Bailey's 50th birthday party, which was to take place in the Tithe Barn at Stanway House in Gloucestershire.

While getting ready for it on the Saturday evening, I suddenly made the awful discovery that I had left all my black shoes in London. What to do? I never thought of investigating if any of my neighbours had a pair that might fit; or, if I did, was either too embarrassed to ask, or thought it best if they were not to know of my absent-mindedness. So, without further ado, I jumped in the car and raced down to the Winchcombe town centre, to its one and only shoe shop, just before closing time. However, on arrival, I was to discover that they only sold footwear for ladies and children. At the time there were also two charity shops in the town, though one of them had already closed and, amazingly, the other was still open and, as luck would have it, they did have one pair of men's black shoes. There had to be a snag, of course, and it was that they were size 8 whereas I needed a half-size more or a pair of 9's. But "needs must when the devil drives". I managed to squeeze into them with the greatest difficulty and gladly parted with £8 – for me almost the price of a new pair in those days – and returned home a happy man to continue getting ready.

While nobody paid any attention to my footwear at the party, at the same time people were much too kind to pass any remarks about my limp.

The following weekend I returned the shoes to the charity shop as a gift – I think I was still limping then – and no doubt they were soon sold to another customer for a further £8.

I will not have a word said against charity shops.

A BRUSH WITH HER MAJESTY

Thursday 22 July 2004 was the first day of the second test match at Lord's Ground: England v West Indies. As usual I walked from Chester Court to Lord's and made my way to my usual seat on the ground floor of the pavilion, just in front of the Committee Room.

Some time after lunch and before the tea interval, the Queen and Prince Philip arrived and Her Majesty sat just behind me in the Committee Room. I noticed that HM was given some tea and placed the cup and saucer on a ledge just in front of her. She then chose a small cake but found that the plate was too large to fit on the ledge so she placed it on her lap. Very soon afterwards Robert Key (of Kent) reached his maiden test hundred and, as normal on such occasions, the MCC members rose to applaud. I'm not sure whether HM intended to stand up or not but in any event she couldn't as she had a cake and plate to contend with. She did not seem very amused at this point. Prince Philip, on the other hand, stood at the back of the Committee Room, talking to Tom Graveney, that year's President and some other Committee members, and I presume was enjoying some rather stronger beverage than tea.

After the tea interval the Queen and Prince Philip were escorted down to the pitch by Roger Knight, then Secretary of the MCC, and Tom Graveney to be introduced to the teams. Following this short interruption play resumed for the final session of the day and the royal couple slipped quietly away.

The following morning, after I had driven from London to Cheltenham, my neighbour there, Doug Potter, asked if I had received many phone calls the previous evening. On being puzzled by the question he explained that immediately after Robert Key reached his century and waved his bat in the air in acknowledgement, the TV cameras showed the pavilion crowd standing and honed in on the Queen and me. This incident, he said, was shown at the end of each BBC and ITV news bulletin that day. I had not realised it as the shots must have been taken from the far side of the ground. Lucky I wasn't doing something of a personal nature at the time.

Later that weekend, when I got back to London on the Sunday night, there were two messages on my answering machine from ladies enquiring if I had seen my photograph in Friday's *Daily Mail*. I had not, but next day took steps to obtain a copy of the photo from Associated Press (free to me as I was in it) and it later became my Christmas card for 2004.

At Lord's, July 2004

WEDDING SPEECH

While rummaging through a mountain of paperwork in August 2019, I was amazed to discover the text of a speech I had delivered at the marriage of Quentin and Louise Crivon in Belfast in March 1965, a mere 54 years previously; and to think I didn't even know (or I had forgotten) that such a document existed.

One of the best man's duties used to be to read the telegrams – in the days when there used to be telegrams – from friends and family members who were on the other side of the world and unable to attend the celebrations. My usual procedure was to read the messages and, at the end, just for a bit of devilment, I would read some fictitious ones. They went along the following lines: "finally we have some congratulations from the Prince of Wales and the Duke of York – and from a number of other pubs in Oxfordshire (or wherever)".

My speech in Belfast went as follows:

Mr Chairman, Quentin and Louise, Ladies and Gentlemen. When Quentin asked me the other day if I would reply to the toast to the visitors, I enquired whether there were to be many speeches. 'There are eleven in all', he replied, 'and you're the last.' That conjured up an impression of a cricket match with the speakers as the batsmen. Secretly I hoped that some of the batsmen might play long innings so that the team could declare without the need for me to go in to bat. But no such luck and here I am.

At a time when politicians and business people on both sides of the border are leaning over backwards to be friendly to each other, it is perhaps appropriate that Quentin and Louise should play a part in healing a forty-year-old wound, and we are fortunate and lucky enough to be here today as witnesses.

I am reminded of the story of De Valera who was walking home alone in the early hours one morning. His eyesight was not too good and, as he was crossing O'Connell Bridge in Dublin, he went too near the parapet and toppled over it and into the River Liffey. His cries for help were heard by three young men returning home from a dance and within a minute they had dived, fully clothed, into the river and saved him. After the old man had recovered and got his breath back, he told the men who he was and invited them around to his residence in Phoenix Park so that they might be thanked and he could show them his gratitude. The three men duly arrived at the Presidential residence and were shown into the library where the President was waiting. He thanked them and said he would be only too glad to help in any way possible. 'What can I do for you?', he said, turning to the first man.

'Well, I've never been to an All-Ireland hurling final at Croke Park and I'd love to be able to get a ticket for it'. 'Certainly', said Dev, 'I'll send you an invitation so you can join me in the Presidential box at the match when the time comes.' 'And what about you?', he said, turning to the second man. 'Well, I've always wanted to join the police force but I could never get in because my feet were too big'. 'Don't worry', said Dev, 'you can start in the force next Monday with the rank of Superintendent'.

Then came the third man, and he asked if Dev could commute a death sentence on him. Dev showed particular interest in this man, believing him to be a Republican. 'Well', said the man, 'I'm a member of an Orange Lodge in Portadown, and when I get back home tomorrow and they hear that I have saved De Valera from drowning, they'll shoot me on the spot'.

Coming in as the tail-end Charlie at number eleven, I suppose I ought to follow the example of a famous Lord Chief Justice at a Bar Council dinner. He announced that he had prepared two speeches, one short and one long, and he proposed to give them both. The first was "thank you" and the second was "thank you very much". However, if I left it at that, we visitors might be accused of ingratitude towards Mr and Mrs Franks, our host and hostess, who have spared no effort in making our visit to Belfast this weekend a most memorable and enjoyable one. To them, and on behalf of all of us visitors, I can only say "thank you" and "thank you very much indeed".

RAIN STOPPED PLAY

One of the joys of the English cricket season is the BBC's radio commentary conducted by the amazing Test Match Special team.

Even when play is not possible due to rain or bad light, the commentators have a special gift for talking most interestingly about almost nothing. On one such occasion I recall John Arlott speaking with great feeling about a bluebottle climbing up the inside of the studio window and we listeners hung on his every word, issued as usual in his Hampshire burr.

Then there used to be the inimitable Brian Johnston thanking Mrs Walker of Wisbech, or whoever, for sending the team a delightful chocolate cake. In fact on most days one female listener or another would deliver a cake to be consumed during the tea interval – and of course the cake was described in great detail.

At another time, on the morning of an England-Australia test match at Lord's, there was a fine drizzle which looked as if it might continue for the rest of the day. However, undaunted, the Test Match Special team carried on with their discussions about all manner of things and I am sure that if there had been no play for all five days of the Test, they would not have been found wanting for words.

When I switched on the radio on that last drizzly occasion, the topic of conversation under discussion was unusual ways in which cricket matches have been stopped. Not for them players being hit by balls and carted off to hospital, or umpires fainting in the heat. These were close to being ordinary stoppages.

Trevor Bailey, the great England and Essex all-rounder, however, was telling a story about a county match in which he had participated between Glamorgan and Essex at Cardiff. He related that when changing ends, the umpires suddenly realised that the scorekeepers' box was empty and there was nobody keeping the score – so play was halted while the absences were investigated. While this was happening, one of the scorekeepers raced back to his duties having, it was assumed, been answering the call of nature. There was no knowing what had happened to the other scorekeeper but one was deemed sufficient for the match to continue.

After half an hour or so, Tony Lewis, ex England and Glamorgan captain and later a President of MCC, turned up in the BBC's commentary box at Lord's and apologised profusely for his late arrival due to very heavy traffic in the approaches to St. John's Wood.

During the delay he had been listening to Test Match Special on his car radio and said he was particularly interested in Trevor's story. He remembered the occasion very well as he had been present at that match. In fact he was due to play but could not do so owing to a knee injury, so he had been asked if he would act as Glamorgan's scorer. Trevor Bailey had been most discreet in not mentioning his name on the radio but the story was, in fact, true and more extensive than Trevor had indicated.

Tony then related how matters were proceeding normally on that first morning – slowly as cricket matches usually do – until, all of a sudden, his fiancée rushed into the scorer's hut. They had been having arguments that morning and the lady hurled her engagement ring at the scorebook, before storming off in a huff.

She left the ground, with Tony in hot pursuit, and he eventually caught up with her at a car dealer's showroom where she was just about to sell their jointly-owned car.

However the story had a happy ending, he said, and things were soon patched up. He and his fiancée got married and, at the time he told the story, they had been together for something like 28 years.

A few years later I met Trevor Bailey at a reception and told him how much I had enjoyed his story. He agreed it was one of the best but was disappointed that so few of his friends had heard it at the time. They were either travelling to Lord's or chatting to their friends while waiting for the rain to stop.

THE HOLIDAY OF A LIFETIME

You know the scene. A sunny, late spring Sunday morning in a pretty London street for a drinks party with smart-casual guests and designer labels aplenty.

Don't know how I came to be invited.

While talking to some fellow guests, an old friend came over and enquired if I would be interested in joining three others to make up a bridge four for a week or two near Denia, about halfway between Valencia and Alicante. As it was a part of Spain unknown to me, and always up for a challenge, I expressed interest and was then introduced to the other three: Pauline, Peter and another David. They seemed very pleasant, probably were much better bridge players than me – in which case maybe I would learn something – and we agreed to meet up a few weeks later to discuss the trip and perhaps settle on some dates.

When we did meet I discovered that the others were planning a two-week holiday whereas I was only interested in one. However this did not present an insurmountable problem as they were thinking of driving down there from the UK whereas my thoughts were of flying; and as it would take them two or three days to drive down, and the same to get back, they thought they could meet me at Valencia airport and deliver me back there again at the end of the holiday.

We would be staying at the apartment owned by the parents of one of them – attractive in itself as it meant a considerable saving on hotel bills. So far so good.

I wasn't deterred by the fact that I couldn't get on a direct flight to Valencia. However, my travel agent said I could fly to Barcelona and then get a train from there to Valencia but, as it was going to be the height of the summer season, he strongly recommended I book a seat on a train. Again, no problem.

On arriving at Barcelona airport I got a taxi to the railway station and spent some time looking for my carriage with its booked seat. Eventually on finding it I discovered that the carriage contained ten seats, five facing each way, but there were already 12 people in the carriage plus some babies on their mothers' laps. None of the occupants spoke any English (or if they did, they never admitted to it) and I spoke only four words of Spanish, so there was nothing I could do but stand in the corridor for the duration of the journey which I recall lasted for almost three hours.

On arrival at Valencia station my spirits were raised somewhat when I saw that my new friends were there awaiting me and they escorted me out to the car park. There I was surprised to find them driving a local hire car instead of Pauline's BMW. Didn't you hear, they said, that Pauline was involved in a car accident at Kingston Hill while she was collecting Peter and the other David, her car was damaged and had to go to a garage. As a result David's father who was a member of a villa owners' club managed to get them cheap flights to Valencia (something, remember, that I couldn't obtain) and they had then hired a car at the airport.

That wasn't all the bad news however. On arriving at Denia they had gone out to a nearby restaurant for a celebratory dinner, intended to cheer Pauline, who was very concerned about the state of her car and worried about whether it would be repaired by the time she returned home, but the meal had resulted in Pauline getting food poisoning and feeling so lousy that her only interest was to get back home as quickly as posssible. When leaving the station, we would be going straight to the airport so she could catch her plane to Gatwick. Clearly there would be no bridge – and of course I would be expected to pay a share of the car hire for my week in Denia. On the other hand the weather would be good and I could look forward to some sightseeing, so things could be a lot worse. Little did I realise that very soon they were.

The following evening we went to the same restaurant where Pauline had been poisoned and I ordered the recommended paella, a local speciality as all the rice was grown in that part of Spain. I really did enjoy the meal – at least until the early hours of the following morning, when I sprung out of bed and just made it to the loo. I didn't realise at first that I had contracted the same illness that had caused Pauline to return home. So ill did I feel that I dared not leave the apartment in case I had an "accident", and a doctor had to be summoned to my bedside. David and Peter were there to take the prescriptions to the pharmacy, and it took a full four days before I recovered sufficiently and felt confident enough to venture out on my own, for a little walk around the vicinity on the day before returning home. On my little walk, however, I happened to go behind the restaurant where I'd eaten and found a smelly and stagnant pond where members of the kitchen staff were to be seen scrubbing those familiar large copper paella dishes.

Ever since when I order paella I do so only if I know for certain that there isn't a stagnant body of water behind the restaurant; and I did wonder if the owner of the restaurant wasn't in some way in cahoots with the owner of the pharmacy because I can't imagine that Pauline and I were the only two who suffered.

Wasn't it that wise man Robert Louis Stevenson who wrote "to travel hopefully is a better thing than to arrive", but even he failed to mention the Denia paella.

I never did get to visit the nearby surroundings, apart from the station and airport at Valencia at that time, though I did visit Valencia some 40 years later and was amazed by the transformation that had taken place in the city in recent years. The River Turio, which had frequently flooded, damaging properties, orange groves and paddyfields, had been rerouted and a new City of Arts and Sciences created in the old river-bed. New buildings including an opera house, exhibition halls, a science museum and gigantic aquarium, all designed by leading architects Santiago Calitrava and Felix Candela, have turned the area into one of Spain's leading tourist attractions with, as far as I could see, not a paella restaurant in sight.

BUDAPEST

This was an unseasonably warm day in Budapest. I was on my first visit there, with friends Leonie and Nicki, and that evening was due to visit the splendid opera house which was all of three minutes walk from the apartment in which we were staying.

The story goes that when the city burghers wished to build a new opera house in about 1880, Ferenc Jozsef, who was the Austro-Hungarian emperor at the time, decreed that it must not be larger than the opera house in his beloved Vienna. Getting over the shock of this requirement the Hungarians obeyed the decision, but instead made sure that their new creation, which opened in 1894, if smaller would certainly be even more ornate than the splendid Austrian version.

Looking forward to seeing Handel's "Xerxes", I noted that the performance was due to start at 7 p.m. but that the doors would only open at 6.30 p.m. That barely left time for me to admire the inside of the building and have a pre-show drink. Furthermore, I was advised that coats, brollies and other paraphernalia must be deposited in the cloakroom and not kept on one's lap or under the seat, as allowed in most other theatres that I'd visited. However, as the weather was good and the evening likely to be warm, carrying a coat was not likely to be a consideration.

How wrong I was. At about 4pm the skies opened and it began to rain. Not any old rain but a downpour – even a deluge – and it was so heavy that the street drains were unable to cope with the flood. From the apartment windows the streets around had suddenly become rivers, and the many pedestrians who had been much in evidence ten minutes before had suddenly disappeared. More like Gluck than Handel, I thought: the gods are truly angry.

As the rain continued with no end in sight, a change of plan would be required. There would be a very long wait in a queue at the cloakroom and the promise of an even longer one at the end: certainly no drink would be possible before the performance or admiration of the building.

I regaled my friends with a story of a delay caused by rain in London about 35 years previously. Having planned to listen to a Prom concert on Radio 3 (or was it the Third Programme then?) after work, there was very heavy traffic on the Euston and Marylebone Roads. Cars were unable to move because windscreen wipers couldn't cope with the heavy rain and drivers couldn't see much further than their noses or at least their car bonnets.

Eventually I got home after 7.30 p.m. and switched on the radio before making myself some supper. I was surprised to hear music that had not been scheduled at the concert being played and, after about ten minutes or so, a continuity announcer interrupted it to say that the concert had been delayed because the eminent soprano due to perform had been unable to get from her hotel to a waiting taxi. The alternative music continued and a little while later the announcer interrupted it again to say that the soprano was now on her way. About 45 minutes later than planned the concert eventually started – and apart from cricket or tennis, that was the only time I had ever experienced a performance being delayed by rain.

Back in Budapest, just as suddenly as the rain had started at 4pm, it stopped at 6.15 p.m. so, reverting to plan A, I went off down Andrassi Street without hat or coat but with much relief. Getting to my seat in good time for the performance, I noticed that 7pm came and went, and so did 7.15 and 7.30. There was no sign of any action apart from an audience whispering and moving restlessly in their seats. This gave me time to spot that there would be only a small period orchestra of perhaps 20 players who would occupy the left-hand side of the orchestral pit – and the right hand side had been covered over by an extended stage. As my seat was on the end of a row on a left-hand aisle, I was centrally located behind the orchestra and in an excellent position to hear the music.

More than half an hour late, the lights dimmed and the overture began. The leader of the orchestra was a lady who was standing up to play and conduct with her bow. To me this was not unusual because often the conductor in early music concerts conducted from the keyboard.

Sometime later I was conscious of a latecomer stealing down the aisle beside me in the dark. He seemed to be heading for the front row but when he got there he stepped over a barrier into the pit and took over the conducting. Peter Oberfrank the conductor had arrived, whereupon the lady leader resumed her seat.

I doubt if many people present noticed this incident or whether it was reported in the Hungarian press. It may even be a regular occurrence at the Budapest Opera, and as I don't speak Hungarian, I never did get to see any of the reviews. Oh, and by the way, the performance and production were both most enjoyable – and the reason the stage had been extended as described earlier was to enable two sports cars (one bright red and the other yellow) to be driven on stage and off by the soloists. Xerxes and Handel would have been amazed.

I hope the management remembered to take out motor insurance.

THE ELYAN COLLECTION

In a sense, the Elyan Collection began with Laurence Elyan (1902-1991). Uncle Larry was born in Cork and entered the British Civil Service in 1918, at the end of World War I, and remained in London until the Irish Free State was created in 1922. He was then given the choice of remaining with the Board of Trade in London or transferring to the 'new' Irish Civil Service based at Dublin Castle. He chose Dublin and remained there until his retirement in 1960. In London he had become involved in amateur dramatics and he continued this interest in Dublin. He performed with the famed Abbey and Gate Theatre companies and, in time, was considered the leading amateur actor of his day, although he was never sufficiently confident of his abilities to embrace acting full-time.

Because Larry had a regular income from his employment, he was able to afford the rent of a flat and, over the years, a number of his artistic friends would ring his doorbell when they were evicted from their digs for non-payment of rent. Amongst those who camped on Larry's floor were Cyril Cusack and Frank O'Connor, two of his closest friends and, later, two of Ireland's leading figures in the arts.

When Larry retired in 1960, he decided to go abroad and gave me the contents of his flat which included a small collection of books. some theatre programmes. newscuttings and correspondence. Because of my interest in first editions, signed copies and private press books, I decided to attempt to assemble all of Frank O'Connor's works, other than the copies acquired from Larry. As O'Connor was also a friend of my parents, this was very much a labour of love, but how I wish I had asked him to inscribe the copies I collected when he came to visit us at home in Cork.

Over a period of almost 40 years, I concentrated on Irish authors such as Samuel Beckett, Padraic Colum, Eva Gore-Booth, Sean O'Casey, George Russell, James Stephens and W.B. Yeats. The publication dates run mostly from about 1890 to 1990 and it is gratifying to think that the books assembled over four decades comprise one of the best collections of Anglo-Irish literature anywhere.

The collection is particularly strong on poetry but also covers fiction, drama, essays, short stories, biography and autobiography. There are also items of literary criticism, some interesting letters and a number of important theatre programmes including the Abbey Theatre's first production in 1904. The books are illustrated by Arthur Rackham, Harry Clarke, Jack Yeats and Willy Pogany, with many privately printed in limited editions and some fine bindings.

There are in the collection complete runs of literary magazines such as *The Dubliner/Dublin Magazine, Nonplus, Envoy* and the *Kilkenny Magazine*.

The collection includes a full set of Cuala Press books, produced on a hand press by W.B. Yeats's sisters in limited editions and sometimes illustrated by Jack Yeats, their famous artist brother. The press started as the Dun Emer Press in 1903, changed its name to Cuala Press in 1908 and continued right up to the 1970s when Liam Miller, founder of the Dolmen Press, was in charge.

A little known fact is that I myself founded *The Dubliner* while an undergraduate at Trinity College, Dublin in 1961. Four years later we came to an arangement with Estella Solomons, the eminent Irish portrait painter, who permitted us to assume the title *The Dublin Magazine* which had been founded by her late husband, Seumas O'Sullivan (Dr James Starkey) in 1923. I am proud that we published so many major Irish literary figures over a period of 13 years until we ceased publication. Closure was not due to insolvency but to the fact that I couldn't find anybody to edit the publication – not surprising perhaps when the post didn't carry any remuneration.

For a time we were the only significant Irish literary magazine in existence. Among the authors published were Austin Clarke, Padraic Colum, Paul Vincent Carroll, Cecil Day Lewis, Monk Gibbon, Seamus Heaney and Frank O'Connor. We also published some slim volumes of verse under the New Square Publications imprint.

In book collecting, my objective from the outset was to collect what I liked rather than attempt to build an all-embracing collection; thus the books listed represent the interests, or whims, of one individual.

The collection is naturally strong on writers from Cork – Corkery, O'Faolain and O'Connor, for example – because that was my home town. At the same time it is very weak on Liam O'Flaherty because on the only occasion we met (at the Royal Hibernian Hotel in Dawson Street, Dublin, alas now no more) he was quite drunk and fell off his bar-stool into my arms.

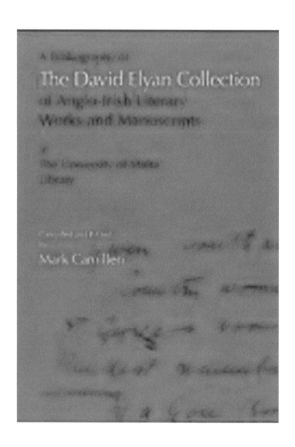

I also witnessed Brendan Behan and Patrick Kavanagh drink more than was good for them but I liked Kavanagh's poetry so most of his works are included.

Irish intellectual patriots such as Thomas MacDonagh and Joseph Plunkett, who were shot by firing squad following the 1916 rising, are represented by some scarce items, as is Terence MacSwiney, Lord Mayor of Cork, who died on hunger strike in prison in London. A book of sketches of Abbey Theatre personalities by Grace Gifford, Joseph Plunkett's fiancée, is there along with an original letter from Sir Roger Casement, a hero to the Irish and a traitor to the British, who was also executed, among the letters and manuscripts.

Hardest of all to find were some of the Cuala Press volumes and I had to wait more than 25 years before being able to acquire the last handful of items. For some reason they never appeared in booksellers' catalogues, at auction or in bookshops.

Overall, I'm glad I collected when I did. The task would be much more difficult (and expensive) nowadays, if not impossible, because so many of the books in my field have been acquired by university or other institutional libraries, particularly in America, and having been acquired these books will remain behind closed doors forever.

I am delighted that the collection in its entirety has found its way to an unlikely home in Malta and it is my hope that, apart from its use as a basis for occasional exhibitions, it may prove a valuable research resource for future scholars in Malta and from abroad. The books have at last ended their journey.

Laurence Elyan, on stage at the Gate Theatre, Dublin

THE EARRINGS

One evening attending an opera at the Royal Academy of Music with some friends, during the interval I met another old friend, PTF, who was also there with a new girlfriend. I asked them if they would like to come back to my little flat at Chester Court afterwards for a light supper. They agreed. After we had waited for some time, PTF and P eventually arrived and apologised for being late because P had lost one of her earrings, and they had to wait for the auditorium to be emptied before they could search in the vicinity of their seats with a borrowed torch, but they had no luck. I asked what it had looked like and P showed me her remaining ring. Oh, I said, on the way out I nearly trod on something I thought was a silver drawing pin. I picked it up so nobody would step on it and placed it on a nearby ledge – and left it there. PTF immediately raced back to the Academy in an effort to retrieve it before it closed and returned half an hour later with the missing earring. Hurray.

While he was away I mentioned that I thought I had met P before at a luncheon party in a country house, given by Carol Wheeler, granddaughter of Sir Mortimer – possibly 20 years previously. This was not what PTF wished to hear when he arrived back; that a friend of his had met his new girlfriend before he had.

The following day P phoned to thank me for the hasty meal, my assistance in recovering the earring and mentioned that PTF had doubted our meeting so long before.

She invited me to supper, we remained friends and she visited me for some walking weekends in Winchcombe. P was also a very talented textile designer with her own studio in Elvaston Place and visited USA each year to promote and sell her designs. On the first visit to Winchcombe she congratulated me on my bedroom curtains, which had been bought, rather cheaply as I recall, from Marks and Spencer because they had been designed by some important designer and were somewhat iconic. That was good to know, so that when I later moved from Winchcombe to a flat in Cheltenham, and the curtains no longer fitted, I put them into storage rather than throw them out.

It is funny how it always seemed to be sunny on those summer days while walking along paths through the Cotswold cornfields or on Bredon Hill; and it is funny that a little earring could possibly play a part in a friendship.

Following on from the last episode, the next earring remains irretrievably lost.

In September 2007 I went to the Boyne Valley in Ireland with members of the Isle of Man Natural History and Antiquarian Society (founded in 1879). After we had returned from a trip to the Hill of Tara, once the headquarters of the High Kings of Ireland, I was approached by Felicity Cain who inquired when I would next be visiting Malta. In about a month's time, I answered, while wondering why she had asked.

In fact somewhere on the Hill, a massive mound with splendid views all around, she had lost an earring, which had been a gift from her husband, William, purchased on a visit to Malta some years previously. She wondered if I would be able to find a replacement. Ever the optimist, I didn't see a problem. A month later, with the remaining earring tucked safely away on my person, I arrived in Malta but hadn't a clue where to start my search

As luck would have it, I was having lunch with Leslie Agius the following day and acquainted him with my problem. He knew as little about jewellery as I did, but suggested I speak to his next-door neighbour who happened to own a jewellery shop in Valletta. Mr Azzopardi whose family, like mine, were once Sephardi Jews from Spain, and in his case had escaped at the time of the Inquisition, settled in Malta well before the Knights arrived in 1530.

He looked carefully at the ring, held it up to the light, and hesitated before announcing that the jeweller who had produced it was no longer in business. However all was not lost as he knew the man who had bought his equipment and remaining stock, and he had a shop not far away.

On visiting the purchaser of the equipment, and explaining my predicament, he too looked most carefully at the earring, held it up to the light, and announced that he didn't any longer have any of the same size in stock. Again all was not lost because he said he had some other branches in Malta and it was possible that one of them might have a matching earring. He asked me to wait while his assistant phoned around to make enquiries. Eventually he came back to say we were out of luck (or rather I was), but he had a suggestion to make: that if I were to purchase a pair of the smaller earrings, which he had in stock, he would clean the larger one and turn it into a matching pendant. What did I think? Well, to be truthful I didn't know what to think. I had no authority from Felicity to purchase a new pair, nor did I know if she would be the slightest bit interested in acquiring a pendant. In the circumstances I took an instant decision and agreed to the jeweller's suggestion. The worst that could happen would be me ending up with a pair of earrings for myself.

When I got back to the Isle of Man and recounted my exploits to Felicity, to my relief she was very pleased with the arrangement I had entered into. A few nights later I bumped into two ladies who played in the local symphony orchestra with her and they remarked how pleased she was with her new acquisition.

I suppose that many years from now some metal detectorist, working on the Hill of Tara, will discover the missing earring and wonder if he has discovered some medieval gem dating back to the High Kings of Ireland – and puzzle about how it got there from Malta.

DOUBLE, DOUBLE TOIL AND TRAVEL

Overall I suppose my travels by train, plane or bus have been at about average frequencies except that the plane and train/boat trips have increased in number substantially since I came to live in the Isle of Man at the end of the 1990s.

Most of the journeys will have been uneventful, boring even, with lots of hanging about. At a guess far more of my trips will have arrived late as opposed to being on time, and of course they hardly ever arrived early. However, a handful of journeys stand out for their peculiar nature and the amount of angst they caused me.

Take that Flybe trip from the Isle of Man to Luton, for example. After we got airborne I overheard the Dutch gentleman in the seat behind me ask the stewardess if she knew how he could get from Luton to Stansted as he was booked on a flight to Rotterdam later in the day. She wasn't sure if there was a direct coach link between the two airports and if not he would have to get a train to Kings Cross, take the underground to Liverpool Street and then get another train to Stansted. About 20 minutes later the captain announced that owing to fog at Luton he was going to have to divert to Southampton. After that I heard no more from the Dutchman, nor do I know how, or if, he ever got to Luton and Rotterdam.

Meanwhile on arriving in Southampton we were told that under aviation regulations we had to be conveyed to our original destination, whether or not that is where we wanted to go, and regardless of the fact that 61 out of 64 passengers desired to go to London. After our bags had appeared, we were to wait while coaches were arranged for the three hour journey to Luton. Not liking the sound of this, as soon as I was reunited with my bag I fled as quickly as I could to the railway station which was conveniently situated next door to the airport arrivals hall. More than half of the passengers followed me to the queue at the ticket office.

While we waited for the train to arrive an announcement was made that it was running 16 minutes late owing to a fox on the train. We passengers looked at each other. Had we heard correctly? About five minutes later the same announcement was made again, so there was nothing wrong with our hearing. Once on board I asked the train manager (a euphemism for the ticket collector) how a fox could possibly get on board as they were hardly large enough to press the button to open a door. It's not as if they were large apes or brown bears. The answer was that the train had originated in Bournemouth where all the doors had been left open for some hours while the train was being cleaned.

On another occasion in London, when there was very stormy weather up North, I was due to get a train to Liverpool and the boat to Douglas. Knowing that the boat did not sail in rough weather, I phoned the Isle of Man Steam Packet Company to ask what I should do. They said they could book me on the boat from Heysham if I could get there in time for the 2.15 p.m. sailing as that particular craft sailed in almost all weather. I rushed to Euston and got the first train to Lancaster, aware that in those days – not so long ago – there were enormous problems with antiquated signalling systems to say nothing of the famous "wrong sort of leaves on the track".

We made good time until we got to Staffordshire where the train came to a sudden halt in the middle of nowhere without any warning. After we had been there for half an hour or more, I went in search of the train manager to find out what was going on (or not as the case might be). The hold-up was due to a signal failure ahead and we were in a queue. Eventually we got going again after about another half-hour and then proceeded to Preston without further mishap. After we had been there for perhaps half an hour, without any sign of moving and no announcements, I again went in search of the manager. This time the delay was due to "changing the crew". Bearing in mind we had arrived in Preston over an hour late, surely the crew would have been ready to board and anxious to make up lost time. I explained to the onboard supremo that I was anxious to get to Lancaster and Heysham where I had a boat to catch. In that case, he said, you ought to get off here and cross over to the platform where the Glasgow train is due in 15 minutes, so off I went shlepping my heavy bag up and down the steep steps of Preston station. When I got there I waited – and watched as my original train pulled out.

On arrival at Lancaster it was already past 2.15 p.m. and I had missed my shuttle train to Heysham. I hailed a taxi and told the driver of my predicament and to wait if the boat had gone because I'd need to get back to Lancaster as the next boat didn't leave for a further 12 hours (at 2.15 a.m.). Amazingly, when we got to Heysham the boat was still in the harbour as it had been delayed by 90 minutes owing to the bad weather. What a relief. It wasn't a relief for everybody, however, as there were only about 19 places available and some 60 would-be passengers waiting. Thankfully I had already booked. Trips like that, to say nothing of the really rough crossings, must have shortened my life by some years and I even feel unwell sometimes just remembering particular incidents.

Turning next to the Maltese buses, which have created their own adventures and legends until as late as 2010 when all the old, antiquated vehicles were replaced by modern air-conditioned models. Before my time in Malta I understand that buses on different routes were painted different colours because it was said so many of the locals were unable to read. In my time they were all painted the same bilious orange, which was how most of the passengers felt on completing their journeys as so many of the buses were devoid of springs and shock-absorbers and the roads were full of pot-holes. All the buses carried holy pictures and crucifixes up at the front which were presumably of some solace to those on board. The buses were owned by the drivers, who were given governmental loans for the purpose – a crazy system if ever there was one – and they hated giving change or receiving notes.

There was a story of an elderly lady who boarded a bus in Tower Road (Sliema) en route for Valletta and just as she was about to pay the driver, the bus shot forward and she was thrown into the lap of a fellow traveller, dropping her coins which fell through a hole in the floor. When she had been helped back to her feet, the driver demanded the fare before he would proceed. An argument developed in which the passengers took the old lady's side and eventually the bus reversed and a young man got down to look for the old lady's coins. He actually found them, got back on the bus, handed them to the driver and the bus proceeded on its way.

A friend who lived in the Gardens (St. Julians) and did not drive told me of the time her niece arrived from Wales and together they were going to visit some cousins in Mellieha. They went to City Gate (Valletta) and to the usual Mellieha departure stop and searched in vain for a number 44. When they couldn't find it, my friend went to the office situated in the wall to enquire if they had changed the stop. The official said no and waved in the general direction of the stop they had just left. Back they went again but still there was no sign of a 44 bus, so my friend went again to see the official. This time he took her by the elbow to the same stop and said 'there' in Maltese. But she replied that there was no number on the bus. 'Then it must have fallen off ' he retorted and was gone back to his place in the wall.

Another incident which I witnessed, again in Tower Road, involved a large bearded German who got on the bus with his wife and I noticed that he had a ten lira note (about £12) in his hand as he waited to pay. The driver is not going to like this I thought as I sat and waited for the explosion. Sure enough, as soon as the German proffered the note the driver said loudly 'Have you no change?', 'No, I have not', 'Then you must get off ', 'I will not', 'You must have change', 'I am offering you the fare'. This went on for some time with the driver offering asides in Maltese – presumably extremely rude – to those nearby. Eventually three elderly ladies rummaged in their bags and took out some coins which they gave the driver in settlement and after ten minutes or so we were able to proceed on our way without further ado.

Finally, there was the time I was invited to a dinner party in Mdina and went for the Rabat bus to take me there. After a short wait the bus arrived. It was being driven by a thin wiry driver and the only other passenger apart from me was his over-fat son of about 14. After turning to me with a smile and a shout of 'alright?' we were off. Not off in the usual way but more like a bat out of hell. At the first roundabout, a small car which clearly had right of way screeched to a halt and avoided hitting us by inches. Then it was through Floriana like there was no tomorrow and on to Hamrun. There, in the middle of the road, the bus stopped so that the boy could get off. Not a getting off as you or I would understand it; he wasn't going to leave us, but merely to stand in a short queue at the pastizzi (cheese pie) shop and dad was going to wait. I was amazed and looking behind saw the traffic building up. Nobody hooted because nobody realised that the bus itself was causing the hold-up. Eventually the boy got back on board clutching a bulging brown paper bag. Dad again turned to me with a smile: 'You want one?', he shouted. I mumbled something and shook my head. Then we were back on our way to Rabat with a driver intent on making up for lost time.

Surely it is journeys like this that are far more memorable than 99% of our travels?

A collection of the historic Maltese buses.

ROYAL ALBERT HALL

'How did you get your seats at the Royal Albert Hall?' is a question I have frequently been asked. It is a rather long story in that it took some years to come about.

In about 1970 I was introduced to Victor Falk who was a seatholder at the Hall and who was agreeable to selling tickets to friends when not using them himself. I can't remember if his two seats went back to the beginning of the Hall or shortly afterwards. The beginning was 1866 when, in order to finance the planned new building on the site of the Great Exhibition of 1851, it was decided to sell about 25% of the 5,500 seats proposed in the new hall whether in the stalls or in boxes. The seats were sold leasehold for 999 years from 1866, subject to an annual levy rather akin to a service charge at a block of flats. Victor's seats had passed down through his family for a number of generations. His maternal grandfather had two seats which he left to his two daughters – one each. Victor inherited one seat from his mother and later purchased the other from his aunt.

One day he suggested that as I went to the Hall fairly frequently for classical music concerts, it would possibly make sense for me to acquire two seats of my own. Though they didn't come on the market very often, the Secretary of the day kept a list of would-be buyers and although there might be a wait of some years, it wouldn't cost anything to get my name placed on the Secretary's list. That sounded like a good idea, so I wrote to the Secretary, received an acknowledgement and then waited – and waited. That was in September 1975. Some six years later I received a letter telling me that some seats had become available and a pair would cost £4,000. Could I please arrange to inspect them and decide quickly if I wished to proceed with a purchase. I immediately called Victor who confirmed that the seats were well located, not far from his, and the price appeared to be about right. The purchase thus went ahead. Some years later, curious as to who had previously owned the seats, I contacted the Hall's archivist and she checked the records which showed that I was the fourth possessor since the building was erected.

As I write these notes in 2011, some thirty-odd years later, the price of two stall seats has risen to about £140,000 – rather a good rate of return. The funny thing is that I never expected the purchase to be a good financial investment. I hoped of course that I wouldn't lose money if it came to selling them, but the intention was to own a piece of history in one of the most famous concert halls in the world. To date they have provided me with a great deal of enjoyment and too many memorable concerts to mention here.

After some consideration there are one or two events that I would like to mention. The first was in 1992, not long after acquiring my seats, when I received a request from Guide Dogs for the Blind to donate my tickets for a Barry Manilow charity concert at the Hall. I was delighted to be able to support such a worthy cause and, as my employers, AGB, had recently purchased a five seat second tier box, we donated those seats also.

Nearer the time of the concert I received a call asking if I would like to join the charity committee in the Royal Box as a thank-you for my generosity. This was a great surprise because most seatholders had more seats than I did, and surely they hadn't all refused to donate their seats to the charity (or otherwise the Royal Box would have been more than jam-packed with members of the Corporation). Anyway, on the night, I found myself sitting alongside the charity's President, Princess Alexandra. In all the 40-plus years that I have owned seats, I have to confess to only having been to two popular concerts and this one turned out to be most enjoyable.

Some years later the Royal Opera House was engaged in a major renovation exercise and it was running late. Wagner's Ring Cycle had as a result to be moved to the Hall and all four performances sold out almost immediately. I managed to acquire seats in the Council box (situated next to the Royal Box) and on one particular night they were in the front row of four seats. My guest Jacky was sitting next to me and Peta Travis (then a Council member and later President) sat alongside with her sister. We knew in advance that some VIPs were expected that night and extra security measures would be in place. However, we did not know until they arrived at our box that the distinguished guests would be the Duke of Kent and his sister Princess Alexandra.

As they entered the box, Peta leant over towards me and said 'do you think we should offer them our seats'? Before I could answer, Jacky said 'not bloody likely', so we remained where we were. The Duke sat immediately behind me in the second row and it was evident he knew his Wagner very well as he kept tapping his feet in time to the music. Perhaps it was something to do with his German background. During the intervals I conversed with the Princess and you can guess what we spoke about. Why, guide dogs of course.

In 1995 there were plans for a major refurbishment of the Hall and rumours abounded that there would be some big fundraising activities requiring contributions from all of the Hall's 300 plus seatholders (known as members) which would coincide with an application for national lottery funding. It was not a surprise therefore when I received a phone call early in 1996 from the President's office inviting me to lunch at the Hall. The President at the time was John Cleland, a most agreeable person who was also a great enthusiast for the iconic building and its activities. It was an invitation both expected and dreaded in equal measure; part of the 'softening up' process, I surmised, intended to encourage members' donations.

When I got to the stage door on the appointed day, the Chief Executive's secretary came down to meet me and escort me to the luncheon room. On the way I enquired if there would be many people attending. 'Only you,' she replied 'plus the President, Chief Executive and Secretary'. What was going on, I wondered.

On arrival at the Royal Retiring Room, which is used to entertain the Queen or other important dignitaries, John Cleland greeted me, introduced me to John Middleton, Secretary, and Patrick Deuchar, Chief Executive, and asked me what I would like to drink from a bar which had been set up in the corner.

'You must have wondered why we invited you here', John began. I think I just nodded in agreement as I was suddenly unable to speak. 'We would like you to join the Council' he continued. 'David Buxton, our Treasurer, has recently retired from Council and we would like you to take his place. Please say 'yes' as it will make for a much more agreeable lunch'. I was dumbfounded as nothing had been further from my thoughts. So it wasn't about putting my hand in my pocket after all.

Having taken a large gulp of my Bloody Mary (for it was a cold winter's day), I replied that the invitation was a very great surprise and that I would be both delighted and honoured to join the Council.

Having now been a member of the governing body for some 15 years, it remains an honour and I hope this privileged position will continue until my enforced retirement when I reach 75. Little did I realise when purchasing the two seats in 1981 that I would have such close links with the Royal Albert Hall and that a great British institution would become such an important part of my life for 20 or so years.

Originally in 1866 all of the seats for sale were priced at £100 each regardless of where they were located, and it is interesting to note that Queen Victoria paid this same price for each of her seats in the Royal Box. I believe that this is the only Royal Box in the UK which is actually owned by the sovereign, whereas all of the others in theatres throughout the land are merely boxes where the sovereign or other dignitaries sit if attending performances.

Council members were required to seek re-election every three years up to age 75 and it was my turn to retire by rotation at the Annual General Meeting in 2015. As the meeting was in June and I was due to reach 75 the following October, I was unsure whether I should stand for re-election in June or retire at that meeting as it seemed pointless to stand for a mere four months.

To my surprise I was invited to stand again and was told that the rules would be changed before my next birthday so that one would no longer be required to retire at 75. I was amazed to discover then, despite my venerable age, that I 'topped the poll', getting most votes "for" and none "against".

One Trustee got more votes "against" than "for" and so was voted off the Council by the members. In my experience stretching over 35 years, it was the first time this had happened.

The following month the regulations were duly changed so that candidates over 65 could also stand for election for the first time and Trustees on reaching 75 could remain. Thus I was able to continue in office for a further three years.

About this time I was curious to know how I came to be invited to join the Council back in 1996 and asked to see the relevant Council minutes. There must have been other candidates considered, I thought.

I discovered that Council had indeed considered three candidates; the other two being Baroness Darcy de Knayth, holder of one of the oldest titles in England going back to 1332, and Baroness (Elizabeth) Smith of Gilmorehill, a life peeress and widow of the late John Smith MP, leader of the Labour party.

Having been Chairman of the Friends of the Royal Academy of Music I assume that appointment, plus the fact I had considerable business experience and was already a seatholder, must have carried some weight, but I don't of course know for certain. Nor do I know how the voting went at the relevant Council meeting. Eventually I decided to retire at the AGM in May 2018 having completed some 22 years as a Trustee and witnessed so many changes during that time.

When I first attended concerts, it is hard to believe in this day and age, people were allowed to smoke in the Hall – and at boxing tournaments large cigars were very much in evidence.

Council members at the Royal Albert Hall in 2010. Professor Colin Lawson, director of Royal College of Music at the Elton John piano.

Greeting Baroness Thatcher at the Royal Albert Hall, February 2008

BARONESS THATCHER

When my photograph was taken with Lady Thatcher at the Royal Albert Hall in February 2008, we cannot be said to have known each other, although we had met a handful of times over the years.

There were a few occasions when I was introduced to her at City of London functions, along with many other individuals, and then again when she opened a new building for AGB Research at Hanger Lane, Ealing.

Over the period of her premiership from 1979 to 1990 I was of course able to observe closely her performance as PM which, during her reign, went from ground-breaking change to complete chaos.

She will of course go down in history as Britain's first female Prime Minister and the person who was to take on the trade unions, which were so powerful at the time, and see them defeated, along with her predecessor and rivals – Edward Heath, Harold Wilson and Jim Callaghan – while remaining in office for so long. As she herself said outside No. 10 Downing Street, after being driven from office – and into retirement – "after eleven and a half wonderful years".

In 1979 the coal miners were strong enough to hold the country to ransom under their leader, Arthur Scargill, whose ambition was to preserve jobs for miners and their children at any cost. The fact that "going down the mines" was one of the most degrading tasks imaginable; working in semi-darkness, underground, and often unable to stand upright, and leading to all sorts of skin and respiratory diseases, didn't matter to Scargill. He wasn't at all concerned that miners' children should be better educated and in consequence not need to follow their parents below ground.

At that time there were also other industries which were in drastic need of modernisation including the newspapers where, again, the unions exerted great influence and went on strike at the drop of a hat, and sometimes it seemed just to be provocative.

I recall an incident at the Telegraph where it was the "regulation" that a member of the electricians' union was required to switch on the printing machinery so that the printers could produce the papers. However, one evening the electrician's car broke down and he failed to appear in the printing department on time. After hanging about for an hour or so, it was decided that one of the printers should press the switches, and the presses began to roll.

Then, when the printing was in full swing, the electrician appeared – and, irate, immediately switched off the machinery! After sitting in his office for a further hour or so, he considered he had taught the printers a lesson and everything was switched on again. That lesson resulted in the Telegraph losing some 200,000 copies of the newspaper that night.

The newspaper managements were powerless in the face of this strength – and terrified at losing the following day's sales on the basis that nobody was interested in buying and reading "yesterday's news".

The old press families who had inherited their newspaper businesses – the Kemsleys, Camroses, Beaverbrooks, Rothermeres, Astors and the like – were not equal to the struggle. After all, they had already made their money and received their titles – for they were known as "the press barons" – and, one by one, they sold out to a new generation of proprietors who had no intention of lying down and being trampled on.

For some reason at that time Australians and Canadians always seemed to be willing purchasers. These newcomers were keen supporters of Mrs Thatcher's tough, new conservatism which she called "popular capitalism" and, together, they moved from Fleet Street to outer London and from the ancient hand-setting of type to the new linotype and monotype technology. The changes required far fewer print workers and removed the need for hundreds of tons of newsprint to be moved by lorry into central London every day and then out again in the form of newspapers, with all the traffic congestion that caused around Fleet Street.

However, Lady T could also be very stubborn and the introduction of the disastrous Poll Tax very nearly caused the collapse of her Government before its very embarrassing withdrawal. By that time she dominated her cabinet and found it increasingly difficult to accept any criticism as her judgement became more and more unreliable. If only she had stepped down after six or seven years she would be remembered as a really great PM.

Now for the anecdotes.

In November 1979, some six months after she became Prime Minister, President Giscard d'Estaing paid a state visit to London and was entertained at No. 10 Downing Street. Mrs T (as she then was) greeted him at the front door and escorted him upstairs. On the way he paused to admire two of the fine paintings looking down at him: one of Viscount Nelson by Lemuel Abbott and the other of the Duke of Wellington by Sir Thomas Lawrence. "We have paintings in the Elysée Palace of Napoleon and his generals just like these" he said to the Prime Minister. "They are not at all like these", she replied rather tartly. "You must understand that these gentlemen here were winners!"

Some years later she was hosting a reception for the British athletes and officials who had recently returned from the Olympic Games. She didn't know any of them but it was pointed out to her that one of those present was Sebastian Coe, who had attended a Conservative party conference or two and had recently been adopted as the Conservative party candidate for Falmouth and Camborne at the next General Election.

When he was introduced to her she asked him how he had fared. He said something like "I came second in the 800 metres, Prime Minister", to which she replied "Oh, Mr Coe, I think you will find that in politics there are no prizes for coming second".

Years later, John Antcliffe, President of the Royal Albert Hall at the time, had invited Lady Thatcher to a performance of "Tosca" at the Hall on 28 February 2008 and he had invited me along also to offer some support. It was a most memorable occasion, not just because we were entertaining an ex-Prime Minister but because that afternoon, she confided in us, she had been to 10 Downing Street to have afternoon tea with Gordon Brown, then the current Prime Minister.

That evening, on arrival at the Hall, her driver let her out at the entrance used by the sovereign where there was a private lift to the Grand Tier, and John was telephoned to say that she had arrived and was on her way. We waited and waited by the lift in vain. Eventually

John said he had better go down and look for his guest. Of course no sooner had he set off than Lady T arrived, presumably having struggled up the stairs. As there was an official photographer in attendance, and as we didn't wish to keep the good lady waiting for her host, I was asked to do the honours and give her our official welcome. Eventually John returned and was no doubt relieved to find that all was well.

Lady T said that when the photographs were available she would be more than happy to sign copies for us. Unfortunately, and sadly, John died suddenly not long afterwards and we never did get them signed.

My memories of Lady T that evening outweighed my memories of "Tosca" though I do recall a most enjoyable evening all round.

DOREEN

My sister Doreen died on the evening of Wednesday 26 November 2014 in a care home at Bembridge on the Isle of Wight, aged 70. Less than three months previously a cancer specialist from Portsmouth, on his regular visits to his patients on the island, told her that she had terminal cancer and should 'think in terms of months'. Doreen's cancer first became evident when, at the end of 2011, she was found to have a cancerous kidney, which had to be removed. The operation was successful and she was told that she could expect to make a full recovery and that there was no reason why she could not live for a long time with one. There were regular check-ups from then on but six or so months later "spots" were discovered on her liver and lungs. She and we understood that these were not life-threatening and for a year that remained the position.

However, in the spring of 2014 the spreading had started. At about the same time her husband, Henry, who had suffered from skin cancer for a decade or more, himself became ill and in May of that year had to go to the Royal Marsden Hospital in London to have a brain tumour removed. Initially the operation appeared to have been a success but this was not the case and he began to suffer from various side-effects. He returned home to the Isle of Wight but passed away on 8 August 2014. Doreen and he had been married for over thirty years, a second marriage for each of them, and his death came as a great shock to Doreen, on top of her own health worries.

When the specialist told Doreen that her form of cancer had turned aggressive, it was fortunate that her daughter Sarah-Jane just happened to be staying with her at the time and was present when the medic shocked them both with the "terminal" message. Could it be that the advancement of the cancer was a consequence of the shock of Henry's demise? We shall never know. At the funeral in Bristol some days later, I recalled Doreen's life and the fact that I had known her for all of her 70 years. In fact I could even remember when she was born.

I was then three and a bit and Mum and Dad were concerned that I, having been an only child and the centre of their attention for those years, might feel put out with the appearance of a rival for their attention. Mum said 'aren't you lucky: you will soon have a little friend to play with'. That sounded fun and I looked forward, as they did, to the new arrival. What a disappointment. Instead of a little brother or sister to play with, what arrived was a small, helpless baby that only slept and cried. Some years later, when I was interested in football, cricket and table tennis, Doreen showed absolutely no interest whatsoever in any of these sports. In fact she had no aptitude or interest in any sport. Her childhood was devoted to ballet and it must be said that she was pretty good at it, performing regularly with Joan Denise Moriarty's Cork Ballet Company.

Joan was a family friend and soon Dad with his carpentry skills was much in demand as a scenery maker. His friends who knew him as a macho male who liked his drink were amazed at how much he enjoyed his involvement with the ballet. He did confide in me once that in his teens he went with some friends to a ballet in Cork. For a joke one of these friends produced an ancient rag and every time one of the soloists stretched out her legs he tore the rag noisily. This proved great amusement for the friends but horrified the rest of the audience and after this had happened a few times all of them were thrown out.

Doreen attended Rochelle School in Cork, established in 1829 by Huguenots who had been silk weavers in France. They had even planted mulberry trees in the grounds though we never saw any silkworms. Surprisingly, the headmistress then was Miss Hester Watson who had also been Mum's headmistress when she attended the school. After Miss Watson retired during Doreen's time there she was succeeded by Miss Elizabeth Coulter who later became a distinguished head-mistress at Sherborne Girls School in Dorset.

On leaving Rochelle, Doreen went to Institut Ascher, a boarding school at Bex les Bains on the eastern side of Lake Geneva. This had been recommended to Mum and Dad by some family friends (the Botschko's) who lived in Montreux. I can't remember why but I was deputed to accompany Doreen to Bex. We set off the day after my 21st birthday, flying to Geneva, taking the train to Montreux for the weekend, and then another train to Villars on the Sunday. At the station there we were met by a lady taxi driver, the first time I had encountered one, and immediately I was in a quandary: was she or I supposed to carry Doreen's suitcase which weighed a ton? Leaving Doreen behind, I then set off to meet up with friends and explore Milan and Venice before heading down to Nice. In case you think I was made of money, I must emphasise that I had worked hard and long hours at Eskimo Frozen Foods in Cleethorpes to pay for my holidays.

At the end of the academic year in Switzerland, Doreen returned to Ireland and Dad managed to find her a job at Switzers department store in Grafton Street in Dublin. It greatly helped that Dad knew the manager there, James Chapman, who I recall had a most elaborate moustache along the lines of Salvadore Dali's. Because Doreen now spoke good French, she was much in demand in the store to converse with French-speaking customers who were delighted to find someone who could understand their requirements and answer their questions.

While at Switzers she met Harold Woolfe, then a dental student at the Royal College of Surgeons in Dublin. After he graduated they got engaged, married and moved to Manchester. My memories of this time are a little hazy but I think they lived, firstly, in Chorlton-cum-Hardy – I loved the name – before moving to Brooklands in Cheshire where Harold soon became involved with the nearby Sale rugby club and before long became chairman of the house committee (which I think meant the bar).

After some years Harold established a weekend practice at Cemaes Bay on Anglesea and as this expanded so did the idea of moving there permanently. However, they decided to send Joe, their son, to school at Clifton College in Bristol and soon realised what a lengthy journey it was. Before long they sent Sarah-Jane, their daughter, to the nearby Clifton High, only to discover that half-terms of both schools did not always coincide. On the basis that "if you can't beat 'em, join 'em", the solution was for the parents also to move to Bristol, so they bought a lovely period home at Westbury-on-Trym. After Harold's untimely death, Doreen met Henry Harris, who worked for a technical publishing company and, after a number of house moves in the Bristol area, they decided to move to Bembridge. There Henry continued with his masonic interests and Doreen, by now a keen gardener, became secretary of the Bembridge Horticultural Society. Together they took part in musicals and Gilbert and Sullivan operettas, and were active in arranging Jewish social events and occasional services on the island. Doreen's passing came as a great shock to me, I having always assumed that as the elder sibling I would be the first to meet my maker. It will take me quite some time to realise that she is no longer around or at the end of a telephone line. She will be remembered as a kind, considerate and helpful person who delighted in assisting and entertaining others.

Mum, Dad and Doreen at Molly Quirk's Glen, Isle of Man, 1980s.

EASTER RISING 1916

Elsewhere I have described my gift of books and letters to the University of Malta Library in 2000, since when a number of people with an interest in Anglo-Irish literature have visited the collection, sometimes for research purposes and at other times out of curiosity. Then, in 2015, I received a request enquiring if it would be in order for some of the books by W. B. Yeats to be removed to the National Library in Valletta as the Irish Ambassador, Pádraig MacCoscair, was planning to organise a seminar and exhibition there celebrating the 150th anniversary of the birth of W. B. Yeats, Ireland's leading poet. I readily agreed to the request because one of the purposes of the gift was to enable the material to be exhibited whenever and wherever possible, rather than remain hidden away on the University Library shelves.

Some months went by and I heard no more. I wondered whether the Ambassador's plans had been thwarted or whether he had decided to go ahead with the seminar but without the books. As I was going to be visiting Malta in the Autumn, I thought I would wait until I arrived there and then make enquiries but in the meantime the weeks were going by and, as we got closer to November, the chosen time for the exhibition, the less time there would be to organise anything.

To my surprise I discovered that the seminar was going ahead but without an exhibition. It appeared that though the Ambassador had reserved the dates, he had been unable to confirm them as he was awaiting a commitment from the powers that be in Dublin and, in the meantime, the National Library was under pressure from another organisation that was ready to go ahead. This other organisation turned out to be the Italian Cultural Institute which required the space for an exhibition celebrating the 750th birthday of Dante Alighieri.

Even I had to admit that probably Dante's 750th birthday was of greater international significance than Yeats's 150th; and although Yeats had been awarded a Nobel prize for literature, there is little doubt that had Nobel prizes been around in Dante's time, he was also certain to have been awarded one.

When I spoke to the Ambassador, he thought that perhaps we could have the exhibition separately in the following year, but I pointed out that 2016 would be the centenary of the Easter Rising in Dublin and, moreover, there was a good deal of material – letters and books – in the Elyan Collection relating to the Rising and the leading participants.

After the Ambassador had inspected the material in the University Library he had to agree and so the planning for Easter 2016 commenced. He contacted the Department of Foreign Affairs in Dublin for assistance with storyboards and the like and the National Library was able to turn up Maltese newspapers of the time.

By way of background, the Easter Rising was organised by members of the Irish Volunteer Force and the Irish Citizen Army. It was to be timed for when the British Forces were engaged in fighting on the Western front in France and Belgium, and the intention was to mark the end, finally, of the long period of British rule in Ireland with the creation of an Irish republic. The participants were well-educated individuals, certainly not riff-raff, and included university lecturers, trade union officials and teachers. Among the best-known participants were Sir Roger Casement and Constance, Countess Markievicz, the sister of Eva Gore-Booth, Thomas MacDonagh and Joseph Plunkett. Casement was a British civil servant who had become an Irish nationalist, Eva G-B was a published poet and her sister was an artist, both members of a prominent Anglo-Irish family and good friends of Yeats and of Lady Gregory, while MacDonagh and Plunkett were university lecturers and poets who between them had published more than a dozen volumes of poetry and literary criticism.

From the start the Rising was badly organised and managed by people with high ideals but little understanding of military matters, all made worse by an inadequate supply of weapons and ammunition, and supported by no more than 1,000 combatants including a number of women. Although the hostilities initially caught the British off-guard, very quickly troops were sent over from England and the Rising was put down within a week, resulting in 240 people being killed, some 2,600 injured and more than 200 buildings being destroyed or severely damaged. The leaders were quickly court-martialled, found guilty and sentenced to death. This rough justice received considerable adverse publicity worldwide and particularly throughout the British Empire.

Some 15 people were executed by firing squad. One of them, James Connolly, a trade union leader and elected to Douglas Corporation some three years previously, had been severely injured in the fighting at the General Post Office and, as a concession, as he was unable to stand, was blind-folded and tied to a chair before being shot. The Countess Markievicz was sentenced to life imprisonment but, being a lady, was quietly released a year or so later. MacDonagh, aged 38, was married to Grace Gifford and had two young children. She was an accomplished artist who produced a much sought-after book of sketches of Abbey Theatre actors among other works. Her younger sister Muriel was the fiancée of Joseph Plunkett, aged 29 and son of Count Plunkett, and as another "concession" she and Joseph were given permission to marry on the eve of his execution. The controversial nature of some of these deaths horrified the public to such an extent that the British Prime Minister at the time, Herbert Asquith, decided to call a halt to all future summary executions in Ireland.

The failed Easter Rising produced a number of famous poems by Yeats and his contemporaries (who had been sympathetic to the attempt) and, despite its failure, it nevertheless had the effect of leading to the creation of the Irish Free State in 1922 and, eventually, to the Irish Republic which remained in the British Commonwealth until 1948. Ireland's attempted rebellion also led the way for many other nations in the Commonwealth to gain their independence in the years that followed.

Thanks are due to Pádraig MacCoscair for his considerable efforts in mounting the exhibition which greatly helped to raise awareness of a major landmark in Irish history and an event that hardly merits a footnote in the history of Britain.

Looking forward, although I will not to be around in 2039, there will then be a second chance to celebrate W. B. Yeats on the centenary of his death with a fitting tribute.

Ambasáid na hÉireann
Embassy of Ireland

19
20 16
ÁR COMÓRTHA
CÉAD BLIAIN
Centenary Programme

1916
rising

14th – 25th March 2016

Selected
personalities
and their
writings

Exhibition of documents,
illustrations and writings by
personalities associated with
the Irish 1916 Rising drawn
from the University of
Malta's Elyan Collection

National Library of Malta Opening Hours:
Monday to Friday: 08.15 hrs – 17.00 hrs
Saturday: 08.15 hrs – 13.15 hrs

University of Malta Library
Il-Biblijoteka tal-Università ta' Malta

GLOUCESTERSHIRE

My marriage to Gloucestershire took place in 1974 after my brief relationship with Suffolk had come to an end. To me Suffolk was my favourite county: not too far from London, with attractive villages, characterful cottages and some large "wool" churches. It was also on the coast even if that meant the cold North Sea as so accurately portrayed in Britten's Sea Interludes from "Peter Grimes". However, the journey from London was horrendous with long tailbacks, particularly on Friday evenings, but as a new airport was planned at Maplin-Foulness, it would only be a few years before there was a new motorway from the City of London to Southend which was calculated to knock at least an hour off the journey. It was to be the M4 of the East. Unfortunately the wildfowl lobby outmanoeuvred the Government by claiming that the lengthy construction work and the noise from a new airport would drive away all the birds; and as the locals were none too happy either about the proposal, the plans were dropped. However, it is my belief that migrating birds are very competent at finding alternative resting and nesting places, and numerous other locations along the coast were plentiful. Away went my hopes in that direction: if the Government were dropping their plans, I was forced to drop mine.

At first I thought I'd found my ideal cottage right in the centre of Stow-on-the-Wold ("where the wind blows cold" as the rhyme goes). However after reaching agreement on price a surveyor friend travelled down with me from London to give the place the once-over. To my disappointment he pointed out a number of structural defects which would have created difficulties in obtaining a mortgage; and so it was again back to the drawing board.

Shortly before the surveyor's visit, in the spring of 1974, I was in Stow with a girlfriend and there appeared to be a lot of activity in the main square. It seemed that an ancient oak tree, dating back to Charles I, was very rotten and on its last legs (or trunks?) and the parish council decided it should be chopped down. This caused consternation among the local population who looked upon the tree rather as Gibraltarians look on their macaques. A compromise was reached whereby it was agreed that a local tree surgeon would be engaged to lop off all the obviously decaying branches, but the trunk would be retained and perhaps new shoots would spring forth in due course.

On that Saturday morning, before we arrived, the tree surgeon had climbed the tree and was in the process of removing deadwood when one large branch broke away and fell on his head, killing him instantly (on what happened to be his 20th birthday). The council members met instantly and decided finally that the tree must be felled before it could do any further damage. We waited in the square while all the nearby cars were removed by the local police and a tractor arrived with chains to be wrapped around the poor old tree. Eventually there was a great deal of creaking and groaning as the great old oak toppled sideways with a loud crash and an enormous cloud of dust. It had been very rotten. The stump remained and I think there is now a plaque to mark the sad occasion.

On the way back to London along with my surveyor, he mentioned that he had a friend (don't they all?) who ran an estate agency in Bourton-on-the-Water and Winchcombe and he might possibly have something of interest for me. I knew Bourton and found it a bit too "touristy" for my liking, but I had never been to Winchcombe. A week or so later, along with Ray Parsons of the Dickensian-named Bloss, Tippett and Taylor, we visited a number of properties in the vicinity.

At the time I was living in St. Mary's Mansions in Paddington so moving my search westwards made sense; and although Gloucestershire was at least 30 miles further away than Suffolk, the journey actually took less time. After spending many weekends visiting Cotswold villages, I eventually found a cottage I liked at Coates Mill, an old corn and later a paper mill, on the outskirts of Winchcombe which met my requirements. And though I didn't know the area well, the discovery of Cheltenham after having exchanged contracts proved to be a surprise and an added bonus. Some seven miles from Winchcombe, Cheltenham proved to be well-connected with its motor links to Bristol, Birmingham and Cardiff, each about an hour away, and less than two from London.

In fact not long after I moved, my parents were due to stay with my sister, Doreen, and her family at their weekend home in Cemaes Bay, Anglesea, and hoped to visit me from there. They could go by train, or more correctly trains, as they would have had to change at Crewe and Birmingham and the overall journey would have taken some five hours. They then discovered that there was a coach service which went direct to Cheltenham in about three hours with only one (comfort) stop at Shrewsbury.

Cheltenham also seemed to be about the 'right' size for me: not too big and not too small. It had a fine old Frank Matcham theatre, an excellent tennis club, the East Gloucestershire (of which I was a member for more than 30 years) with excellent grass courts, and was in the centre of an area with a strong choral tradition, thanks to Elgar, Holst and Vaughan-Williams who had all grown up in the vicinity. And no doubt their early interest in music owed a lot to the Three Choirs Festival, Britain's oldest, which went back to the 18th century.

My desire to participate in local community activities proved difficult, almost impossible, because I was working in London and only had weekends in the locality. There were thoughts that I might be able to help as a volunteer with the newly-created Gloucestershire and Warwickshire Steam Railway Company, which was hoping to do in 20 or 30 years what Dr. Beechings "cuts" had undone in one hour, that is to close the line between Winchcombe and nearby towns. However, with a small garden to look after and tennis at the East Glos, they had prior claims on my time. My help instead became financial rather than manual and I became a shareholder in the fledgling company. Three decades later, the line now runs all the way to Broadway, which was the original intention. The company makes good profits which are all ploughed back into the business, it carries over 100,000 passengers a year and is a major tourist attraction in the area.

Also in 1974 I read in a local paper that the Vicar of Wyck Rissington had produced a limited edition of porcelain mugs to celebrate the centenary of Gustav Holst's birth with all (or any) profits going to church funds. I contacted the Vicar and arranged to pay him a visit, though I didn't know then that Holst on Sunday mornings used to cycle there from Cheltenham to play the organ in the church, a distance of about 15 miles. When I got there and had bought some of the mugs, I was invited to see the drawing room where, on one occasion after Holst stayed for lunch, he then played the piano at the childrens' Christmas party. I don't think the room had changed in any way since the 1890s: the same wallpaper, the sepia prints and photographs and of course the same piano.

I presented one of the mugs to the Cheltenham Museum and later, when the Museum's collection of Holst-related artefacts were transferred to Holst's birthplace house, I went along to see if the mug had survived the trip. It didn't appear to be there and the suggestion was that it had got lost en route, a journey of less than one mile. I presented a replacement, after which the original was found so hopefully they now have two examples.

In the 1990s the new University of Gloucestershire was keen to acquire hand-printed books and ephemera produced by the Whittington Press, established a few miles from Cheltenham in the grounds of Whittington Court. The Press was founded by John and Rose Randle in the 1970s and they asked me if I would consider donating some of my material to the University. Having agreed I also thought I might donate my collection of first editions by James Elroy Flecker, Cheltenham's most famous poet, to the University Library. His father, Rev. Dr. W. H. Flecker, had been the first Headmaster of Dean Close School but his son died prematurely of consumption at the age of 31 in 1915. He achieved some success before his death with "The Golden Journey to Samarkand" and much more posthumously with his play "Hassan" and other works. He is best known (to me at least) for 'November Eve':

"November evenings damp and still.
They used to cloak Leckhampton hill."

It was most disappointing that the centenary of his death went unnoticed by Dean Close School, the Cheltenham (Wilson) Art Gallery and by the University, despite my flagging up in advance the need for a major commemorative exhibition.

Also in 2015, a local auction house announced that they were selling an oil portrait of Capt. Henry Skillicorn (1678-1763) with an estimated price of £1,000–2,000. I was particularly interested in this picture as

Skillicorn was a Manxman who played a major role in the development of Cheltenham as a town and particularly as a spa town which people with all sorts of ailments would visit to take the waters. He was also famous for another reason as his epitaph in Cheltenham Minster (formerly St. Mary's parish church) is believed to be the longest in any church in the British Isles. (It is interesting to note that up to Skillicorn's time Winchcombe had a larger population than Cheltenham).

I decided to bid for the picture from the Isle of Man by telephone but dropped out when the bidding got to £5,000 (plus a further 20% commission and VAT). There seemed to be only one other bidder who was intent on acquiring the picture at any cost – who later turned out to be the Friends of the Wilson Gallery. The picture had been hanging in the Queen's Hotel for more than 100 years and when I pointed out to friends that I had been the unsuccessful under-bidder, they all said they were surprised, in the light of the low estimate, that the owners of the Queen's Hotel (the French Accor group) had not as a gesture presented the painting to the Wilson Gallery. If I had acquired the picture, it would have presented me with a difficulty. It was too big to hang at home and I would have had to decide, Solomon-like, whether to pass it on to the Manx Museum in Douglas or to the Wilson in Cheltenham. I hope I would not have come up with Solomon's advice.

Building on my connections with the University resulting from my Whittington Press and Flecker gifts, I suggested to Dame Janet Trotter, then Vice-Chancellor, that I would be interested in sponsoring something of importance relating to the arts or literature. After Janet had taken advice from her colleagues, we hit on the idea of the Cheltenham Illustration Award and a newly-created illustration department, now so ably run by Kieren Phelps who has done a splendid job over the past 14 or so years. The plan to create a new department came at a time when the sculpture department was closing and spirits were low. However, whereas there would have been only a handful or two of sculpture students, there are now more than 160 students working for a BA degree in illustration – a very pleasing outcome.

That is the way of the world. Now if the Government in 1974 had decided to go ahead with a major new road to Southend, what route might artistic developments in Suffolk or elsewhere have taken?

A naughty girlfriend at Stow-on-the-Wold, 1974

Nephew Joe and cousin Renee at Coates Mill, Winchcombe, May 1986

With Anthony Aldridge and Julie Sherwood on a Malvern sponsored walk, October 1980

Mum, Dad, Henry and Doreen at Coates Mill, 1990s

ABOUT ISLANDS

For as long as I can remember, I have been fascinated by islands. As a toddler at the edge of the Lough in Cork, the moorhens and coots escaped my clutches and stones as they shot across the water to the safety of their nests on a small islet well out of my reach. I watched with envy.

Later there were trips by car around Cork Harbour, one of the world's finest, where I could admire from afar Spike Island and Haulbowline. The former had once been a monastery and later a prison, while the latter had been the home of the Royal Cork Yacht Club which was formed there in 1720 and believed to be the world's oldest. Haulbowline is now the headquarters of Irish Naval Services. In my days both were out of bounds but today are very much tourist attractions (which I have not yet visited).

Then, on summer holidays in Schull, in West Cork, where we stayed at O'Driscoll's East End Hotel, we gladly accepted invitations from Teddy Pope to have a day's sailing on his yacht. We travelled to Cape Clear, the southernmost point in Ireland, or to Sherkin Island nearby, and once went as far as the Fastnet Rock to view the yachts taking part in the Cowes-Fastnet race rounding the lighthouse before heading back in the general direction of Cornwall. How I marvelled that anybody could build a lighthouse on such an isolated rock amid fierce seas and ferocious winds. Before automation, who would have wanted to be a lighthouse-keeper on such a God-forsaken spot?

Later again, at Trinity, my friend John Barker thought it would be a good idea for us to buy an island. Why not if you can afford it? John was full of good ideas but to me this seemed one of his better ones (particularly as I loved islands). We were dissuaded from our first attempt to buy a property out in the Atlantic because of the unpredictability of the weather, which might have led to us being stranded there for days or even weeks. I remember reading of lighthouse-keepers having their Christmas post and food delivered some time in February, and my memories of the Fastnet Rock were not too encouraging.

So instead we began in 1963 to look "inland", that is to say for an island on a lake. Soon we were heading in the direction of Lough Key at the Northern end of the Shannon, near the town of Boyle, where we visited the local estate agent and auctioneer who doubled up as a publican.

He happened to have just what we wanted: an uninhabited island of about 11 acres called Stag. There was however just one problem. The previous summer a Swiss family had agreed to buy it and although a local solicitor had prepared a contract for the would-be purchasers, it had not been returned. The auctioneer said he would now make contact with the Swiss family to ascertain their intentions. To his surprise and our disappointment they responded by returning the signed contract with the required deposit. We were back at square one.

However he said he would keep a look out for something suitable for us and, sure enough, the following year he phoned me to say that Bullock island, all of 15 acres and the biggest on Lough Key, had come up for sale. Although uninhabited (apart that is from a flock of goats), the island had been home to a community of French monks of a White Canon order for some hundreds of years. They had built a church and a number of outbuildings, now sadly ruined, and were supposed to have been self-sufficient. Some of them were buried there and their graves remained though covered with brambles and bracken.

In the Irish famines of the 1840s they found they could no longer carry on and returned to their mother order back in France. After their departure, most of the buildings were dismantled and the stone conveyed to the mainland where it was used to build a folly called Cloontykilla Castle which has recently been restored. At the time of the famines, it was the task of enlightened landowners to use their farm workers to build follies on their land as there was no farm-work available and the owners of the Rockingham estate, of which Lough Key formed a part, were no exception.

Quite near to Bullock island is the ruin of castellated McDermott's island which has been in the ownership of the McDermott family for more than 500 years. When we bought Bullock, it was owned by The McDermott of Moylurg, descended from and head of the Irish McDermott clan, but working in 20th century employment as a stockbroker in London.

There is an interesting story told of one of his forebears, an earlier McDermott who had an attractive daughter called Una, or Una Bhán (Una the Fair). Her father was called away from his island castle to fight some wars and, worried that his daughter was interested in a local reprobate called Thomas Costello (otherwise known as Thomas the Proud), he incarcerated her on the island during his absence with instructions that she was not under any circumstances to see the proud Thomas. However, while he was absent Thomas used to swim over to the island to serenade and converse with Una from outside her window via a grill and this continued for some time until eventually Thomas became ill and died. Una was so upset by his death that she pined away and died herself not long afterwards of a broken heart. On his return to the island her father relented and allowed both Una and Thomas to be buried alongside each other on another island, Trinity, on the lake.

The story ends with two trees which grew out of each of their graves and eventually became entwined as one.

W.B. Yeats has written a poem about Una, and Dr Douglas Hyde, first President of Ireland, has written about the story in his "Love Songs of Connacht". Hyde was himself from Roscommon, the county where Lough Key is located, and he said that one evening he went to the lakeside to find out whether the story about the trees was true or not but as it was getting dark he couldn't find a boatman willing to take him over to the island.

Much later I had the opportunity to visit the island and can confirm that the story of the trees, unusual though it might be, was absolutely true.

We considered building a fishing lodge on Bullock and obtained outline planning permission for it, but a combination of the damp, the lack of services, and John and I becoming disinterested in the project meant that the plans were abandoned and we decided to leave the island as a bird sanctuary – much to the relief of the birds. Oh, and I nearly forgot to say that the cost of purchasing the island was £800 plus £40 fees.

Now, moving further afield, there were holiday visits to Majorca, Corfu and all of the Ionian islands, Mykonos and Ios in the Cyclades, Madeira, the Canaries plus three visits to the Azores. Have you met anybody who has been to the Azores even once?

The first of all these overseas visits was to Majorca where I went with James Dudley and Peter O'Clery, who had been two university chums. We must have been mad – not because we went there, but because all three of us turned up in dark suits with rolled umbrellas and wearing bowler hats in stifling heat. You should have seen the looks we got from the reception staff and our fellow guests when we turned up in our hotel in Cala Mayor. Looking back on it now, we must have set the trend for stag and hen parties thirty or more years hence because whenever I go through Heathrow or Gatwick departure lounges nowadays there seem to be lots of men in drag or young ladies in wedding dresses, though admittedly nobody with bowler hats or rolled umbrellas.

In 1987 after I left AGB and was seeking a holiday home in the sun, an article appeared in the *Financial Times* one Saturday mentioning that Malta might again become a popular destination for Brits if the opinion polls were right and Dom Mintoff's Labour party lost the forthcoming election. They duly lost and that autumn I set off on an exploratory trip to see what the place was like. It obviously attracted me because while there I agreed to purchase a house in St. Julians, once a small fishing village but now a burgeoning tourist resort with lots of noise and traffic.

As reported earlier it became a popular house for my friends to visit and my visitor's book contains the names of more than 50 guests, some of whom came to stay more than once, which I consider to be a good sign.

Despite all the sunshine, the sea views and the local multi-coloured fishing boats, the crass amount of building work going on all around me eventually got on my nerves. The postcards made people envious but they did not of course convey the noise or the dust that I and my neighbours had to endure. So some 23 years later I decided to sell up and move to a slightly more tranquil location in Floriana where the walls are 30 inches thick and the outlook is over the Mall Gardens which, hopefully, will never be built on – or at least not in my lifetime.

When I arrived in Malta I didn't know a soul but found that it was possible to make friends quite quickly. Because so much of life is out-of-doors, one didn't have to wait for lunch or dinner party invitations to meet people. Instead there were barbecues where much greater numbers could be accommodated so even if you only met a host or hostess a few days beforehand, another person or two added to the guest-list made no difference to the catering arrangements.

There have always been lots of concerts and art exhibitions to be attended as well as operas at the beautiful baroque Manoel Theatre in Valletta, believed to be Europe's oldest, and you'd be surprised how often one meets other "regulars" before events or during the intervals. Over time I got to meet Paul Xuereb, University Librarian, and Peter Vassallo, Professor of English who, when they heard I was looking for a home for my collection of rare Anglo-Irish literature, promptly presented the case for Malta being their repository. We soon came to an agreement and today the books and letters are housed in the University Library where they are subject to restricted access and I'm sure are very happy.

Some years later I was invited by the retired Rector, Rev. Professor Peter Serracino Inglot, to join the Board of the Mediterranean Institute, a part of the University which he chaired. I can best describe the Institute as the home of all the small "orphan" faculties such as music, anthropology, geography and theatre studies; and consider Fr. Peter as possibly the most talented person of my acquaintance. Though primarily a priest and a philosopher, he was also a writer of poetry and of books on a great variety of subjects as well as of opera libretti. I'm not sure if he ever tried his hand at painting but I have no doubt that he would have made a success of it.

He even played a major role as a member of Malta's team negotiating her entry into the EU. On one occasion he travelled back to Malta early one morning from Brussels and went straight from the airport to a Mediterannean Institute meeting at "the farm" which was his office at the University. I think he found it amusing to give each of us a copy of the draft EU constitution which had just been produced and suggested we should study it closely.

I remarked that I had been impressed on reading in the local papers that the Malta representatives had obtained agreement for Malta to have 5 MEPs in 2004 and rising to 6 from 2006 onwards. That gave Malta one MEP for every 80,000 people based on a population of 400,000. In Britain on the other hand there was one MEP for 750,000 to 800,000 people and the constituencies were so large that not many people knew who their MEPs were or where to find them. That clearly would have suited the MEPs very well as most of them didn't wish to have any contact with their constituents, other than at election time. On the basis of the British representation, I said, Malta would only be entitled to half of one MEP but I being such a kind person would have rounded the figure upwards and awarded Malta one full MEP.

Fr. Peter looked at me rather sadly and said: 'David, all we had to do was ask for the same as Luxembourg already had'. In fact, though Luxembourg is about 8 times larger than Malta, the population was then only slightly larger. That explained why, when any British PM criticized the EU, the PM of Luxembourg was always the first person to immediately jump to his feet and rush to its defence.

I first visited Luxembourg in 1961, when I went to Brussels for the World Trade Fair, and found the place full of coal mines and slag heaps and with so much smog that it would have given London a run for its money. On my last visit some 40 years later I saw the amazing transformation that had taken place, thanks to a considerable inflow of EU money. Now the place was spotlessly clean with attractive tinted glass buildings and beautifully manicured parks with black swans.

Elsewhere I have used the phrase "punching above one's weight" but this phrase can certainly be applied to the Isle of Man. This little dot in the middle of the Irish Sea, possessing the oldest continuous parliament in the world, created by the Vikings, is not a member of the United Kingdom or of the European Union. Farming, fishing and tourism traditionally have been the main occupations, but nowadays tourism has fallen back with the advent of air travel meaning holiday-makers can get to sunny places comparatively easily, with their good weather and, often, cheap booze. Tourism seems to have largely been replaced by online gaming and the production of thermostats for electric kettles and blankets, meaning that at least the Manx can keep warm during the overlong cold winters.

The people are very generous and as far as I can judge from the number of appeals I receive, about a quarter of the residents are members of charity committees dealing with all manner of things from a rest home for retired horses to orphanages in Nepal. The island has also given a disproportionate amount of support to Great Britain in two world wars, both in terms of men supplied and lost, and of ships and men at the time of the D-Day landings in 1944. Two of Britains leading sculptors, Brian Kneale and Michael Sandle, were born or educated on the island, and both have been members of the Royal Academy. An increasing number of leading European cyclists have learned their sport on the local roads and some choirs have been invited to sing in far away places such as New York and Malta. However the transformation of a redundant church into an arts centre in Port Erin as a labour of love by John Bethell, aided by considerable local voluntary support, must register as a major achievement as it now holds a number of well-known festivals each year and acts as the venue for music concerts and broadcasts on the BBC's Radio Three. There is a surprising amount to do on this little dot.

The fascination with islands continues into old age. I haven't yet been to the Caribbean, where there are so many, or to the Pacific, where there are even more. Probably I will never get to see them but for now I am happy spending my time largely in the Isle of Man with regular forays to Malta and elsewhere. Among my worries on islands, particularly if they are small, and some of my favourites are very small indeed, is what happens if you are ill , how far away is the nearest hospital and are you likely to die before you get there. I'll never know the answers.

The President of Malta

requests the pleasure of the company of

<u>Mr David Elyan</u>

to a reception

on the occasion of his conferment of

the Degree of Doctor of Literature *Honoris Causa*

on Monday, 12th March, 2001 at 6.00 p.m.

at The Palace, Valletta

Dress: Lounge

R.O. Tel: 231350

With Anne Dillon-Carrigan on Bullock
Island, Lough Key

Bullock Island, Lough Key

Mum and Dad in their garden, Castletown c.1990

The Mall, Floriana, 2012

My home in Douglas, 2019

SCHWANENGESANG (SWAN SONG)

When my father was a lad during the First World War, every town of any size in Ireland seemed to have a brass band and he and his friends liked nothing better than to march behind their favourite, the Cork Butter Exchange Band. His ambition was to learn to play an instrument so that he too could become a bandsman and march with a purpose. It wasn't to be. His mother instead insisted that he should become a cabinet maker and do something useful with his life. It didn't prevent him learning ballroom dancing and he became a very good dancer indeed. So good in fact that he put me to shame, not that it would have been too difficult, and was able to dance very well right into his eighties.

I wasn't interested in brass bands, nor was I any good at dancing but I did have a secret ambition. Possibly due to seeing too many post Second World War films, I aspired to become a tap-dancer. You had a love scene in a film and then, for no obvious reason, the two protagonists without any warning would commence the most furious piece of tap-dancing imaginable with hands waving in time to the music. The nearest I got to any of that was joining the school choir where we rehearsed Christmas carols and some dreary, long-forgotten tunes though there was just one that I will always remember. Indeed how could I forget it, for it was the rousing hunting chorus from Carl Maria von Weber's opera "Der Freischütz". Now I grant you it is a very loud and noisy tune – but suitable for little boys at the time (or at any time)? Much, much later I discovered that Weber (1786 –1826) was no slouch at writing operas and became the most popular composer of the day following the success of "Der Freischütz", though none of that would have been of interest to me then. Indeed I was to learn that he actually died in London while staying with a friend in Great Portland Street, just a stone's throw from my flat in Albany Street, albeit 140 years before.

While taking no active part in music-making, I nevertheless had a good "ear" and could tell an exceptional singer from the run-of-the-mill, and even an exceptional prospect; so much so that I was able on numerous occasions to recommend young singers to opera company managers and casting directors with a fair modicum of success. No doubt I would have achieved more if I had German contacts and not merely British ones; as compared with Britain's four or five opera houses, Germany has more than 100, no doubt all well supported by their Government.

One thing that has always fascinated me about singers was that in popular music the singers are instantly recognisable, largely because they are associated with the songs they sing. As soon a you hear the song, you know it is being sung by, for example, Bing Crosby, Frank Sinatra, Elaine Paige, George Formby or the Beatles. Opera on the other hand doesn't quite work like that. Apart from maybe 5 or 10 singers, you have to be a "professional" to be able to tell the differences, based on certain voice characteristics and the known ranges. These tests certainly mark me down as an amateur and I have listed here the voices that I (and I suspect most others) can immediately recognise: Kathleen Ferrier, John McCormack, Maria Callas, Janet Baker, Juan Diego Flores, Luciano Pavarotti and a few others whose early recordings give them away. My favourite arias? In general I prefer female to male voices and it has been said, with regard to Richard Strauss, that nobody has written so well for the female voice. In his case he had his wife Pauline's voice in mind when composing. Now from what I have read about him, Strauss doesn't appear to have been very appealing as an individual (except perhaps to Pauline), but nowhere nearly as bad as Wagner; and Pauline doesn't appear to have been a bundle of fun either. Felicity Lott once told me that when she was appearing in a Strauss opera in Vienna, Richard's grandson, Christian, asked if he could call to see her. She was a bit concerned about the visit but had no reason to be as they got on very well. As he was leaving he said 'I wish my grandmother could have been as pleasant as you are'. Notwithstanding the above, my favourite arias have to be the great female trio from "Der Rosenkavalier" involving Octavian, Sophie and the Marschallin; Strauss's "Four Last Songs" which were first performed in 1950 not long after his death, and Purcell's "When I am laid in earth" from "Dido and Aeneas" (1689). The latter libretto was by Nahum Tate, a graduate of Trinity College, Dublin, who was regarded as the least illustrious of all the poet laureates before or since.

While I don't believe in a "life hereafter", I have to confess it would be so enjoyable to meet up again with so many old friends, if only to hear them point out any inaccuracies in my serendipitous tales, and listen to my favourite tunes.

CHRONOLOGY

1940   Born Cork

1945   Cork Grammar School

1958   Trinity College, Dublin (TCD)

1962   BA, BComm; 1965 – MA

1967   ACCS, ACIS; 1976 – FCIS

1966/70 Stock Conversion & Investment Trust
        Rainbird Publishing Group
        The Observer

1970   Company Secretary Gordon & Gotch Holdings plc

1972   Fellow Royal Society of Arts (FRSA)

1974   Company Secretary AGB Research PLC;
        1980 – Director (to 1988)

1978   Liveryman Worshipful Company of
        Chartered Secretaries

1983   Underwriting Member of Lloyd's

1991   Member Post Office Advisory Committee
        (POAC) (to 1998)

1992   Secretary and Director Bankside Gallery (to 2009)

1993   Chairman Friends of Royal Academy of Music (to 2000)

1996   Trustee and Council Member Royal Albert
        Hall (to 2018)

1999	Hon. Associate Royal Academy of Music (Hon. ARAM)
2000	Hon. Fellow University of Malta
2001	Declined OBE
	Director Manx Public Art (to 2007)
2003	Director Mediterranean Institute (to 2012)
2004	Trustee Fenton Arts Trust (to 2011)
2008	Hon. Fellow University of Gloucestershire
2009	Consultant Santander Charitable Foundation (to 2011)
2012	Trustee Manx National Heritage (to 2017) Hon. Member Royal Watercolour Society (Hon RWS)

Lives remembered

Patrick Seale

David Elyan writes: A less well known period in the career of Patrick Seale (obituary, Apr 30) at The Observer came when he headed a new venture called Observer Books and Features, with the objective of creating a literary agency to utilise the talents of Observer writers. Patrick was easily distracted and noticed the phenomenal success of The Observer's new colour magazine in offering rocking chairs by mail-order to its readers. What could be promoted as a follow-up?

The idea of marketing original graphics was suggested. At the time the usual print run was about 50 to 70 signed and numbered copies, which typically sold for about £50 each. Patrick, however, planned much larger editions of perhaps 500 copies which could be sold for £12 or £15 each. The Observer Art scheme got off to a promising start with Richard Hamilton's Kent State. This was followed by specially commissioned prints from Eduardo Paolozzi, Joe Tilson, David Hockney, Patrick Procktor and Elizabeth Frink, all of which sold well. Then an agreement was reached with Brenda Rawnsley to sell her unsold school prints by French artists: Braque, Dufy, Leger, Matisse (a paper cut-out) and Picasso.

Eventually thousands of prints were sold for about £15 each. Today, 40 years later, some of these individual prints resell for thousands of pounds. There must be many elderly Observer readers who are unaware that they owe Patrick Seale a considerable debt of gratitude.

Lives remembered

Lord Howe of Aberavon

David Elyan writes: You mentioned that Lord Howe's capacity for hard work was partly based on his ability to make do with only three or four hours of sleep (obituary, Oct 11). I can confirm the accuracy of this statement.

When in opposition from 1974 onwards, Sir Geoffrey (as he then was) became a non-executive director of AGB Research and his office was next door to mine. One morning, shortly after joining AGB, the BBC 8am radio news reported comments by Sir Geoffrey when addressing Newcastle-upon-Tyne Chamber of Commerce the night before. Imagine my surprise then on getting to the office at 8.45am and finding Geoffrey already there and dictating to his secretary.

Lives Remembered

Brenda Rawnsley

David Elyan writes: When in 1971 Brenda Rawnsley (obituary July 4) wrote to the Hon David Astor, then Editor of *The Observer*, asking if the newspaper might be interested in purchasing her print publishing business, the letter eventually found its way to me. It would have been both easy and sensible to reply that we were not interested, but something made me contact Mrs Rawnsley. Even as I was about to ring her doorbell in Motcomb Street, I wondered what I was doing there.

An hour or so later Brenda asked if I would like to see her framing operation. Not wishing to appear ungrateful for her liquid hospitality, I agreed. On enquiring about some parcels in a corner, I was told: "Oh, those are our French prints by artists such as Braque and Picasso. They didn't sell very well. In fact, I have probably had to throw away more than I sold because they got stained as a result of a leaking roof." Fascinated by what I was hearing, I returned to the flat above the gallery where Brenda told me about the trip to France in 1948 to track down a handful of leading French artists and persuade them to produce prints for sale to schools in England. The story had never been written about and there were many photographs taken on the visit.

The following day I recounted Brenda's story to my colleague, Patrick Seale, who determined that *The Observer* must publish the story and offer to sell the remaining prints to our readers. What Brenda had been unable to sell at £1 each, we offered at £15 each. Within a few weeks we had sold the lot and I believe Brenda received as much from the sale of these prints as she was expecting from the sale of the business, including the lease and her entire stock.

She and I later collaborated in writing *The Story of School Prints* (1990). We last met in March when we toured the Pallant House gallery's school prints exhibition. She was so alive and alert for her 90 years.

Sir David Willcocks

David Elyan writes: The Bach Choir's centenary concert at the Albert Hall in April, 1976, when Sir David Willcocks (obituary, Sept 19) conducted the Bach Mass in B minor was followed by a party at the Royal College of Music near by.

Sir David invited a number of notable people (without prior warning) to take part in an entertainment. I recall David McKenna, then chairman of the choir, singing *Rule Britannia* covered by a white sheet and holding something resembling a harpoon; and Dame Janet Baker being invited to sing the Beatles' song *Yesterday*. Needless to say, she performed admirably, much to the delight of Sir David and the rest of us.

Victoria de los Angeles

David Elyan writes: Your obituary of **Victoria de los Angeles** describes her wonderful artistry, her "charismatic personality and knockdown charm". Ample evidence of these qualities was provided by her Usher Hall recital in the summer of 1957. Her recital took place on a Sunday afternoon and at the end of the programmed items the applause was so lengthy and so loud that she was not allowed to leave the stage. The resultant encores with much further applause lasted longer than the original concert — and only terminated when the manager of the Hall went on stage and pleaded with the audience to leave as the audience for the evening symphony concert was already outside and could not be admitted. What a bravura performance by a diva at the height of her powers. My only regret is that the programme she inscribed for me is lost.

Sir Colin Davis

David Elyan writes: Your obituary failed to mention Sir Colin's considerable contribution to both the Royal Academy of Music and the Royal College of Music. On those occasions when he agreed to conduct their concerts and operas, he delighted students and audiences alike with his professionalism and humility. And of course the Academy and the College were always assured of a full house.